A most timely and highly signi
a Western audience at the prese
of gifts: personal, long-term immersion in an Islamic society, detailed understanding of the rise and development of Islam, awareness of the sensitive political issues at the present time, clear biblical and theological bearings, and (perhaps most of all) a real respect and love for Muslims. Mike Kuhn is exceptionally well qualified in all these respects, and this book deserves a wide circulation.

—COLIN CHAPMAN
Author, *Whose Promised Land?* and *Whose Holy City?*

So many books on Islam have been authored by theoreticians or academicians with little or no experience encountering the followers of Muhammad. Mike Kuhn incarnated his life and witness in the Middle East for many years. Kuhn's love for Muslims shines throughout this volume. His assessment of the current "clash of civilizations" is one of the best I have read. Kuhn's readable writing style at times reinforces one's presuppositions and at other times is provocative, even jolting. This is a book not to flippantly peruse, but rather one to thoughtfully interact with. It has my highest commendation.

—PHIL PARSHALL
Author, *The Cross and the Crescent* and *Bridges to Islam;* SIM missionary at large

Today Muslims have taken the place of the Communists as the symbol of the antichrist for Christians. This book is a biblical vision that explores how we can overcome a spirit of animosity toward others who are different—regardless of their creed or race. This book is definitely a "need to read"!

—MAZHAR MALLOUHI
Author, *A Sufi Reading of the Gospel of John* and numerous Arabic books and articles

Written in an erudite and yet highly readable style, Kuhn's book will challenge many sacred cows of evangelicals. Prophetically and comprehensively, with the experience of having lived in the Arab world for almost two decades, Mike Kuhn will get you thinking about your view of Muslims, eschatology, and how best to present the One who is more than a prophet to Muslims.

—DR. DAVID LUNDY
International director of Arab World Ministries and author, *Servant Leadership for Slow Learners* and *Borderless Church*

Kuhn writes in the prophetic mold and will not tickle readers' ears by riding the popular wave of demonizing Islam, but neither does he ignore the issues that concern many Christians today. Kuhn's remedies are born out of his experience in Muslim homelands, and he offers the third way so desperately needed to diffuse fears and tensions in a growing world culture of alienation and aggression. Dare to read it and be challenged and maybe transformed.

—CHRISTINE MALLOUHI
Author, *Waging Peace on Islam* and *Miniskirts, Muslims and Mothers*

FRESH VISION
for the
MUSLIM WORLD

An Incarnational Alternative

Mike Kuhn

Biblica Books
from InterVarsity Press

InterVarsity Press
P.O. Box 1400, Downers Grove, IL 60515-1426
World Wide Web: www.ivpress.com
Email: email@ivpress.com

*InterVarsity Press® is the book-publishing division of InterVarsity Christian Fellowship/USA®, a
movement of students and faculty active on campus at hundreds of universities, colleges and schools of
nursing in the United States of America, and a member movement of the International Fellowship of
Evangelical Students. For information about local and regional activities, write Public Relations
Dept., InterVarsity Christian Fellowship/USA, 6400 Schroeder Rd., P.O. Box 7895, Madison, WI
53707-7895, or visit the IVCF website at <www.intervarsity.org>.*

All Scripture quotations, unless otherwise indicated, are taken from the Holy Bible, New
International Version®. NIV®. *Copyright ©1973, 1978, 1984 by International Bible Society. Used
by permission of Zondervan Publishing House. All rights reserved.*

*Unless otherwise noted, Qur'anic quotations taken from The Meaning of the Glorious Qur'an by
Muhammad Marmaduke Pickthall.*

*Quotations marked "Yusuf Ali translation" are taken from The Holy Qur'an: Text, Translation and
Commentary, translated by Abdullah Yusuf Ali.*

*Hadiith quotations taken from Sahih al-Bukhari, translated by Dr. Muhammad Muhsin Khan,
vols. 1–9, published by Dar Al Arabiya, Beirut, Lebanon.*

Originally published by Biblica. Published in 2009 by Authentic.

ISBN 978-0-8308-5655-8

Printed in the United States of America ∞

Cataloging-in-Publication Data is available through the Library of Congress.

P	17	16	15	14	13	12	11	10	9	8	7	6	5	4	3	2	1
Y	27	26	25	24	23	22	21	20	19	18	17	16	15				

CONTENTS

FOREWORD

In my youth I used to skip over the foreword, assuming that it was an extra or a decoration and not really an important part of the book. Over the years I learned better! My challenge now is to motivate you to read rather than to skim this foreword, because I have something very important to say about the author and indirectly about this book.

First I must explain my background. I come from an Arab Christian family that goes back to first- or second-century Christianity. I was born in Syria, lived a good part of my life in Lebanon, and served God as a missionary with the Navigators in Egypt from 1975 to 1990. My family and I planned to stay in Egypt the rest of our lives, but in September 1990 I was blacklisted and given ten days to leave the country. Since then my family and I have been living in Colorado Springs, and we carry U.S. citizenship. Part of what I do is teach on a regular basis an intensive course called Islam in the Twenty-first Century at several seminaries in the United States and Canada.

Mike Kuhn knew me before I knew him. Years ago he read one of my books on Islamic fundamentalism. He lived in Egypt after we left, and he co-labored with my best friend there. He was blacklisted and expelled from Egypt as well. Here in the States I connected with him face-to-face in November 2007 and have continued to get to know him. As I was reading through the manuscript of this book, I often found myself identifying with Mike's experiences, but more importantly with his *attitudes, ideas,* and *perspective.* Then a thought came to mind: This man one day could become one of my soul mates.

I have known some missionaries in Muslim countries who tended to have a condescending attitude, fearing that they might get contaminated by the culture and the theology of the Muslims. I have known other missionaries who lived in Muslim countries with the attitude of the journalists; they were not "fully there" because their minds were occupied with their friends and donors back home. The experiences they were having served as potential stories or photos for their next newsletter. Mike is not like that at all. He was fully there.

That is only one reason why I think Mike is the right man to write on Islam, Muslims, and Arabs. Here are some others:

I know only five Americans who have really mastered the Arabic language. Mike is one of them. He was able not only to connect with the people at a heart level but also to get into the writings of Islam in the original language. This makes a huge impression on Muslims.

Mike is completely free of any bitterness against Egypt, Islam, or Muslims. He was unjustly expelled from Egypt and blacklisted, yet there is not even a trace of resentment in his attitudes. There is no chip on his shoulder.

He is very well educated in the history and theology of Islam. He studied not only the Qur'an but also the Hadiith and the culture and geopolitics of the Muslims with whom he lived.

Mike has deep roots in evangelical Christianity and is a patriotic American (his father is a Marine Corps veteran), yet he has become an insider among Arabs and Muslims. Therefore he is very qualified to interpret to Western Christians the "strange" phenomena of Islam and Arabs. There are not many people who can do that.

Mike is *not* an armchair theologian or an armchair missiologist who appointed himself as an expert and is playing a role. Mike left behind in the Middle East a sustainable ministry. As you read through this book, you will get to meet his Muslim friends with whom he shared the love of God.

He is a man of courage. As you will see in the pages of this book, he dares to get into issues that very few evangelicals dare to get into. He addresses these issues biblically and in a scholarly manner.

Mike disagrees wholeheartedly with replacement theology, and in this book he challenges Christian Zionism, which is hindering our ministry to 1.4 billion Muslims around the world. His argument is not with dispensational theology as such; his criticism is of Christian Zionism.

Lesslie Newbigin, an Anglican missionary, returned home from England after forty years in India and found that England had drifted away from a Christian consensus toward a pluralistic worldview. Newbigin suggested fresh vision to the church. Like Newbigin, Mike Kuhn returned to the States after being away among Arab Muslims for twenty years, and this book offers *fresh vision*.

As I was reading the manuscript, I was on a journey. Reading the book brought back cherished memories of my time in Egypt. The contents of the book refreshed my heart and vision to the degree that I decided to make this book required reading at the seminaries where I teach. At another time, while reading, I thought of all the people to whom I would like to give copies. This book is *necessary* and *timely*.

—Dr. Nabeel T. Jabbour
Author, *The Crescent Through the Eyes of the Cross*, *Unshackled and Growing*, *The Rumbling Volcano*, and *The Unseen Reality*
www.nabeeljabbour.com

ACKNOWLEDGMENTS

So many have contributed to this book, whether directly or indirectly, that it will be impossible to name them all. I would like first to express sincere thanks to those who read the manuscript and provided constructive feedback:

Donna Smith and Mike Jacobson are friends and colleagues whose insight into the Arab world and the reading audience was invaluable.

Mike Reimer's keen editorial eye and incisive understanding of the history of the Middle East saved me from some embarrassing oversimplifications.

My own family—Margaret, Kenny, and Jeff Kuhn—was a source of encouragement, not to mention editorial assistance. I greatly appreciated Jeff's insight into North American culture and the state of the church.

Phil Parshall and Nabeel Jabbour read the manuscript, and both men gave me encouragement at a moment when I felt this book might never see the light of day. I am indebted to them and continue to look to them as role models of incarnational followers of Jesus.

My home church, Cedar Springs Presbyterian, patiently allowed me to test many of these ideas in teaching and preaching. How patient and encouraging you have been! Special thanks to Marty Holder and Doug Messer, who read the manuscript very early in the process. Piers

Vander, thank you for your encouragement to keep pursuing the vision of this book.

For twenty-two years I served shoulder to shoulder with a number of men and women with Arab World Ministries and other organizations. I could never adequately express my thanks to these brothers and sisters for their example of self-giving love. Most would not wish me to mention their names as they continue to serve in Muslim lands. Some have already heard their "Well done." Know that you have left your mark on me. I am grateful.

Kasr Dubara Evangelical Church, you paid me the great honor of accepting me into your fellowship and interpreting to me your fascinating culture and history. Thank you for your faithfulness, for accepting a *khawaga* (foreigner) and treating him as a brother. May you stand tall among the lampstands.

To M. F. and Barbara Kuhn, who gave up their son (not to mention their grandkids) without regret for those many years, your constant love and guidance are the stuff of life. You are highly treasured, and I am confident your reward is great in this life and the next.

To those few whose names cannot be mentioned here, you have loved Christ more than family and lands. You were my real teachers. Your mothers and fathers, sisters and brothers continue as Muslims, yet you have been called out. I can never forget you, and I will continue to carry you in my heart wherever I am. Thank you for your laughter amid dire circumstances, for your faith against all odds, for your courage. The ideas in this book owe more to your persevering faith and authentic incarnation than any other single source.

Finally, to Stephanie, my true companion in this journey; to Bethany, Hannah, and Emily, who make the journey a delight; and to Jake, my newest son (by marriage to Bethany), words cannot express how grateful I am for each of you. I love you all.

PART I
A VISIONARY PARADIGM

How do human beings change? Jesus asked his disciples to "open [their] eyes and look at the fields! They are ripe for harvest" (John 4:35). Essentially, he was asking them to embrace a new vision of reality. Undoubtedly, the physical objects within their field of vision would remain the same. What would change was their ability to see what Jesus himself saw. Perhaps Jesus still asks his followers in our day to open their eyes—to get a new vision. Might he challenge us to see the Muslim world in a totally different light?

Vision has power to change the soul. We take the first steps on the road to change by getting a new vision.

CHAPTER 1

CASTING A
NEW KIND OF VISION

A wet, rainy night in England always had a soothing effect on my soul—like a balm on an open sore. A friend had simply laid a couple of DVDs out on the table. I sensed sleep would not come easily after our conversation, so I picked one up.

Beyond the Gates of Splendor. The title alone was enough to get my attention.

As a college student I had read *Through Gates of Splendor.* Many factors conspire to lead a young man into missions, but Elisabeth Elliot's book had definitely left its mark on me. The appeal of these five missionaries-turned-martyrs was not so much their death, noble as that was. It was that they were real people, real men. They laughed, loved, thought deeply, played with their kids, and lived their lives for something great. Some suffered a sense of inadequacy; the exuberance of others could reach the point of irritation. Reading about these athletic, gifted men (and their wives) had given me hope. If they could die for their cause, just maybe I could live for it.

Two Stories

The DVD turned out to be a documentary with heart—the story of Steve Saint, son of one of the missionaries martyred by the Waorani people of Ecuador (sometimes referred to as the Auca Indians) in the 1950s.

What a strange visitation of providence. I was no martyr, but I had just experienced a death of sorts.

A Story of Exile

An American who had made my home in the Middle East for long years, I now found myself in England as an exile—deported from Egypt and blacklisted, unable to ever return.

Fulfilling my mission in Egypt meant more than delivery of a message. It meant an entering into life—not an easy task—and I make no claim to have done it perfectly or even well. We (my family and I) spent the early years peering through the window at a culture and people we aspired to know and love. At some point the window mysteriously opened, and we were pulled through. The people of the Muslim world became our neighbors and friends. We laughed at their jokes, waited in their traffic jams, wept at their funerals, and cried for joy at their weddings. We tried ever so hard to see things from their perspective. Our motives were sometimes viewed with suspicion. We had moments of discomfort and longing for "home."

To outside observers the language seems the insurmountable barrier; however, it is merely the key that unlocks a door to a new culture. After opening that door we found a confusing matrix of family values, economic systems, and political and historical realities that simply could not be assimilated in a day. Suffice it to say that I was a transplant—growing deep roots in an adopted culture. My neighbors and friends delighted to hear me speak warmly and positively of their country. They were all too aware of its many inconsistencies and defects. Yet here was an American referring to their country as his country by adoption. I meant it, and I think that pleased them.

Then on the night of September 18, 2005, returning home on a flight from Africa, I was not allowed back into Egypt. Internal security police had blacklisted me. I was escorted to a holding room and kept under guard and questioned intermittently that entire night.

During one interview the plainclothes officer behind the desk asked me my profession, and I replied, "Pastor." Egyptians have difficulty distinguishing the sounds of *p* and *b*. (They are wonderful jokesters, those Egyptians, and often tell how their president returned from a visit to the United States and strangely insisted that his name be written on every door in every public place. The American president, he said, had his name on every door (*push—Bush*!). So my interlocutor, mystified by the name of my profession, began to repeat it over and over with a *b* rather than a *p*. As the humor of being referred to as what sounded like *bastard* in this climactic moment began to sink in, I had to smile.

In Middle Eastern culture magnanimity and generosity top the list of virtues. That night two Pakistanis and three Egyptians shared my incarceration. We were served no food, but just after dawn prayers, a stocky Egyptian woman showed up and offered to bring sandwiches and tea for a small fee. Various ones placed their orders while the two Pakistanis slept at the other end of the room. I questioned the Egyptian guard about how long they had been there and if they had eaten. His nonverbal response let me know these troublemakers were not worth the effort. Taking my stand on the high ground of Arab magnanimity, I replied, "But these men are our guests" (asserting myself as though I actually had rights!). The Egyptian begrudgingly agreed that the Pakistanis deserved to eat, as they were, after all, guests in "our" country.

One of the Egyptian captives gave rather evasive answers to his interrogators. At one point he was invited into an adjacent room. Shocking shrieks and screams of confession amid the unmistakable thud of blows landing on flesh assaulted our midnight stupor. Confusion. Disconnect. Could it be that the young Egyptian man sitting beside me five minutes ago was the centerpiece of a torture scene? He returned later to reoccupy his place on the bench beside me, weeping, his eyes and face swollen and red, his head now between his knees. I noticed red streaks going down his neck and marveled at the vulnerability of man to his greatest adversary—man.

The next morning as I was taken to the British Air office to buy a one-way ticket out, I asked my escort if I might phone my wife, who had been awaiting my return all night with no news. Middle Easterners are masters of body language. My escort made no reply but simply rubbed his fingers across his thumb. I slipped him a ten-pound note and was allowed to use the phone at the British Air desk to inform my wife that I would not be returning home. As far as I knew then, and as far as I know now, I will never return to Egypt.

A Story of Martyrdom

Just a few weeks later, I sat up that rainy night in southern England, listening to Steve Saint relate the story of his father's heroic death, and I experienced the power of the words "They being dead yet speak." Rachel Saint and Elisabeth Elliot responded to that terrible event in a way that defies our comfort-seeking culture. They waited. They prepared. When the time came, they moved in and lived among the very tribe that had taken the lives of Rachel's brother, Nate, and Elisabeth's husband, Jim.

The vicious tribe had defied the friendly advances of peace-loving missionaries and speared them mercilessly, seemingly on a whim. The world was left with the perplexing question, why? Could any sense be made of their martyrdom? A sense of *aha!* developed as reports proliferated about the conversion of the Waorani Indians. A neat, evangelical resolution of the tension of martyrdom was found in that faith birthed deep in the jungle. Yet as Elisabeth Elliot has pointed out, such neat and happy endings are seldom satisfying: "A healthier faith seeks a reference point outside all human experience, the polestar which marks the course of all human events." That polestar is an inscrutable and immutable God—"I will find rest nowhere but in his will, and that will is infinitely, immeasurably, unspeakably beyond my largest notions of what he is up to."[1]

I suppose we could stop there. Certainly no one can deny the mystery and lack of neat resolution in the current tension between the Western world and radical Islam. If God is up to something, most of us are at a loss to discern it. But one focus of this book is to suggest that God is, in fact, up to something. Although the tension will not resolve into a neatly packaged scenario, the current world conflict has all the makings of a symphony, admittedly discordant at times, but led, nonetheless, by a master conductor. Our world is not madly spinning out of control while our God fretfully bites his nails.

You and I will find our purpose and our peace as we rest in a God who, as C. S. Lewis said of Aslan, is not safe but is good.[2]

Another moral of the story of the Ecuadorian martyrs readily commends itself. The treachery of the Waorani, while real, masked a more basic motivation—fear. It is no psychological secret that those most vulnerable and abused often act most savagely and treacherously. Elisabeth Elliot recorded that the Waorani people speared foreigners simply because they feared being cannibalized. Rather than be eaten, the tribe attacked. Their provincial view of the world did not allow them to trust the kind advances of those who meant them no harm. They had no grid other than that of jungle warriors through which to process the missionaries' gifts and acts of kindness.

A large yellow "bird"—an airplane—had allowed men who covered their white skin with funny clothes to penetrate Waorani territory. For centuries the dense jungle of Ecuador had been impenetrable. Some of the Waorani had left the jungle never to return, but this was the first advance into the Waorani's homeland. Who could say what such an advance would produce? These jungle Indians, face-to-face for the first time with people they supposed to be cannibals, feared for their lives. Perhaps they were more justified than we have been led to believe, as foreigners of a less-kind disposition may well have abused their simplicity. Much as a wounded animal bites the hand that would help it, so the Waorani struck out in fear.

Satellite and Internet technology have penetrated the Muslim world to a degree unknown heretofore. The presence of Western military in the Muslim world causes tremendous uncertainty and suspicion. While living in the Middle East, I was privy to incessant waves of conspiracy theories, most of which had to do with Zionists and Westerners holding the reigns of world events and directing them for the benefit of a privileged few. Incredulous, I listened to these elaborately detailed schemes of world dominance. I now realize that fear, similar to that of the Waoranis of Ecuador, dominates the worldview of much of the Muslim world. Just as the Waorani tribe murdered in fear, so radical Muslims are striking at anything associated with the West.

To fear the unknown is not a one-way street. In the West I often hear sweeping generalizations about the Middle East, Arabs, and Muslims: "Those people are killing each other. Don't they know they can trust us? Why are they so filled with hate? We've always upheld justice and returned the country to its people after we leave. We even help rebuild the country." It's a common malady of humanity that we see our own (or our group's) intentions as noble and pure while we are skeptical, if not downright antagonistic, toward the motivations of others.

In a class I taught recently in the United States, where I now live, I was asked why "the Muslims" are always killing each other. The reference was to the Sunni-Shiite tension in Iraq. My reply? "Good question. Let me help you see it from their side. I lived in a Middle Eastern city of eighteen million people. Yet for all the overcrowding and irascible problems of that city, it was a relatively safe place to live. Murders were fairly rare. Contrast that with any large U.S. city—Los Angeles, New York City, Miami. Middle Easterners hear the statistics of violence in the United States and ask me, 'Why are the Americans always killing each other?' Yes, there is persistent violence in Iraq between Sunnis and Shiites these days, but in vast areas of the Muslim world people live in peace and go about their daily affairs. They want to find better education for their children, make their payments on their house, afford a better car. Their concerns are much like yours."

Surprise! Or maybe not.

Incarnation

There is an opposite reaction to fear. The word I will use to describe this reaction is *incarnation*, derived from the Latin *carnis* (flesh) and *in*—"in flesh." In Christian parlance it is most often used of Christ as he took on humanity (human flesh) and lived among us.

In the case of the Waorani of Ecuador, Rachel and Elisabeth adopted much of the Waorani way of life. They *incarnated* among them, learning the tribe's language, eating their food, being exposed to their illnesses. In brief, the women lived among the tribe, embracing much of the tribe's life and culture. The tribe, in turn, learned and embraced much from the women, including the message of God's love and grace.

The incarnation of the gospel, for all its benefit to the Waorani people, came at great cost. We are fortunate to see the resulting faith of the primitive tribe, but we also do well to remember the immense price that was paid. The process of incarnation is costly, yet it is the messy work to which Jesus has called his followers. Perhaps a vignette from Jesus' life will further illustrate.

A Modern-Day Samaria

Despised and hated people groups are not new to the world scene. In Jesus' day the despised people group was the Samaritans, a type of Jewish half-breed. From the perspective of the purists, they had corrupted the law, rejected the prophets, and deformed worship; they were an "unclean" people. At one point the Samaritans offered to help the Jews rebuild their temple after their return from exile. The Jewish reply was simply, "You have no part in this work" (see Ezra 4:3). Accordingly, the Samaritans attempted to frustrate and halt the reconstruction of the temple by inciting King Artaxerxes against the project. As if that weren't enough, when the Samaritans later built their own temple on Mount Gerazim, they dedicated it to pagan deities! (Imagine that—rival temples in the Middle East worshipping different gods!) When Jewish leaders sought the supreme insult to cast at Jesus, they simply said, "Aren't we right in saying that you are a Samaritan and demon-possessed?" (John 8:48). In brief, Jewish antagonism toward the Samaritans was political and religious, historical and contemporary, with all the elements of a modern-day ethnic rivalry—spiced with accusations, hatred, even warfare.

The story of Jesus' encounter with a Samaritan woman has inspired Christians for centuries. We would expect Jesus to have a different attitude about the Samaritans, but his disciples, steeped in the prevailing view of their day, couldn't understand it.

The Gospel of John relates Jesus' journey through Samaria on his way to Jerusalem. He sent his disciples into a nearby village to buy food while he waited near a well. A Samaritan woman came to the well alone, in the middle of the day. As the story unfolds, we see that she had a history of immorality and that she had given up on the institution of marriage—in some ways a very modern woman.

The disciples returned and were amazed to see Jesus doing something no Jewish rabbi was permitted to do in a public place—conversing with a woman. This Samaritan woman became one of the early New Testament missionaries as she scampered off to tell the people of her village, "Come, see a man who told me everything I ever did. Could this be the [Messiah]?" (4:29). The disciples urged

Jesus to eat, but he replied, "I have food to eat that you know nothing about" (4:32).

Think about that. Jesus referred to his interaction with a Samaritan woman as his food. Food is what sustains and gives strength. For most of us, food is a nonnegotiable. We do what we must to obtain it because our existence requires that we eat. Yet Jesus clarified for the disciples: "My food…is to do the will of him who sent me" (4:34). Amazing, really! Jesus could heal the blind, raise the dead, and cause the deaf to hear. When he commanded the winds and waves to be still, they calmed. His teaching caused thousands to throng behind him and cling to his every word. Yet his food was this—conversing with an immoral woman from a despised people group.

The woman returned with the village representatives in tow. Jesus used imagery common to the time: "Do you not say, 'Four months more and then the harvest'? I tell you, open your eyes and look at the fields! They are ripe for harvest" (4:35). In effect, "Get a new vision. Look at this differently. Lift up your eyes! See it the way I see it."

Given this unusual dialogue, we have to infer that Jesus was immensely satisfied with the reaction of the Samaritan people. In fact, he delayed his journey a full two days while many of the Samaritans came to believe in him as the Savior of the world. Although the text is not explicit in this regard, we assume that he stayed in the homes of the Samaritan people, eating their food and enjoying their camaraderie. It's as though he'd just enjoyed a good meal or brought in a copious harvest. He found the Samaritan reception of his mission and himself to be fulfilling.

In much the same way that Rachel Saint and Elisabeth Elliot entered the world of their brother's and husband's murderers, so Jesus moved freely among a people who would normally be the object of hatred and animosity among his people, the Jews. Many Jews intentionally avoided traveling through Samaria as they went from Galilee to Jerusalem; Jesus chose to go through Samaria. He chose to sit by a Samaritan well. He chose to engage a needy Samaritan woman and found immense joy in a warm reception by her despised and hated people. Beyond that, he stayed with them, sleeping in their homes and eating their food, for two more days.

We do not know if the disciples "got it," if they really changed their perspective on the Samaritans. It may have taken some time. In the book of Acts, we learn that the Samaritans heard the gospel message from Philip (not one of the original disciples); Peter and John traveled into Samaria and witnessed the Holy Spirit transform the Samaritans into Jesus-followers. So the disciples did "get it" later if not on that trip through Samaria.

Have we gotten it? There is, after all, a modern-day Samaria—a people who have corrupted our holy faith, moved around our holy sites, occupied our holy land. I daresay that many of us would avoid traveling through their land. To sit down and share a meal with them is not something we've considered.

Consider it now.

Confronted with a Choice

You and I are confronted with a choice. On the one hand is the path of isolation, fear, alienation, and self-preservation—a well-worn road. Its rhetoric is comforting and its landmarks reassuring. We know that we are in the right because so many of our friends are going along the same road, offering their encouragement. The alternative path is clearly less traveled. It calls for self-awareness, empathy for the other, and deep listening. Although excruciatingly difficult, its summit is the peak of incarnation.

Which will it be?

If you're on the path of self-preservation, you won't need to look far for affirmation. For instance, in 1998 Samuel Huntington wrote *The Clash of Civilizations and the Remaking of World Order,* in which he portrayed an Islamic resurgence and analyzed the historic tensions between the Islamic East and the West. Huntington's provocative thesis led many to believe that future conflict with the Muslim world was inevitable. Although a religious enemy, Islam was an all-encompassing way of life, often referred to as a worldview, including the political, economic, military, educational, social, and religious dimensions of society.

Rather than quell the rhetoric of enmity, recent events have only reinforced it in the minds of many thinking people. September 11 was the capstone event that isolated Islamic radicalism (sometimes referred to as *Islamism*) as a potent and threatening enemy of Western democracy. However, events prior to 9/11 and since that time have confirmed the suspicions of many. Just prior to his demise, Abu Musab al-Zarqawi, a Jordanian leader of the Iraqi insurgence, declared that his fighters had broken the back of the American military presence in Iraq. While many see this as idle bravado, there is no doubt (at the time of this writing) that the insurgence continues to wreak havoc with the proposed U.S. plan of establishing a democracy in this crucial Muslim country.

Iraq is not the only focal point of this tension with the West. The reemergence of the Taliban (the fundamentalist Islamic militia in Afghanistan); the electoral victories of the Islamist parliamentarians in Egypt and Gaza; suicide bombings; Ahmedinejad's persistent enrichment of uranium while calling for Israel's destruction; bomb-ings in Bali, Madrid, London, Sharm El Sheikh, Dahab, Amman—all of this and much more point toward an impasse in relations of Western democracies with the Muslim world. Small wonder that many conclude that the Islamic worldview is the present threat to the Western democratic ideal. If you will, the Muslim world is a modern-day Samaria.

Since my return to the United States, I've been rather alarmed by the fact that the discussion of the issue of Islamic radicalism among Christians differs little from what I hear in conservative media. I wonder, are the conservative media moguls now spokespersons for Christ's kingdom? In our present world, torn as it is by conflicting interests that erupt into bloody attacks, should not Christ-followers have a unique voice? Is there no fresh vision of the Muslim world rooted in the values of Christ's kingdom? Is our only option to con-front the Muslim world and eliminate the threat? Can the mind-set of confrontation give way to incarnation?

I hear you saying, "Wait a minute. They started it! I just want to live my life in peace." It sounds like an acceptable personal reaction to the Muslim world. Unfortunately, it is not credible because of it being individualistic and naive. And believe it or not, I've heard the same line from many acquaintances throughout the Muslim world. They're tired of all the killing. They'd like to live and let live.

I believe there is an alternative. It is the second path—the path of empathy, self-awareness, deep listening, and *incarnation*. Those who choose such a path will be few, and while they are not the only candidates, I suggest that good candidates for the second path are those who are resolved to follow the way of Christ. These people will recognize immediately that they must "take the plank out of [their own] eye" before they can "see clearly to remove the speck from [their] brother's eye" (Luke 6:42). They know that the option of retreat into a materialistic revelry of passivity is not workable. Nor will they be so naive as to think that they will mystically join hands with Muslims and go walking into the sunset of tolerance and pluralism. They will know instinctively that reconciliation does not come cheaply.

In the case of the Waorani tribe of Ecuador, a band of Christ-followers embracing the commission to make disciples of all nations established links of peace with the primitive tribe. It was done at great cost—loss of life. Yet no one could deny that the principles and values Jesus taught were the key ingredients allowing a successful incarnation of his kingdom to take place. The determination to forgive a murderer, the passion for Christ's reign of peace, the fierce commitment to human dignity—all these equipped those Christ-followers with the tools they needed for effective incarnation.

We are in a similar position with radical Islam. Clearly, radical Muslims make no apology for acts of violence perpetrated on innocent, even well-meaning, people. To many Westerners the intention of radical Islamic groups to eradicate Israel and other enemies of Islam leaves no legitimate option but confrontation or in some cases elimination. This somber reality cannot be denied. Kill or be killed seems to be the order of the day in the Middle East. While it is indeed illegitimate to lump all Muslims together as radical Islamists—a deeply inaccurate reflection of the complex and multivaried nature of the Muslim world—still the violent intentions of Islamic movements such as Hezbollah (Lebanon), *jihad* (defense of the religious state), Hamas (Palestine), al Qaeda, and Wahabism (Saudi Arabia) cannot be denied. In such an environment, armed conflict may be inevitable. But is there another way? To state the question differently, what is the unique perspective of a Christ-follower individually and the kingdom of Jesus collectively to the current conflicts of the West with the Muslim world?

◆ SEEKING FRESH VISION ◆

The premise of this book is that there is an alternative response to this threat that goes beyond the response of confrontation offered at a state and political level. This alternative response is exemplified in Jesus' approach to the Samaritans and the reaction of Rachel Saint and Elisabeth Elliot to the Waorani people—the response of incarnation. Elliot and Saint were motivated not by vindication of their husband's and brother's deaths but by passion that Jesus Christ receive his rightful place of glory and honor among the Waorani people. Their response mirrored Jesus' joyful encounter with another despised and hated people, the Samaritans.

Such a response is by no means easy and requires a passionate and radical commitment to Christ. But this is no blind fanaticism. It also calls for a patient and painstaking understanding of people who see reality radically different from us. It requires a good deal of self-awareness for overcoming the natural tendency of fear toward self-preservation. Finally, it involves a careful evaluation of long-standing beliefs that may have become fetishes to a false tradition.

So if you are growing more skeptical about the possibility of eliminating the Muslim threat, and if you are looking for a unique response birthed out of the values of Christ's kingdom, then this book may have something to say to you. I make no claim to providing the final word but hope merely to open the discussion by proposing a

radical and incredibly challenging response to the Muslim world—
the alternative response of *incarnation*.

PART II
A HISTORICAL PERSPECTIVE

The complex web of Christian-Muslim relations is not a recent phenomenon. In order to adopt an informed response to the Muslim world, Christians need to understand the historic advance of Islamic civilization and its impact on Christian peoples. The reality is that Christians also resorted to militaristic responses and thereby contributed to the current impasse. The lesson of history is to adopt kingdom principles of response instead of the knee-jerk reaction of self-defense.

CHAPTER 2

A HISTORY OF COMPLICITY: WHO, ME?

Now here's a thought-provoking question for you: Could it be that we (primarily, Christians) have been complicit in the development of religious tyranny in the Muslim world?

I hear you saying, "Come on, you can't be serious—Western Christians to blame for what is happening today in the Muslim world? Give me a break! Is this a case of no good deed shall go unpunished? Haven't we Western Christians sent missionaries to Muslim lands? Haven't our governments given massive amounts of money and assistance to these countries? You can't be serious."

I recall the comment of my Cairo landlord as we discussed the intricacies of Muslim-Christian relations through the centuries. His perspective gave me pause for thought: "You Christians have treated Muslims far worse than Muslims have treated Christians." First of all,

I failed to appreciate his tendency to lump Christians and Europeans together. Second, I didn't agree.

No one wants to be blamed for something for which he or she bears no direct responsibility. I am not suggesting that you and I are to blame for what is happening. What I am asking is whether Western Christians have in any way been complicit in the current situation of the Muslim world. Jesus recognized in his contemporaries the same tendencies that were present in their forebears. He clearly told them, "Your forefathers . . . killed the prophets, and you build their tombs." His warning to them is absolutely chilling: "This generation will be held responsible for the blood of all the prophets that has been shed since the beginning of the world, from the blood of Abel to the blood of Zechariah, who was killed between the altar and the sanctuary" (Luke 11:48–51). He emphatically pointed out how his contemporaries were perpetrating the same murderous acts and that they would be held responsible. It must have been a shocking wake-up call for the Jews of Jesus' day to hear a viewpoint so radically opposed to their self-understanding.

Examining history can be a very self-congratulating act: "Look what they did in the era of ignorance. Look how far we have come!" It can be an academic exercise of observing events from a safe distance, with no sense of personal involvement whatsoever. As we take a look at some high points and sore points of Muslim-Christian interaction, let's be aware of Jesus' warning to his contemporaries. We may be repeating history unawares.

Christians and Muhammad

Our first stop in the history of Muslim-Christian interaction is the founding prophet of Islam, Muhammad, who lived from 570 to 632 CE in the Arabian Peninsula.

As a young man Muhammad was deeply disturbed by the polytheism of the Arab tribes. He began to associate with a group of monotheists (known in Arabic as *hunafaa*). His eighth-century biographer, Ibn Ishaq, stated that Muhammad was taught by Jabr, a Christian, as the two met on a hill called Al-Marwa, overlooking Mecca. This Jabr may have been an Ethiopian. The same biographer relates the story of Muhammad meeting Bahira, a Syrian monk, on a caravan journey with his uncle while still a youth. Bahira recognized that Muhammad possessed an innate greatness and warned of his future enmity with the Jews.[1]

Muhammad's practice was to spend extended times of meditation and prayer in a cave outside the city of Mecca. When Muhammad first received his call to prophethood in the Hira Cave, he had deep reservations about the experience that had taken place. As the *Hadiith* (the written traditions enshrining Muhammad's sayings and actions)[2] tells the story, Muhammad was visited by a luminous be-ing (in Islamic understanding, the angel Gabriel) who commanded him to "recite." The word could also be translated "read." To which Muhammad responded, "I am not a reader." The being then replied, "Recite in the name of your lord who created, created man from a clot. Read and your lord is the most beneficent."[3] Thus began the prophetic revelation given to Muhammad known as the *Qur'an.*

Muhammad returned from the Hira Cave quite perturbed in spirit. In fact, with his heart still racing from the experience, his first words to his wife, Khadija, were, "Cover me, cover me." He then related to her that he feared for himself. Khadija assured Muhammad that he was a virtuous man and that Allah would never disgrace him. She then proceeded to take Muhammad to her cousin Waraqa bin (the son of) Naufal.

This man Waraqa bin Naufal is an enigma in Islamic history. According to the Hadiith, he had become a Christian[4] in the pre-Islamic period. We do not know much about the nature of Waraqa's faith. The Hadiith tells us that he "would write from the Gospel in Hebrew as much as Allah wished him to write."[5]

What we do know about Waraqa is that he was the second voice of affirmation of Muhammad's prophetic call, Khadija being the first. What he affirmed in Muhammad was the original vision in the Hira Cave. He strongly buttressed Muhammad, saying that the revelation he had received was the same as the angel Gabriel had given to Moses. Furthermore, he predicted Muhammad's rejection by his own people and expressed regret that he would no longer be alive to lend Muhammad strong support in his hour of need. Waraqa was an old man and died before Muhammad's revelations took shape.

Roughly six hundred years had transpired between Pentecost and Muhammad's prophetic call. The Christian church had passed through a period of intense persecution at the hands of the Roman Empire and had risen to become a prestigious religion of Rome, whose capital was now Byzantine Constantinople (modern-day Istanbul, Turkey). The presence of Christians in the Arabian Peninsula is confirmed by Waraqa bin Naufal. Waraqa was likely an adherent of Nestorian Christianity,[6] considered a heresy by the early church councils. He was, nonetheless, a man who evidenced desire for the things of God. Perhaps we could see him as a type of many in the Arab world today—people who have a zeal for God, a desire

THE CHRISTIAN BYZANTINE EMPIRE (6TH CENTURY)

to know and understand, and yet have limited access to credible sources of information. Waraqa lives on in today's Muslim world. Samuel Hugh Moffett, professor of ecumenics and mission at Princeton Theological Seminary, suggests three reasons why Muhammad never became a Christian:

First, there was no Bible in Arabic. Missionaries had translated the Scriptures into other Asian languages, such as Syriac and Chinese, but not Arabic. Some church leaders knew Arabic, and it seems that translation could have progressed.[7] Much of the church's energy seems to have been expended in discussion of important doctrinal issues related to the nature of Christ.

Second, Christianity in the Middle East was a sad portrayal of disunity. Muhammad must have had some awareness of the angry divisions of the faith in his area, represented by Nestorians, Monophysites,[8] Chalcedonians, and heretical sects. Popes such as

Justinian, ruling from Constantinople, had attempted to unify the church's understanding of crucial doctrinal issues, especially the nature of Christ. Inevitably, churches that diverged from the orthodox position resented what they viewed as coercion by the powerful See of Constantinople.

Third, Christianity at that time and place was associated with imperialism. There was the Byzantine Empire to the north, which was Christian. The Persian Empire, flanking the Arabian Peninsula to the east and south, was largely Zoroastrian but with a notable Nestorian Christian population. The two empires had been at war for nearly a century (540–629),[9] and both sides lay exhausted and vulnerable. Neither empire could have anticipated that the real threat that would end both their ascendancies was being birthed by the prophetic call of an Arab caravan leader named Muhammad.

By 650 Mesopotamia, heart of the Persian Empire, had fallen into Muslim hands. Carthage, the Byzantine center in modern-day Tunisia (North Africa), fell to Islam in 697. The first attacks on Constantinople came in the early eighth century (717–718), although the city would not be ruled by Muslims until several centuries later.[10]

The picture that emerges is instructive. Muhammad had personal contact with people who were known as Christians. He may even have received extensive instruction from Christians. Although he viewed his own prophetic revelations as consonant with the former revelations to Moses and Christ, he moved beyond these to look for a new dynamic that would unite the Arab peoples in a faith in one God. He called this new dynamic Islam.

Conclusions on Church History

Drawing conclusions from history is complex and often suffers from our modern-day biases. Nevertheless, three conclusions seem inevitable from a superficial observation of the history of the church in Muhammad's day.

First, and most obvious, is that the church must devote itself to the final commission of Jesus—to make disciples of all nations. The marginalization of the Arabs and the failure to effectively teach the gospel of Christ in Arab lands continue to plague the church and the world until today.

Second, the church has a regrettable history of clothing the gospel in political power. Constantine's attempts to unify the church through church councils were a double-edged sword. On the one hand, standards of theological confession were established and continue to serve us well today. On the other hand, those standards became a tool in the hand of the empire to enforce standardization. The Greek and Latin doctrinal formulations of the early church, when clothed with political power, effectively snuffed out the divergent formulations of the Copts, the Syrians, and the Nestorians. These Eastern churches resented this theological heavy-handedness that translated itself, in their experience, into religious imperialism.

The fact is that the divergent views of the nature of Christ lived on in the area, although variations of language and culture have added to the complexity of identifying those divergences precisely. The problem was not the divergent views but the resentful division of church factions because of the imposition of a particular view by the more powerful churches. In fact, this kind of theological heavy-handedness made many of the churches in the Middle East long for a new master to take the place of the old Byzantine Empire (one reason

Islam met with little resistance as Christian Western Asia quickly fell to Islamic invaders). It also led to confusion among the Arabs as to who Jesus really is. While it is difficult to suggest an alternative to history, it is instructive to ponder what might have been the result if families of churches had respected each other's theological divergences and allowed time and dialogue to effect rapprochement.

Third, we must learn from this history that the kingdom of Christ transcends earthly kingdoms. It is a costly error when his kingdom becomes associated with a mere earthly power, no matter how just and right that power may seem to its adherents.

Are we guilty of the same? Is the church today enmeshed with political establishment such that other peoples and civilizations receive our overtures as heavy-handed imposition rather than gracious cooperation? Do we maintain our societal and civilizational identities at the expense of the kingdom of Christ? Are we Western Christians or Christians who happen to live in the West? Are we American Christians or Christ-followers who happen to be from the United States? Can the world tell the difference?

The Forward Movement of Islam and the Church of Augustine

Our second stop in this brief historical overview is the church of North Africa, whose most famous spokesman was Augustine. Although Augustine predated Islam, the church of Augustine existed throughout North Africa in the seventh century when the armies of Islam entered North Africa, resulting in a deep-rooted conversion to Islam that remains until today. The immediate question is, Why did this church with access to prominent theologians of Christian history such as Tertullian, Cyprian, and Augustine give way to Islam and fade out of existence?

A Missional Misstep

The church in North Africa did not die overnight. It suffered a slow death brought on by many contributing factors. One factor cries out for our attention in this overview.

Very simply, the church of North Africa was a Latin-speaking church; its theology and teaching were carried on in the language of the church of Rome. The urban centers of North Africa, such as Carthage, were occupied by Latin speakers in those days. However, the smaller villages and countryside were not nearly so latinized; the languages spoken in these areas were indigenous strains of Berber, such as Tamazight and Imazighen. There are good indicators suggesting that the church had extended well into the Berber areas of North Africa and was no longer a uniquely Latin church. Still, the teaching, correspondence, and theologizing of the church took place in Latin; and its leaders were Latin speakers.

While discussion of the faith probably took place in the local dialects, the Scriptures were never translated into the indigenous languages. Even Latin copies of the Scriptures were hard to come by in those days. The result was a compromised faith. The church was dependent on word-of-mouth discipleship. There was no systematic training of the local populace based on the truths of Scripture. Rather, the church of that day relied on a Latin-speaking, celibate leadership. The local believers (Berber speakers) who aspired to leadership in the churches must have felt it far beyond their reach.

The invasion of Arab armies effected a massive defection of church leadership from North Africa over a period of many years.

The Latin-speaking leadership of the North African church found it easier to return to its compatriots on the northern side of the Mediterranean than to hold fast amid the challenge of training an indigenous leadership for the North African church. As shepherds progressively abandoned their posts, the sheep were left defenseless and vulnerable. Thus conversions to Islam ensued, such that all that remains today of the historic churches of North Africa are artifacts and ruins.

North Africa: A Heritage Rich in Faith

The church of North Africa has often been referred to as the church of the martyrs. Cyprian himself was beheaded for his refusal to offer sacrifice to Roman deities. The account of his death stands as a memorial to one faithful shepherd who paid the ultimate price.

Another account tells of Perpetua, a young woman of Carthage, born to status and wealth uncommon to young women of her day. Her father had acquired his wealth in the service of Rome and was known as an outstanding and magnanimous citizen of the city. He had labored to afford his daughter the best education possible. Baffled by her refusal to renounce her newfound faith, he carried his grandson, Perpetua's son, in his arms as a final plea to his daughter to renounce her reckless ways. She asked, "Father, what do you see there in the corner of the cell?"

"It is a water pot."

"Could it be anything else?"

"No."

Perpetua responded, "Nor can I be anything other than what I am—a Christian." Her final days were spent nursing her son in her fetid prison cell, praying for him.

Perpetua's good friend, Felicitas, who was pregnant, entered prison with her and prayed to give birth before the date of their execution, as pregnant women were customarily spared.

The two young women along with three young men died in the arena after being mauled by savage beasts. A young Roman soldier was ordered to end Perpetua's life. When he failed to kill her efficiently, she steadied his sword to her breast by her own hand.[11]

The historic church in North Africa provided some of the most articulate theologians in the history of the church, as well as some of the most stunning tales of martyrdom. Its heritage stands tall among the scenes of church history. Yet history has revealed two failures. First, the church of that day failed to truly indigenize in every area, including worship, teaching, and translation of the Scriptures. Second, church leadership was held aloof and inaccessible to the local Berber population.

Perhaps we can best honor the legacy of the North African church by determining that these failures will not happen again. Much has been done to provide the Scriptures in local languages and dialects. That good work must continue. Care must also be taken that church leadership is effectively and quickly passed on to the local people of North Africa and the rest of the Muslim world.

Many more like Cyprian, Augustine, Perpetua, and Felicitas are waiting in the wings. Will they find us ready to stand with them as they establish the church among their people?

◆ SEEKING FRESH VISION ◆

I began this chapter by asking if Western Christians have played a role of complicity in the development of religious tyranny in the

Muslim world, and I noted the chilling response of Jesus to the religious rulers of his day as he held them responsible for the persecution and murder of prophets perpetrated by their forebears. The answer to the question may become clearer in subsequent chapters. For now, it is sufficient to note the attitudes and actions of our forebears during the early ages of Islam.

First, the message of the gospel was unclear to Arab peoples. They had no Bible. They also lived in the shadow of theological controversies that made no sense to them. Second, the theological contributions of the surrounding churches had been marginalized and undervalued by the prevailing Byzantine church. The early Islamic conquests in the Levant and Egypt found Coptic and Syriac churches at odds with Byzantine churches over papal loyalties and doctrinal disputes. For many, the Muslims were preferable to the domineering Byzantines. A third attitude is a missional misstep with overtones of ethnic superiority. The Berbers of North Africa were not enfolded into the leadership of the mighty North African church. As the Islamic conquests advanced through North Africa, the Latin church leaders gradually abandoned ship, leaving a shepherdless flock.

Additional Resources for Chapter 2

Daniel, Robin. *This Holy Seed: Faith, Hope and Love in the Early Churches of North Africa*. Harpenden: Tamarisk Publications, 1992.

Latourette, Kenneth Scott. *A History of Christianity: Volume I, Beginnings to 1500*. San Francisco: Harper, 1975.

See also books listed at the end of chapter 3.

CHAPTER 3

GIVE BACK MY HOLY LAND!

Our next stop on this historical survey is a sore point of Muslim-Christian relations: the Crusades.

Modern-day reaction to the Crusades in the Muslim world is legendary. Being an American Protestant, I was only vaguely familiar with these religious wars of the Middle Ages. For me (and I suspect for most Americans) they had virtually nothing to do with my faith and practice of Christianity. Was I ever in for a rude awakening!

The symbol of the cross embodies our most cherished convictions. It is a symbol of peace triumphing over violence, of humility putting arrogance to route, of reconciliation between God and humanity. My first recollection of the cross was a large one my grandmother kept in her bedroom. The cross invokes all we hold dear as followers of Christ.

As a student of Arabic, I soon learned that translating words is relatively simple; what's challenging is translating the correct connotations. The word *cross* in Arabic is *saliib*. The Crusades are known in the Arab world as *the wars of the cross-ites* or *the cross-wars*. Why cross-wars? The simple answer is that the Crusaders came to the Middle East from Europe with the symbol of their faith, the cross, emblazoned on their shields and banners. It only made sense that locals began to call these invaders *cross-ites*. An amazing irony of history stripped away the connotations I associated with the cross for a large percentage of humanity—the Muslim world! The casual referral by a U. S. president to Gulf War II as a crusade raised the ire of the Muslim world for the simple reason that it was translated into the word *cross-war*.

No doubt the cross really was central to many Crusader aspirations. Often the motivation for participating in the Crusades was the redemption of one's soul, although of course this was before the days of Martin Luther's insistence on justification by faith. Regaining lands taken by Muslim invaders clearly served as motivation also. When early Crusaders took back Jerusalem, the Crusader crown, they perceived their victory as a token of divine approbation and blessing on their cause. However, the crown was lost again.

The film *Kingdom of Heaven* portrayed the Muslim hero who recaptured Jerusalem. I remember viewing this film in a theater in Cairo. Saladin's appearance evoked sighs and whispers of admiration from the crowd. Saladin (known in Arabic as Salah al-Diin) may be second only to Muhammad in Islamic society as the epitome of manhood, courage, valor, and magnanimity. A wise military strategist and statesman of Islam, Salah al-Diin was admired for his courage and moderation in the craft of war. He retains pride of place for having rid the Holy Land of the cross-ite scourge. He was remarkably lenient toward the Crusader population as well.

And, yes, Jerusalem (in Arabic *al-Quds*, meaning "the Holy") is a holy place for Muslims. Muhammad related how he had been miraculously transferred from Mecca to Jerusalem and raised up from there through the seven heavens to see visions of the glory of Allah. It was in this miraculous midnight journey that Muhammad received divine permission to limit the number of required daily prayers for Muslims to five. He also led the prophets in prayer and even records having seen Jesus in the third of the seven heavens. The magnificent Dome of the Rock was built to commemorate the site of Muhammad's transport into heaven.[1] Its construction on the temple mount fuels contention between Muslims, Jews, and Christians to this day.

Muslims took Jerusalem and other major Christian strongholds such as Damascus and Alexandria within thirty years of Muhammad's death. Byzantium and its capital, Constantinople, were feeling the heat of the Islamic advance. Constantinople stood fast against early Islamic incursions but grew weaker through the centuries and eventually called on the Western church to help secure pilgrimage routes to Jerusalem, the ostensible kickoff of the Crusades.

Having begun by successfully recapturing Jerusalem, the Crusades ended some two hundred years later in ignominy, at least for the European invaders. The Christian lands that had been retaken were lost again to Muslim armies. History records not only that Muslims were estranged by the Crusader armies but also that the wars did irreparable harm to relations between the Eastern and Western branches of the church, including the Fourth Crusade when Catholic armies sacked Constantinople and placed a Western king on the throne. Jews had also suffered a hideous fate at the hands of the Crusaders. Although conceived in a spirit of pious devotion, the Crusades remain a blight on the history of the medieval church.

Contemporary reactions among Western Christians typically abjure the Crusades as Christian zeal gone awry. Protestants and evangelicals may tend to plead innocence, such as the friend I spoke with recently who smiled and said, "Those Muslims just don't realize that the Crusaders were not real Christians, do they?" On the other hand, some Christians have taken seriously the need to redress the wrongs perpetrated by the Crusades. A recent tour of Western Christians through the Middle East to apologize for the wrongs done was well received by Middle Easterners, even though they detected a note of irony in the apologies—given the presence of Western military throughout the Muslim world.

Although the Crusades ended centuries ago, Muslims are convinced that the old enmity has reared its ugly head. As a guest in the Muslim world, I had no sense of continued antagonism toward the Muslim world or any desire to retake territory (actual land) for Christ or the church. However, my Muslim friends keenly perceive an ever-present attempt to regain influence over Islamic lands. They see it in the Western media that flood into Islamic countries. They see it in the predominance of the English language for purposes of travel and business. They see it in U.S. military bases in the heart of Islamic countries such as Kuwait, Qatar, and Saudi Arabia. Most of all, they see it in the state of Israel, which in their opinion exists under the protective shade of Western nations such as the United States and Great Britain.

For many Muslims the tiny state of Israel is a twentieth-century foothold for a new Crusader effort: the cross-ites have returned and have taken Muslim territory. I'll return to this delicate subject, but it is important, if we wish to gain some appreciation for the Muslim perspective, to establish the link between the Crusades and the modern state of Israel. Most of us in the West would never make such a link. But in the minds of Muslims, that link is simply self-evident.

Two Examples of Islamic Largesse

While living among Muslims, I was exposed to a slightly different reading of history. For me the Renaissance period, which sparked astounding advances in various fields of scientific and artistic endeavor, resulted from an awakening within Europe, the culmination of religious, political, and social forces that ultimately led to the European Enlightenment—a massive leap forward in human civilization. The Protestant Reformation was part of the broad sweep of this cultural and intellectual movement. Never had I considered that the Muslim world may have played some role in this positive momentum. I viewed the Muslim world as repressive and regressive, offering little to human civilization in the way of cultural advancement. My view was arrogant.

Islam and the Renaissance

Imagine my shock at learning from my Muslim friends that the fuel of the European Renaissance was an Islamic Renaissance. Granted, some of my Muslim friends vastly overstated their case. Nevertheless, upon reading the history a little more attentively, I understood that Islamic civilization did make a notable contribution to the revival of science in Europe. The Renaissance was sparked by a return to Greek thinkers who had largely been lost to European civilization during the medieval period. Just how did that Greek thought reappear among European intellectuals?

Two Islamic cultural hubs flourished during the medieval period. One, the Abbasid Empire, was based in Baghdad. The second was based in southern Spain (Andalusia) and retained the name of a former Islamic empire based in Damascus, Syria—the Umayyad Empire. In both Baghdad and Cordoba, science and literature, medicine and poetry, philosophy and theology were all the rage. Intellectual activity was cresting while Christian Europe languished in its Dark Ages. Muslim intellectuals tout the virtues of Abbasid Baghdad and Umayyad Cordoba as centers of profound scholarship and religious tolerance as people of other faiths (Christians and Jews) held posts of eminent prestige.[2]

The notable contributions of these two Islamic cities include medicine (sterile surgical techniques were being pioneered in Baghdad), astrology, philosophy (Averroës—known in Arabic as Ibn Rushd—was from Andalusia), mathematics (*algebra* is an Arabic word, and the West borrowed its numeric system from the Arabs), law, and agriculture (Spanish agricultural terms are often derived from Arabic). To sustain this intellectual thrust, great effort was expended in translation. The Abbasids drew on Persian, Indian, and Greek sources, while Umayyad Cordoba became the most enlightened city of Europe in the ninth and tenth centuries, engaging in the translation of various works of antiquity.

It was returning Crusaders who brought news of Abbasid advances back to Europe. Cordoba's library proved to be a channel of vibrant scholarship that flowed back into Europe to help spark the Renaissance. Greek thinkers such as Aristotle made their way back into Europe through Arabic translation, thanks to the foresight of Muslim scholars. Sicily, which had been Islamic until the Normans overtook it in the eleventh century, was another conduit through which Muslim science made its way back into Europe.

The Decline of Islamic Cultural Centers

These two great Islamic cities, Baghdad and Cordoba, went into decline. Andalusia was plagued by dissension from within. The Reconquista (reconquest) of Spain by Christian Europe terminated the presence of Islam in the Iberian Peninsula but not completely until 1492, when the last Muslim stronghold of Granada was vanquished. Muslims were banished from the peninsula. In the same year Jews were either banished or killed during another embarrassing episode of church history—the Spanish Inquisition.

The history of Andalusia is remembered fondly by Muslims and often upheld as the epitome of Islamic tolerance and pluralism. The Christian Reconquista combined with the Spanish Inquisition showed extreme intolerance on the part of Christian Europeans. The Abbasid Empire, now weakened by the Crusades, suffered its most devastating blow at the hands of Mongol invaders who later converted to Islam. At the high point of Abbasid prestige, there was relative tolerance for Christians in the empire. As the Abbasid rule began to fragment, cases of discrimination and persecution against Christians increased.

Perhaps my Cairo landlord (mentioned at the beginning of chapter 2) had Andalusia and the Abbasids in mind when he insisted that Muslims had been more fair and open minded in their treatment of Christians than Christians had been in their treatment of Muslims. I certainly do not wish to suggest that relations between the two faiths were rosy as long as Muslims were in power; far from it. Countless examples of political and religious tyranny lie on both sides of Muslim-Christian interaction. However, the Abbasids of Baghdad and Umayyads of Cordoba provide refreshing counterexamples and continue to serve as a rallying point for reform-minded Muslims even today. It is important that Christians recognize their contribution.

Two Exceptions from within Christendom

While the medieval church was detained with wresting "Christian" lands from the hands of Muslims, there arose two refreshing individuals who perceived their mission to Muslims to be of an entirely different nature.

St. Francis of Assisi

The forbearance and virtues of St. Francis of Assisi are legendary. He lived in the thirteenth century during the time of the Crusades. Along with his piety and recognition of the hand of God in every detail of creation, St. Francis demonstrated a profound sense of mission. His early preaching moved both men and women to join his ascetic movement, renouncing all material possessions. The Franciscans moved about itinerantly, joining the agricultural labors of their countrymen and singing forth the praises of God as they worked. Francis's devotion and selfless service won the admiration of many as leading men and women of the time voluntarily associated with him in his poverty and itinerant ministry.

Francis lived in a day not unlike our own, when there was much talk of the *Saracen* (Muslim) enemy. Vast armies were recruited to retake "Christian lands," and many saw the salvation of their souls as tied up in this effort to regain lost territory. Lamentably, we do not know more of Francis's perception of the events of his era. What we do know is that Francis made three separate attempts to go to the Muslim world, the first in 1212. A shipwreck prohibited him from making his way to Syria. In 1214 he attempted to go to Morocco but fell ill in Spain and was forced to return home yet again.

Finally, Francis departed for St. Jean d'Acre in May 1219. He had assigned ministry areas to others of his entourage, but for himself he reserved the seat of the Islamic-Crusader conflict so preeminent in his day. He witnessed the Crusader takeover of Damietta (in Egypt). After having preached to the Crusader army, Francis fearlessly crossed over to the enemy camp, and the sultan of Egypt received him favorably. Very little is known about the actual exchange between the two, but it is thought that Francis secured a promise from the sultan that he would treat Crusader prisoners amicably.

Francis traveled on to various sites in modern-day Israel. Although details of his voyage are unknown, it is believed that Francis secured a foothold for the Franciscans in these lands that remains yet today. This suggests that Francis was viewed favorably and trusted even by Muslim rulers who were sovereign in these lands.[3]

What possessed this unassuming saint to believe that he could enter the fray of the Crusades and somehow make a difference? How was it that, living in a time when one's willingness to fight in the way of God was the thermometer of spiritual life, he called on his followers to disavow the use of arms forever? Whatever our view of Francis's spirituality and ascetic lifestyle, he confronts us to this day with a missional view of the Muslim world as unconventional then as it is now. Francis must have believed that the message of the gospel had implications for a centuries-old conflict known as the Crusades. He was courageous enough to proclaim his vision before Crusader and Saracen armies.

Ramon Llull

Ramon Llull, born to a life of ease and luxury, lived in Spain just after Francis and shared with him a vision for the Muslim world. Recurrent visions of Christ on the cross resulted in his conversion to Christianity. Llull promptly sold his possessions, made arrangements for his wife and family, and then devoted himself to his newfound faith and the monastic order of the Franciscans. Perhaps his intrigue with mysticism was the bridge that led Llull into his work with Muslims. He became fascinated with Sufi Islam—a mystical school of thought that focuses on worshipping Allah through experience. As he delved deeper into Islam, Llull began to train others who would be missionaries to the Muslim world. Gradually, he developed principles for Christian interaction with Muslims.

The first principle was to develop effective communication with Islamic peoples through a mastery of their language. He studied Arabic assiduously and taught it to others. (Might I add parenthetically that Llull saw in his day what many mission activists today are slow to understand: an essential aspect of the incarnation of the gospel in a given culture is that it must be clothed in the local language.)

His second principle was to stress philosophy and logic as a means to establishing truth through rational proofs. In his passion to engage the Muslim world, he took on the leading Muslim philosopher of that era, Averroës. Ramon Llull advocated reason as an aid to faith and vice versa. He was convinced that Averroës had made a complete separation of faith and reason and sought to demonstrate that in his mission efforts.

Llull also advocated reform in the medieval church. In his extensive itinerant ministry, he exhorted the church to lay aside its pomp and luxury in exchange for a missionary vision—particularly a vision for the Muslim world. Lastly, he urged that one-tenth of the church's income should be designated to missionary activity.

Ramon Llull made numerous journeys into North Africa, where he debated Islamic scholars. At the mature age of eighty, Llull was still making forays into Muslim North Africa, but during one visit he was stoned with such severity that he died aboard ship on the return voyage to Majorca.[4]

◆ SEEKING FRESH VISION ◆

The Middle Ages saw the fissure between East and West grow into a gaping fracture. The initial thrust of the Islamic conquerors effected the fall of Western Asia, formerly Christian and under Roman rule, into the hands of Muslims. Islam dominated North Africa and the Middle East and threatened the eastern flank of the Byzantine Empire. Already a recipe for cultural and civilizational conflict was being concocted.

Although exceptions existed among the irenic Franciscans and Dominicans of the time, the future did not bode well for Muslim-Christian relations nor for the embrace of Christian truth in the lands that had now come to be dominated by Islam.

A brief survey of history such as this chapter necessarily omits many important elements. The point I wish to stress is that as the religion of Islam comes under increasing scrutiny for intolerance and its failure to provide basic human freedoms to its people, the history of Muslim-Christian relations shows that there were excesses on both sides of the divide; the examples of Christian coercion and violence are numerous and embarrassing. On the other hand, one can find examples of remarkable tolerance on the part of Muslims, given the surrounding culture and worldview.

Perhaps a broader historical perspective will afford Christians more patience as Islamic nations struggle to come to terms with a modern and postmodern world. Jesus' instruction to remove the plank from your own eye before attempting to remove the speck from your brother's eye will serve us well.

Additional Resources for Chapter 3

Mallouhi, Christine A. *Waging Peace on Islam.* London: Monarch Books, 2000. Mallouhi draws from her long experience in the Muslim world, pointing to St. Francis as a model of Christian interaction with Muslims.

Moffett, Samuel Hugh. *A History of Christianity in Asia, Volume I: Beginnings to 1500.* Maryknoll, New York: Orbis Books, 1998.

Riddell, Peter G., and Peter Cotterell. *Islam in Context: Past, Present, and Future.* Grand Rapids: Baker Academic Books, 2003.

Zebiri, Kate. *Muslims and Christians Face to Face.* Oxford: Oneworld, 1997.

CHAPTER 4

TWO WORLD WARS AND A NEW REALITY

A delightful Egyptian proverb reveals much about leadership: "Pharaoh, who made you Pharaoh?" Pharaoh's reply: "No one stood in my way."

The fact is that the Islamic world today is without a clearly appointed leader. That is a sore spot for many Muslims and important for our understanding of the contemporary situation in the Muslim world. Here's how it happened, in brief.

The Effects of World Wars I and II

When Muhammad died, the Islamic nation elected to place authority in the hands of a man named Abu Bakr. This man became the first *caliph*. *Caliph* is an Arabic word that can be translated as "successor." Abu Bakr was followed by three others who, together with Abu Bakr, became known by Sunni Muslims (85 percent of the world's Muslims) as *the rightly guided caliphate.*

Ali was Muhammad's nephew and the last of the rightly guided caliphs. During his rule a struggle erupted for the caliphate, which spawned the Shiite-Sunni controversy. The leadership of the Islamic community moved to Syria under the Umayyad dynasty (660–750). Later, Islamic civilization reached its zenith in the Abbasid dynasty in Baghdad (750–1258). During these epochs Islam was under the guidance of a caliph, a figure who held political and religious authority. Later the caliphate passed into the hands of the Ottoman Turks, who held it from 1512 to 1922.

Events of recent times have led to the disappearance of the Islamic caliphate. Most Westerners do not understand the gravity of that fact. The caliph could be compared to the Roman Catholic pope in terms of his prestige and authority. He was not merely a religious authority. He acted as head of state and was the unifying image of the far-flung world of Islam, referred to in Arabic as the *umma* (nation) of Islam.

Shiites continue to have a different perspective on the caliphate. In brief, their belief is that the leadership of the Islamic nation should remain in the family of Muhammad. Therefore they recognize only Muhammad's nephew Ali (the fourth of the rightly guided caliphs) as the legitimate successor of the prophet. Ali's two sons, Hassan and Hussein, were both killed at war. In the battle of Karbala (680 CE), seventy of Ali's family were brutally killed in war against the Umayyad rulers. A succession of eleven *imams* (leaders of the Islamic community, deemed to be successors of Muhammad) followed them as rulers. The twelfth imam strangely disappeared, and Shiites await his reappearance as the ruler of the Islamic nation.

With the rise of the Ottoman Empire, the Sunni caliphate passed over to Istanbul and remained until the end of World War I. Turkey was on the losing side in World War I. The end of the war signaled the demise of the Ottoman Empire. Its constituent parts were parceled out by the victors of that war, the Allied powers. France had already established colonies in the North African countries of Morocco (1912), Algeria (1830), and Tunisia (1881). Italy set up its establishment in Libya (1911), and the British controlled Egypt (1882). After World War I, Western domination extended its reach, with France taking power in Lebanon and Syria and Great Britain in control of Iraq, Palestine, and Transjordan.

With the end of World War I and Attaturk's establishment of Turkey as a secular state (1924), the thirteen-hundred-year-old establishment known as the caliphate ended. The icon of the once-powerful Sunni Muslim world simply was no more. It did not merely disappear; it was vanquished by the Allied powers, which proceeded to place its nation-states in subjection. Those Allied powers were Christian Europe!

One of Usama bin Laden's videotapes, released on October 7, 2001, contains a reference to the "humiliation and disgrace" suffered by Islam for a period of "more than eighty years."[1] For Muslims, imminently familiar with and intimately related to their history, there was no doubt as to what bin Laden was referring. The abolishment of the caliphate and the fragmentation of the Ottoman Empire were the signal events of the humiliation of the Muslim world.

Although World War I was of a vastly different nature from the Crusades, to Muslims it had the same effect. It brought Islamic territory under subjection to Christian nations. This incredible turn of events pronounced the verdict of history that Islamic civilization was in decline, that the Islamic world no longer held power, and that the Christian West was in a position of superiority. For modern-day Muslims it also illustrates the territorial aspirations of Western (Christian) nations that used their position of authority and military supremacy to rule Islamic territory.

While Europe tended to view itself as the protectors and ad-ministrators of these Muslim nations, the nations themselves most often took the perspective that the intruders were also exploiters. Bernard Lewis points out that even the names given to these na-tions (Libya, Syria, etc.) were constructs of the vanquishing Western powers forcing a geographic identity on a people who had always identified themselves as Muslims and the aggressors as infidels.[2] One by one, these nations cast off European domination. In some cases the Europeans ceded power willingly. In other cases wars of independence were fought.

The Muslim world was in a weakened position during World War II. Its primary role in the war was that of battlefield. Many vet-erans of the war have told me of their sojourn in Morocco, Algeria, or Egypt. The most poignant result of World War II for our purposes is the establishment of Israel in 1948. (Rather than delve into that subject now, let's finish our historic survey. Israel deserves special attention in subsequent chapters.)

Afghanistan and Iraq

It would be hard to overestimate the importance of the war in Afghanistan for Muslim peoples. I am not referring to the post-9/11 war of the United States against the Taliban but to the long incursion of the Soviet Union into Afghanistan (1979–89). A combination of Saudi oil money, U.S. military technology, and Islamic zeal handed the former Soviet Union its own Vietnam and resurrected a ray of hope for Islamists.[3] While Americans viewed Afghanistan as a Cold War victory, Muslims viewed it as a victory for Islam. After all, they had recruited the manpower from Afghanistan and the Arab world to fend off one of the world's two superpowers. In the process *jihad* demonstrated its viability, giving birth to an elaborate system of training guerrilla fighters through camps that combined Islamic piety with military maneuvers. After the Afghan war jihadists returned to their countries having experienced the power of the Islamic cause and fueled with a passion to cast the foreigner out of Muslim lands. The U.S. policy at the time was to provide funding to armed factions willing to resist the Soviet incursion. In Afghanistan, those willing to resist were the Islamists—the forerunners of today's al Qaeda.

Many times I've been asked by Middle Easterners why the United States was so shortsighted as to supply bin Laden and his co-jihadists with arms and training. "Didn't you realize that bin Laden was a snake in the grass and would turn and bite you?" Although I don't offer a ready answer to my friends in the Arab world, I suspect that the U.S. administration was confident that its initiatives toward bin Laden and other Middle Eastern states would be recognized as benevolent. After all, they sought to repulse a territorial invasion by the Soviets.

However, from the perspective of many Muslims, the U.S. occupation of Iraq and its military presence in the Arabian Peninsula are equally as pernicious as the Soviet occupation of Afghanistan. The American objective is to further its own economic interests through the establishment of a free-market economy, and Americans feel strongly that this is a service to the Middle East, but Middle Easterners perceive it as a monopolizing of their limited resources by the power-hungry, consumerist American economy. To them, securing petroleum and other resources smacks of self-service and economic strong-arming of a vulnerable Muslim state. Arabs often suspect the United States of a new kind of imperialism—economic imperialism. Bin Laden's *fatwas* (religious edicts) voice these suspicions, as do the Arab media.

I am neither defending the United States nor lending credence to charges of imperialism leveled at our country. I merely point out that what we assume to be benevolence is most often received as belligerence. The victory of bin Laden's *mujahideen* (guerrilla fighters) over the Soviet Union in Afghanistan has won a lasting admiration from many Muslims. Small wonder that the ideology of jihad seems to be spreading like wildfire through the Muslim world.

Gulf War I

The early 1990s witnessed a direct military intervention of the United States in an Arab Muslim land—the liberation of Kuwait from the occupation of Saddam Hussein's forces. Surely, this was an opportunity for the United States to prove its goodwill by coming to the aid of a weak and needy Muslim nation. Great effort was expended to build a coalition including many Arab nations, some of which sent token troops into the conflict.

There was significant Muslim resistance to the U.S. intervention from the outset. Respected allies such as Jordan and Tunisia refused to lend support to the war effort. Some of the nations that entered the coalition later gave only qualified support. Many voiced their opinion that Saddam was clearly wrong to invade a neighboring Muslim state but that the United States was not justified in its attempt to bring resolution—this was an in-house situation and needed an inter-Arab solution. In the end Gulf War I only compounded suspicion and antagonism toward the United States. The nail in the coffin of Arab and Muslim sentiment toward the United States was that the holy land of Saudi Arabia was used as a staging platform for the aggression against Iraq. America's war would be waged against the flower of bygone Islamic greatness—Baghdad—from the land of the Prophet's birth and Islam's inception. The foreign invasion could not have been more ill conceived, shameful, ignominious. Benevolence was received as belligerence yet again.

As I reflect over my sojourn in the Middle East, the Gulf War was the first occasion I recall experiencing overt antagonism due to my being American. No one I knew was particularly fond of Saddam Hussein, and many would have been happy to see him removed from power. However, there was near universal suspicion that the United States was acting only to secure its own interests. The motivation of benevolence toward tiny Kuwait rang hollow in the Muslim world. The importance of Middle Eastern oil to the national interests of the United States is no secret. The United States, in the eyes of many Arabs, simply could not afford the risk that the oil-laden country of Kuwait would fall into the hands of a tyrant with aspirations to overrun other oil-rich countries. Once again, what most Americans saw as a gesture of nobility was perceived by Middle Easterners to be a fat and spoiled rich kid grabbing the last chicken leg at a picnic and trampling over a dignified grandmother to do it! Of all the Arab countries, only Kuwait remains grateful for the intervention.

9/11: The Muslim Reaction

The epoch-making event 9/11 blew the lid off the boiling pot of relations between the Islamic East and the Christian West. What an incredible time to be in the heart of a Middle Eastern city and try to come to terms with the Muslim reaction! What I offer here is not a scholarly analysis of data but an experiential observation by one American who was desperately trying to understand.

A week ago I was invited to share a meal with a lovely couple whose thirty-eight-year-old son died in one of the towers on that fateful day. What I say here can never mollify the horrific evil that was done that day to thousands of American families as well as many guests living in our country. In no way do I wish to make light of that event or cast it in such a way as to exonerate the murderers. Please understand that is not my desire. I will attempt to portray some of the emotions displayed by Muslims in response to that day and also to give my analysis of that display.

It must be said that some Middle Easterners were horrified at what transpired. I certainly found that to be the case in the Arab Christian church. Our family received calls expressing condolences from some of our neighbors and friends. Some were Muslim. Many were Christian.

In the minds of many Muslims, 9/11 was the revenge of Allah paid out to his enemies. You ask, revenge for what? For things described in this chapter as well as for American support of Israel. In the modern era, Muslim countries have been shamefully defeated by the West. Both world wars saw massive losses by Muslims. Four successive wars with Israel have demonstrated Israeli military superiority—a superiority Israel has taken from its Western allies, especially the United States. An incursion into Iraq by a coalition of primarily Western nations proved that even the most resilient of Arab rulers and armies could not stand up against the magnificent U.S. military machine.

At the end of the twentieth century, the Muslim nations of the world were down for the count. The only point of light on the Islamic horizon was a group of young mujahideen in Afghanistan, originating from all over the Muslim world and led by a fearless Saudi Arabian who managed to use Saudi money and American military technology to fend off a superpower. Usama bin Laden had demonstrated that Allah's wars fought in Allah's way would never lack Allah's blessing. Afghanistan remained a Muslim nation.

A further irritant is the constant assault of Western media on the eyes and ears of Muslim peoples through the Internet, satellite television, and print media. The siren call of Hollywood in Muslim societies purveys immorality and Western materialism in a society that is supremely God conscious and often materially deprived. Numerous times I have listened to Muslim friends' tirades about the deluge of immorality, pornography, and materialism coming from the West. Typically my response is to gently point out that impurity can come to rest only in hearts that are receptive to it—human hearts, whether Western or Eastern. Certainly the Middle East, though typically a more conservative society, has its share of vices. Nevertheless, the common perception in the Muslim world is that licentious media find their source in the West.

Would it not be only reasonable that the jihadists—the warriors of Islam—would make the situation right, restoring the splendor of the Islamic state and establishing Islamic morality? Usama bin Laden had demonstrated the force of jihad in Afghanistan. Now his religious zeal turned on his onetime ally. In a daredevil attempt to restore some sense of honor to a defeated and dejected Muslim world, bin Laden ordered his jihadists to carry out the 9/11 attacks. Their effect exceeded all hopes and dreams. The mighty bastions of capitalism—symbols of American economic superiority—fell to the ground in a burst of flame. The collapse of the twin towers as well as the damage inflicted on the Pentagon brought an immediate surge of hope to Muslims that their civilization would live again. I believe that Usama bin Laden's message to the Muslim world was, "If we fight as Allah would have us fight, we will prevail against any foe"—for many Muslims a convincing message.

9/11: A Victory for Jihad?

Islam is often misread by non-Muslims to refer to a religious belief, one that is largely internal and personal. While this is true, it is a half-truth. The personal-faith aspect of Islam finds a clear parallel in Christianity and is therefore understandable for most Western Christians. However, there is further dimension of Islam—that of a state—that is misunderstood by non-Muslims as it is quite unfamiliar to them.

In this sense, the word *Islam* has "two related but distinct meanings, as the equivalents both of Christianity and of Christendom."[4] In this worldview of a religious state, borders are recognizable and territorial. Armies are the means of defense of those borders. Funds are collected for the support of religious purposes. Finally, defense of the religious state takes on an overwhelming importance. That defense, in Islam, is known as jihad.[5]

We will delve more deeply into jihad in a subsequent chapter. For the time being it will suffice to note that one can hardly read the primary sources of Islam—Qur'an, Hadiith, the *Sira* (or *Life of the Prophet*), and others—without realizing the immense importance of the concept of jihad throughout the history of Islam. The word *jihad* means "struggle or striving." It was the term most often used to depict Muhammad's armed struggle to establish Islam. Muhammad and the caliphs who succeeded him believed in the validity of jihad to establish Islam in the world.

This explains in part the sense of euphoria in the Muslim world as a street-level reaction when the towers fell on September 11, 2001. Jihad had won a great victory. While the hope of reversing the centuries-long decline in Islamic prestige and power remained elusive, many Muslims perceived a jihad-like breakthrough in 9/11. It was a strike back at Western superiority and belligerence. Al Qaeda had resurrected jihad and taken the victory. Perhaps what followed would be a brighter day for Islam. As for the infidels, could 9/11 be the twilight of their day of supremacy giving way to a dawn of descent? This major blow to the American economic goliath gave hope, though little assurance. The superiority of Islam, eclipsed as it was in the twentieth century, could reemerge in the twenty-first century led by the vanguard of the mujahideen. That hope has yet to be snuffed out.

I realize this is an inadequate analogy, but many Americans will remember the race to put a man on the moon during the Cold War era. The United States had been brought up short as Sputnik demonstrated Soviet savvy in space technology. Surely the future lay in the hands of the power that could tame this vast wilderness called outer space! Vietnam saw the American malaise degenerate further still. The 1960s witnessed the advent of a youth rebellion giving expression to a country that had temporarily lost her bearings. I even remember hearing sermons as a child that left me chilled with fear of an unavoidable nuclear conflict with the USSR.

Suddenly news of the Apollo moon expeditions gave reprieve to a country struggling with its own destiny on the world scene. There was a ray of hope, captured in Neil Armstrong's memorable phrase "One small step for man, one giant leap for mankind." America reasserted herself with vigor.

For some Muslims 9/11 represented a vigorous reassertion of Islamic power after more than a century of shameful decline. For the Muslim world the sense of hope was even more palpable than for the United States during the Cold War simply because the decline of the Muslim world was unquestioned. Whereas the reinvigoration of the United States demonstrated its technological prowess, the hoped-for reinvigoration of the Muslim world was of a religious nature. "Islam is the solution"—this catchphrase of the Islamic brotherhood captured the hope of Islamic resurgence. "Our solution will flow out of what is most valuable to us and what most clearly distinguishes us from all the rest—Islam! *Allahu akbar* [Allah is greater]!"

The attack on the prized icon of American capitalism brought a swift response from the American military machine. The United States was in no mood to negotiate, and once al Qaeda was clearly recognized as the culprit, an invasion of Afghanistan became a foregone conclusion. Although 9/11 brought a tangible expectation to the streets of the Muslim world, it was a precarious hope. Bin Laden had clearly overstepped his bounds. Afghanistan, one of the poorest of the world's countries, would endure the rage of a smitten superpower. The Taliban were ousted and power handed to a new Afghan leadership. Like a champion fighter the American military machine made quick work of the Taliban resistance that had seemed so invincible during the war with the Soviets. Alas, for the Muslim world things were not as they seemed. An Islamic stronghold fell swiftly and was occupied by the foreign infidels.

The mujahideen were dispersed. It's anyone's guess where they ended up after the war in Afghanistan. What is sure is that they later made their way into Iraq to carry on their resistance to American superiority.

Gulf War II

If the first Gulf War drew only halfhearted support from a few Muslim countries, the second Gulf War would be actively opposed by the Muslim world. While many Muslim countries saw a real threat in weapons of mass destruction in the hands of Saddam Hussein, no Arab country viewed Saddam in the same category as the Taliban and Usama bin Laden. Saddam was well known throughout the Arab world as a Baathist—a left-leaning tyrant who had exploited religion when it suited him but had little use for fundamentalist Islam.

Many of my Muslim friends saw Gulf War II as the American president's vendetta for the attempt on his father's life and a desire to capture Baghdad as the prize of his presidential legacy. The swift incursion into Iraq that saw Baghdad fall in a matter of weeks was no surprise to the nations of the Muslim world. Arabs chuckled along with the rest of the world as the Iraqi general emphatically declared that Baghdad was not under foreign occupation while CNN showed American tanks rumbling through Baghdad streets even as the general spoke. But it was an embarrassed laugh. You laugh at yourself to avoid further embarrassment—something like that.

The strongman of Baghdad was not strong at all. The American army drove him to hide in a hole in the ground. His only companions were the dollars he had stolen from his fellow countrymen. I can't forget the embarrassment to the Arab and Muslim peoples as Saddam appeared for the first time in public, unshaven and disheveled, his mouth wide open as a dentist inspected his teeth. It was a degrading scene for the deposed statesman, and I believe it symbolized the way many Muslims saw their own society. Once they were strong, very strong. Now the emperor had no clothes. The reality was only too painful. There was no dignity, no honor, no Muslim nation.

Need we mention Abu Ghurayb? Those soldiers were punished quickly and thoroughly for their behavior—I suppose. However, if you think the punishment inflicted on those soldiers somehow expunged the horrific shame of what transpired, think again. As Westerners we tend to think in categories of right and wrong. Wrong is punished. Right is rewarded. Fine. Most Muslim societies have a different way of viewing the world, which has been called *shame-honor*. There is great incentive to avoid shame, and the ultimate good is to bring honor on yourself, your family, your clan, your country. The Abu Ghurayb debacle was shame personified. Arab families watched in horror as female soldiers in American military garb were shown exploiting the nudity of Arab male Muslim prisoners of war. Men who represented the vanguard of Muslim and Arab resistance became the play objects of female soldiers.

Near Mahmoudiya, Iraq, American soldiers watched from their checkpoint station as a fourteen-year-old girl tended the family garden and carried out her chores at her home about two hundred meters from the checkpoint. Because of security risks, her father had refused to let young Abeer go to school. On March 12, 2006, the soldiers changed into black civilian clothing and entered Abeer's house. Her parents and younger sister were taken into a separate room and murdered. Abeer was raped repeatedly by three soldiers. She was shot by one of the soldiers after their brutal deed was complete. The soldiers proceeded to set the house on fire.[6]

I'm sure no sane person would fail to be moved to disgust and pity by the account of Abeer's rape and murder. However, for Iraqis, Arabs, and Muslims, the incident becomes symbolic of American disregard of cultural and religious values. The event takes on collective significance as Abeer's innocence and beauty are set in stark contrast to the evil intentions of her attackers. The shame of rape and murder can never be absorbed by declarations that the guilty will be punished. In the minds of Muslims, the rape of Abeer is tantamount to the rape of Iraq. To say such a thing goes against my love of country and sense of propriety, but I believe it to be an accurate depiction of the way many Middle Easterners view the presence of American troops in Iraq and other countries.

I must add a side note. I hold the men and women of the U. S. armed forces in high regard. My dad is a Marine Corps veteran of the Korean War. I honor his sacrifice and the sacrifice of thousands who have paid the ultimate price to provide me and my family a secure and prosperous society where I am free to express my own opinions and follow my dreams. Furthermore, I know that the vast majority of the American soldiers in Iraq have conducted themselves in an honorable fashion. I honor them. Furthermore, many American soldiers have made a serious effort to cross the cultural divide and befriend Iraqis. The dignity of all these soldiers stands in stark contrast to the ignominy of Abu Ghurayb and the rape and murder of Abeer.

The fact remains that Gulf War II, from a Muslim perspective, epitomized the relentless pursuit of the West to dominate the East. As such, it attracted an insurgency wreaking havoc even today in Iraq. Make no mistake, Muslims are looking on the U.S. presence in Iraq with ever-increasing suspicion. Even the most intransigent U.S.

leaders are beginning to suggest that democracy in the Muslim world will look different than it does in the West. And so it does.

◆ SEEKING FRESH VISION ◆

From this quick survey of recent political events in the Muslim world, I have made the following observations:

- For long centuries, Muslim peoples of the world enjoyed prominence and power, leaving a heritage of notable cultural contributions to world civilization.
- Islamic civilization has been in decline in recent centuries. The twentieth century witnessed a drastic decline for the Muslim world as two successive world wars, the birth of Israel, two Gulf wars, and one war in Afghanistan again and again demonstrated the West's superiority.
- The Muslim world has been the object of a continual assault of Western secular media advocating morals and values repulsive to Muslims.
- September 11 was greeted with street-level euphoria in the Muslim world because Muslims saw in it a ray of hope for an Islamic resurgence.
- Each new defeat at the hands of the West deepens the Islamic sense of shame and also complicates any hope for peace.

We are seeking to find fresh vision for the Muslim world. Fresh vision begins with a look backward. We need some sense of the complex history of the Muslim world and the involvement of the "Christian" West in it.

No doubt you can see that Muslims also have a particular vision or perspective of you as a Westerner. Whether you like it or not, you carry baggage—the baggage of the West. You are seen as a military vanquisher whether or not you wish to be. You are guilty by virtue of association with your own culture, which rightly or wrongly is perceived to be engaged in undying exploitation of the Muslim world.

I hope you are also beginning to see why the Muslim world is striking back at anything Western. You say, "Wait a minute. I don't want to be seen that way. I don't like this." Nor do I. Yet this is the reality of the Muslim world. I discovered it while I lived there, and you will too if you opt for incarnation as opposed to confrontation as a response to the Muslim world.

Viewing ourselves through others' eyes is absolutely essential. Our own self-perception is radically different from how we are perceived by others. Yet to understand how others perceive us is, I believe, the first step in communication and incarnation.

Additional Resources for Chapter 4

Keppel, Gilles. *Jihad: The Trail of Political Islam.* Cambridge: Harvard University Press, 2002.

Lewis, Bernard. *The Crisis of Islam.* New York: The Modern Library, 2003.

———. *What Went Wrong?* New York: Oxford University Press, 2002.

Muller, Roland, *The Messenger, the Message and the Community.* Muller understands the Middle Eastern cultural values of shame and honor. Available from www.rmuller.com.

PART III
A THEOLOGICAL DIMENSION

The Islamic worldview is shaped by an understanding of God, humanity, and revelation that is at odds with the Christian worldview at numerous points. Understanding these distinctions is a key element of developing fresh vision for the Muslim world. It will help us grasp the deep-seated resistance of Muslims to much that is "Christian." It will also enable Christians to articulate a biblical worldview more clearly and attractively.

Finally, this section will examine the need to refine Western affinity for Israel. In brief, how do we love Israel without deepening the perceived enmity of the West toward Arabs? We will also look at related eschatological convictions and how their popular outworking supplies further fuel for the conflict.

CHAPTER 5

YOUR TRUTH OR MINE?

I was young when I made my first forays into the world of Islam—confident, assured, weapons in hand. Raised in rural North Carolina, I was the beneficiary of a deep spiritual heritage bequeathed to me through my grandmother and parents. Our social life revolved around our small church and our friends in that church. I now had a Bible degree from a conservative school in the Southeast—the Bible Belt, to be precise. I knew Greek already at the ripe old age of twenty-two. I was pretty convinced that there were unassailable answers for just about every Muslim objection to my Christian faith. I knew the answers, and I knew how to reference them from my Bible.

Does that sound like arrogance to you? Had you met me in those days, you probably would not have thought so. I certainly didn't feel myself to be arrogant but dependent, and most of my Christian friends would have corroborated my humility and faithfulness. In fact, I had met up with a few Christ-followers who had left Islam and embraced the faith I so heartily believed. My interaction with those individuals served to reassure me of the rightness of the gospel for the people of the Muslim world. I was moved by compassion, and I felt it was a sacred duty, a calling if you will, for me to share the good things I knew. Nevertheless, looking back I realize that I ventured into the Muslim world more to confront than to console, more to teach than to learn, more to impart than to incarnate.

Those early years of encountering Muslims worked on me like sandpaper. I just kept running up against the reality and depth of the Islamic faith and worldview. What I considered to be a garden weed that could be uprooted and disposed of turned out to be a mighty oak, well rooted and impervious to my persistent tugs. In time, I grew to respect it not as ultimate truth, but as an incredibly straightforward and powerful way of understanding God, humanity, and the world. As I listened deeply to my Muslim friends, I began to see why they clung to their faith with such tenacity and how that faith had influenced them so pervasively. I also understood Jesus' words more fully: "No one can come to me unless the Father who sent me draws him" (John 6:44).

Although I found Muslims largely intransigent in their faith and worldview, I have to confess that I found a lot of joy in our rambling discussions. I've been asked how one makes an approach to speaking about the things of God with a Muslim. In fact, I don't know how one keeps from speaking about the things of God with a Muslim!

Someone who obviously didn't know once told me that I should avoid talking about politics and religion with Muslims. In fact, that's about all we ever talked about! Muslims are a God-conscious people. They refer to God constantly in their greetings and leave-takings. They recognize his sovereign hand in their daily affairs. They order their lives around their prayers and fasting and extol those who have dedicated their lives to studying their scriptures and living in accordance. Where the typical Westerner views reality through the scientific notion of cause and effect, Muslims declare *ma sha' Allah* (what Allah has willed). I love talking to Muslims about God, and I hope to do a lot more of it.

You've probably read about the five pillars of Islam and something of the life of Muhammad. While these aspects are essential to understanding Islam, I believe they are the leaves of the tree rather than the trunk or the roots. In the following pages I will attempt to give you a perspective on some lesser-known although foundational theological tenets of the Islamic faith. Again, bear in mind that we're attempting to enter into the worldview of another. If the presentation sounds good, that's a good indication we're succeeding. After all, Muslims wouldn't believe it unless it was convincing.

Transcendence: Allah's Complete Otherness

Laysa mithlihi shay'. This commonly heard Arabic expression is lifted right out of the Qur'an. It means simply, "There exists nothing like him" (like Allah). Probably the second most-often quoted Qur'anic passage in my experience is chapter 112, called the Sincerity Chapter (*surat al-Ikhlaas*): "Say: He is Allah, the One and Only; Allah, the Eternal, Absolute; He begetteth not, nor is He begotten; And there is none like unto Him" (Yusuf Ali translation).

To appreciate the Islamic view of transcendence, you have to understand a little about the religious environment of the Arabian Peninsula prior to Muhammad. Essentially, the various Arab tribes were worshippers of idols, and caravans carried the idols north and south as they made their way through the Arabian Peninsula.

At crossroads and oases in the caravan treks where cubic structures (*kaaba*) had been erected, the Arabs would dismount their camels, unload their idols, enter the cubes, and proceed to prostrate themselves before their idols.

Muhammad and a few others of that era known as *hunafaa*, seekers of the one God, were distraught to see such manifest ignorance in worship. Muhammad was aware of the Jewish faith as well as the form of Christianity that he had encountered in his environment; he knew that God had sent a revelation to those people. Muhammad longed for the one God to send down a revelation for his own people, the Arab people, in a tongue they could understand. Muhammad spent much of his early prophetic ministry disputing with the idolaters of Mecca who refused to recognize the oneness or unity of God (*tawhiid*).

Thus, the Islamic creed became, in all simplicity, "There is no God but Allah, and Muhammad is his prophet." This simple affirmation of the unity of God as opposed to the multiple gods of the Arabian context became the watchword of the nascent faith. To this day the simple power of this monotheistic affirmation is deeply rooted in the soul of Muslims. "Such is Allah, your Lord. There is no Allah save Him, the Creator of all things, so worship Him. And He taketh care of all things" (6:102). The battle cry of Islam and the phrase that introduces the call to prayer, *Allahu akbar* (Allah is greater), reflects the call of the unity and uniqueness of Allah.

Christians also view God as transcendent. Some theology books are almost reminiscent of Islam as they speak of the incomprehensibility of God. However, God's transcendence has been mitigated by the event of the incarnation—Christ's becoming a human being.

This unknowable God has now become knowable. The transcendent has become immanent: Immanuel—God with us![1]

Because Allah is one and because there is nothing that can be compared to him, it is of utmost importance to the Muslims in their thinking and worship that nothing or no one becomes associated with Allah. You may have heard that Muslims do not appreciate or accept artistic representations of God, such as the famous Michelangelo painting on the ceiling of the Sistine Chapel. Some Muslims go beyond this and proscribe any artistic representation of human or animal forms. This tendency is borne out of a zealous desire to uphold the pristine nature of Islam that prohibited the making of forms and shapes that would eventually be used in worship. Worship was to be preserved pure and directed to Allah only, who cannot be compared to any earthly representation.

Additionally, the representation of prophets by artistic forms or icons is forbidden. In the recent Danish cartoon debacle, Muhammad was depicted pejoratively. This raised the ire of the entire Muslim world; Muslims arose with one voice to defend their prophet. Since that event an increasing fervency to defend the Prophet of Islam has been evident. Slogans such as "Anything except you, O prophet of God" (meaning, "We will not tolerate a derogatory treatment of you, O Muhammad") have proliferated.

The Islamic prohibition against the use of artistic forms representing God in worship is not unlike the Protestant Reformers who reacted strongly against the prolific use of icons in the Roman Catholic Church. The Calvinist churches of Europe were known for their austerity and a complete lack of visual artistic expression. For Muslims the great danger of visual images is that they cannot convey truth about Allah because he is deemed to be completely other.

Muslims use the Qur'anic phrase *la shariika lahu* (he has no associate) as another watchword of their faith. By guarding their minds from association of any earthly thing with Allah, they are preserving the purity of their worship and faith. The unpardonable sin of Islam is association (*shirk*). Associating any person or object with Allah cannot be forgiven. "Lo! Allah forgiveth not that a partner should be ascribed unto Him. He forgiveth (all) save that to whom He will. Whoso ascribeth partners to Allah, he hath indeed invented a tremendous sin" (Nisaa' 4:48).

If nothing else, this discussion helps us see that Muslims are very serious about Allah. Devotion to him is of utmost importance. They cannot take liberties with how they conceive of God or how they worship him. For most Muslims, Allah is the transcendent other, the incomparable, ultimate reality—like no one and nothing on earth. Allowing for exceptions such as the Sufis, it is commonly held by Muslims that Allah is unknowable in his essence, although his will is knowable through revelation.[2] Muslim children hear this creed from their earliest days: "There is no God but Allah, and Muhammad is his prophet." Thus begins a conception of Allah that frames and informs the entire life. The transcendence of God affects every aspect of Islamic society. It informs the way business is done, the Islamic view of authority, leadership, and the Islamic family.[3]

Now picture yourself as a person whose deepest conviction about God is that he is other and transcendent and, above all else, that you are not allowed to associate anyone or anything with him. I approach you with the gospel—"good news." God has appeared as a human being. This "Son of God" is "the radiance of God's glory and the exact representation of his being" (Hebrews 1:3). How do you feel about that? You immediately recognize me as the perpetrator of a false religion, and you begin to warn your co-religionists that I am a dangerous person. It becomes apparent that the essence of the Christian faith—God became human being in Christ—is diametrically opposed to Islamic faith. While we can minimize the conflict by not making this doctrine our first point of encounter with Muslims, it remains nonetheless a difficult idea for Muslims to grasp.

I am aware that many have argued that the Christian doctrines of the Trinity and the divinity of Christ do not necessarily contradict the Islamic view of the unity of God (*tawhiid*). They base this on the fact that Muhammad was confronting an unorthodox view of the Trinity in the Arabian Peninsula. While I appreciate these efforts of rapprochement, I conclude that the idea of the incarnation of God among humanity is in flagrant violation of Islamic *tawhiid*. I think it is critical for Christians to recognize that their mandate to make disciples of Christ among all nations—at least in reference to this issue of the fullness of God dwelling in Christ (Colossians 2:9)—puts them at theological loggerheads with Islamic faith and practice.

While efforts at rapprochement may have the appearance of charitable love for Muslim people, Christians will be better served if we understand the depth of the Islamic concept of transcendence and then accept the fact that we are presenting an alternative. Hopefully, as we incarnate the gospel in the Muslim worldview, we will learn to present the alternative in love and with grace—realizing how difficult it is for the Muslim to embrace it. After all, God's immanent dwelling among his people did not end with Christ's resurrection. The Holy Spirit is the mediator of God's presence among his people. "If anyone loves me, he will obey my teaching. My Father will love him, and we will come to him and make our home with him" (John 14:23). If you will, the only convincing proof of God's dwelling among us is us. If Christ lives in us and through us, then the argument against God's immanence is defanged. His presence among his people will be self-evident.

A number of Muslim friends have asked me something like this: "Honestly now, do you really think God was born into this world as a baby, had his diapers changed, scraped his knee, and went to his mother crying for help?" Muslims can, nonetheless, be convinced of the possibility of the incarnation. It happens every day. In my experience it is normally a process of realization through reading the Gospels that a Muslim comes to terms with Christ as the incarnate God. Philosophical and theoretic arguments will do little. But I have noticed with my friends who have embraced Christ that the beauty of God becoming a human being, walking among us, eating our food, and teaching us his ways is immensely attractive. For many it is this very truth, a God who comes seeking his people, that drew them into the fold of Christ. The great British preacher Charles Spurgeon exhorted his listeners that the Word of God is a lion. As such, it needs no defense but only to be released. Muslims who read of Christ in the Gospels—his forgiveness of sins, his miracles, his teachings, his death and resurrection—can begin to understand that Christ was more than a prophet. "No one can come to me unless the Father who sent me draws him" (John 6:44).

Revelation: How Do We Hear from God?

I remember giving the Gospel of Luke to one of my Muslim friends. When I saw him a few days later, he shrugged indifferently and expressed his opinion that this book could not be the Word of God. As I queried him, I discovered the reason: Luke begins by stating that he had conducted careful research in order to put down in an orderly fashion all that transpired concerning Jesus. To my Muslim friend, Luke's prologue smacked of human effort, inspired by careful research and questioning but not by the authoritative voice of Allah. He was not convinced that Luke was of any more value than the daily newspaper.

Christians are not scandalized when they note differences of style, grammar, and even slightly divergent accounts of an event related by different biblical authors. We believe that God spoke through the biblical authors, making use of their distinct personalities, backgrounds, abilities, and preferences. The oversight of the Holy Spirit preserved the Scriptures of the Old and New Testaments as the authoritative Word of God. "Men spoke from God as they were carried along by the Holy Spirit" (2 Peter 1:21). This understanding of God's inspiration has been called organic inspiration, meaning that God used the entirety of the authors' personalities and backgrounds to produce his Word.

The Islamic view of inspiration is significantly different. I have made the mistake of referring to a passage from the Qur'an as the words of Muhammad. This is a serious misunderstanding of Qur'anic inspiration, and I was duly reprimanded: the Qur'an contains none of Muhammad's words but only Allah's words. These words were written on celestial tablets and taught to the prophet Muhammad by the angel Gabriel. The revelation of Allah is often referred to as *tanziil* (what is sent down). The Qur'an is a literal word from heaven. It is for this reason that every letter must be carefully preserved in the original language, Arabic. In fact, translations of the Qur'an are usually titled *The Meaning of the Glorious Qur'an* or something to that effect. They cannot bear the title *Qur'an* simply because they do not preserve the Qur'an in its original language.

The miraculous nature of the Qur'anic revelation is captured in the term *i'jaaz*, which means "inability." The word connotes the inability of human beings to replicate the Qur'anic revelation. Muhammad gave the challenge to his opposition to produce a revelation of similar character to the Qur'an. Muslims maintain that such has never happened, and thus the integrity of the Qur'an is unassailable. "Or say they: He hath invented it? Say: Then bring a surah [a chapter of the Qur'an] like unto it, and call [for help] on all ye can besides Allah, if ye are truthful" (10:38).

This challenge is accentuated by the fact that most Muslims presume Muhammad to have been illiterate. The Qur'an, being a work of literary excellence, could not be the product of an illiterate person. God must have sent it down to Muhammad.[4]

The aesthetic beauty of Qur'anic recitation provides a further experiential proof of its divine origin. Muslims will often be moved to tears by the artistic expression of one who is trained in Qur'anic recitation (*tartiil* or *tajwiid*). In the Muslim world it is very common to hear recordings of Qur'anic recitation being played continuously in businesses, taxis, and homes. Memorization of the text of the Qur'an is highly valued, and young children may memorize the entire contents of the Qur'an (about two-thirds the length of the New Testament) and compete for prizes in its recitation.

This view of inspiration, often referred to as *mechanical inspiration* or *dictation inspiration*, is the default concept with which most Muslims operate. The Qur'an recognizes three other books, in addition to itself, as the Word of God. These three books, in large part, correspond to various portions of our Bible. The *Torah* of Moses is the first prophetic book. The *Zabur* of David, the Psalms, is the second. The third is the *Injil,* or the gospel of Jesus Christ. Certain Qur'anic passages speak very highly of these preceding books.

> 3:3 He hath revealed unto thee [Muhammad] the Scripture with truth, confirming that which was (revealed) before it, even as He revealed the Torah and the Gospel.

> 2:136 Say (O Muslims): We believe in Allah and that which is revealed unto us and that which was revealed unto Abraham, and Ishmael, and Isaac, and Jacob, and the tribes, and that which Moses and Jesus received, and that which the prophets received from their Lord. We make no distinction between any of them, and unto Him we have surrendered.

> 5:47 Let the People of the Gospel judge by that which Allah hath revealed therein. Whoso judgeth not by that which Allah hath revealed: such are evil-livers.

One would think that these passages would lead Muslims to investigate the previous Scriptures. Unfortunately, such is not the case, as the common opinion among Muslims is that Christians and Jews have corrupted (*harrafa*) the Scriptures that preceded the Qur'an. In some instances the Qur'an indicates that it is a replica of the former revelations, only in Arabic: "And lo! it is a revelation of the Lord of the Worlds, Which the True Spirit hath brought down Upon thy heart, that thou mayst be (one) of the warners, In plain Arabic speech. And lo! it is in the Scriptures of the men of old. Is it not a token for them that the doctors of the Children of Israel know it?" (26:192–197).

Christians and Jews are commonly referred to as *ahl al-kitaab* (the people of the book), which is a term of respect. However, Muslims are mystified by the plethora of biblical versions and translations that exist. They find a footnoted biblical text that presents a variant reading of a passage to be inadmissible. Whereas Christians value the scholarly process of comparison of ancient texts, seeing in it the possibility to ascertain, as nearly as possible, the original text, Muslims view it with a great deal of suspicion. It is this scholarly process, in their opinion, that establishes the corruption of the text and points to the Qur'an as the only viable Word of God.

What Muslims are not told is that the text of the Qur'an also contains variant readings, as do all ancient manuscripts. The codification of the Qur'an in recent years, largely carried on by the benevolence of the Kingdom of Saudi Arabia, now holds forth the illusion that the Qur'anic text contains no variants whatsoever. While Qur'anic scholars may recognize the presence of variant readings, most Muslims will insist that no such variants exist.

Thus, the Islamic view of inspiration through divine dictation mitigates against a fair hearing for the Scriptures of the Old and New Testaments. It is an extension of the view of God as the transcendent other. God cannot be likened to anything known by human beings. His word comes to us not in the cloak of human language and personality but as a fixed message, sent down in a divine language. Therefore it is untranslatable and unchangeable.[5]

How does one overcome this sizable obstacle in the path of Muslims to understanding the Bible? Once again, the Scriptures are their own advocate. I recall the testimony of one friend who had been a member of a fundamentalist Islamic group. He began reading the New Testament. Upon reaching Matthew 5:39–40, where Jesus declares, "If someone strikes you on the right cheek, turn to him the other also. . . . If someone forces you to go one mile, go with him two miles," my friend concluded that Christians were serving a different God from the God he had been serving. He devoted his efforts to determining who this God was and, in the end, embraced Christ.

The ultimate proof of the authority and power of God's Word in the lives of Christ-followers is their obedience and submission to it. One friend working in a Muslim country quoted the Bible at great length to validate certain practices such as solitary prayer, fasting, and defending the orphan and widow. Muslims were deeply moved by this man's devotion to Christ, and many approached him to learn more about the Christian Scriptures. Once again, the incarnation of the gospel in and through the people of the gospel speaks powerfully to Muslims.

Man, Oh Man! Good, Bad, or Indifferent?

In Genesis 1–3, Adam and Eve are surrounded by all they need to survive and thrive. They have meaningful work, loving relationships, food and shelter. They even have unobstructed friendship with their creator God. Yet they prefer their own wisdom to God's. That decision is depicted in their eating of a fruit in the garden that God had prohibited eating, the only one he had put off-limits, by the way. That much of the story is very familiar.

You will find the same story in the Qur'an. Adam and Eve have a similar nobility—the angels are instructed to bow down to them. They have innate knowledge of all the world and are able to name all of Allah's creation. Yet there is a subtle but significant difference in the Qur'anic and biblical accounts. In the Qur'an, after the transgression

Adam received words of guidance (*huda*) from his lord. Allah then repented toward him and said to him, "Get thee down."

Guidance. Did you get that? What came from God as a result of Adam's transgression was guidance.

Although one could point to other Qur'anic passages, this one is particularly instructive concerning Islam's understanding of the nature of humanity. The biblical account has God promising that the "seed of the woman" will crush the head of the Serpent—the Enemy of humanity; the Qur'anic account has Allah sending Adam words of guidance and then sending Adam himself down to the earth, albeit with enmity. Other passages in the Qur'an refer to Adam's defect as weakness. One verse states that Adam forgot.

The biblical view is that what resulted from the Eden event was enmity between God and humans, which God checked by pronouncing enmity between humanity and the Serpent and then proceeded to counteract through the unfolding promise of the "seed of the woman"—Christ. It was a cosmic treason of which the couple was guilty, which would become the defining event of the biblical revelation culminating in redemption—the reconciliation of humanity to God through the cross. The Qur'anic view is that man acted out of his weakness and that Allah sent him guidance, to which he responded. Man proceeded to descend (a geographic descent from paradise) to the earth in order to carry out the will of Allah there, but the eating of the forbidden fruit, in Islamic understanding, does not require any more of the divine than that Allah give corrective guidance to the erring couple.

To put it bluntly, humanity is not estranged from Allah by sin. Man is separate from Allah as Allah is transcendent other. But there is no moral chasm that prevents Adam and Eve from living the life

God intended for them to live. In Islam, humanity is not afflicted by an incurable disease known as sin. Now this statement needs some qualifications. Muslims do believe that human beings sin. The Qur'an uses many words to refer to sin and makes it clear that all human beings sin. However, sin derives not from man's desire to usurp the place of God, as is the case throughout the biblical revelation, but from man's inherent weakness as a creature of the dust.

Once again, as I've interacted with Muslims, I've grown to appreciate the implications of such a view and the ready rationale that commends itself manifestly to most Muslims. Let me try to explain.

Christians often refer to their understanding of humanity's state of sinfulness before God as original sin, inherited from Adam and Eve. They sinned; we are their children, and like them, we sin. We, who are alienated in Adam, are reconciled in Christ—a new Adam. (Admittedly, to explain this doctrine fully would need more than a paragraph. Our purpose is to see the import of this doctrine for our interaction with Muslims.) The Muslim then rightfully asks, "How? How is it that I inherited guilt for a transgression that took place thousands of years ago? This simply is not just. Allah would not obligate me for sins committed by my forebears. I am responsible for my own sin."

I have wondered why a religion and worldview that is so corporate in nature would take an apparently individualistic turn at this point. The Muslim senses deeply his own responsibility before God. He knows that he cannot live on his father's or mother's piety. He himself or she herself must demonstrate the good works that befit Islamic faith. I have been impressed with Muslim young men who would not participate in Islamic prayers because they knew their private lives did not correspond to Islamic teaching. Rather than fake piety, they defer, saying that later in life (after they marry), they will begin to pray.

There is a deep sense of individual responsibility for the Muslim. He does not view himself as dead in trespasses and sins, in the words of the apostle Paul (Ephesians 2:1). He knows that he can make the right choices—to pray, to fast, to recite the Islamic creed, to participate in the *hajj* (pilgrimage to Mecca), and to give alms. These good works prescribed by Islam are Allah's guidance (*huda*) for the Muslim. Individuals are neither dead in sin nor in need of redemption; rather, they are weak, forgetful, and in need of guidance.

The Christian concept of original sin seems like passing the buck for many Muslims. Being convinced of human depravity, I have spoken at length with Muslims about my own inability to fully keep God's law. Like me, they have experienced the constant propensity toward self-indulgence. Unlike me, they do not recognize this as an inherent state of rebellion against Allah. They view it as a natural consequence of being a creature. Only Allah is without this weakness; human beings are by nature weak and fallible.

You can probably surmise how a Muslim feels about the statement that human beings are created in the image of God. God cannot have an image. We cannot reflect something that is utterly transcendent and different from ourselves. This dynamic tension of Christianity that human beings are innately noble and yet hopelessly fallen seems to be overdone in the mind of most Muslims I have spoken to. They cannot see why I don't just admit that, as a creature of the dust, I am weak; I am not in rebellion against Allah; I have not chosen another master; I just wander off the right track occasionally and need to be brought back to the way of Islam—the way of submission to God.

Once again, this concept of man's weakness as opposed to his fallen nature permeates much of the Islamic worldview. I have noticed that Muslims on an individual level often appeal to the weakness of their human nature as an excuse for their behavior. A commonly heard Arabic word on the streets of the Middle East is *ma'alesh,* roughly translated as "not on me" or "not my fault." Often it is used as a half apology: "I'm sorry." But the intent behind the word seems to be more a deferral of responsibility than an owning of it.

At the risk of oversimplifying, I believe it is fair to say that sin, for Muslims, is a serious but superficial problem requiring guidance from Allah. Sin, in the biblical worldview, is alienation from God incurring the curse of God—"for when you eat of it you will surely die" (Genesis 2:17). Death then is more than physical expiration. It is spiritual alienation, a cutting off from the source of life—God.

In conversing with Muslims, I generally find better acceptance if I preface my words with something like, "The prophet Jesus taught . . ." Jesus applies the law at the level of our inner motivations. Few commit murder, but who can claim to be free of hatred? Some claim to be free of adultery, but Jesus teaches that lusting is adultery at the heart level. Can anyone claim innocence of lust or envy? Do we consistently love God with all our heart, soul, strength, and mind? "The things that come out of the mouth come from the heart, and these make a man 'unclean.' For out of the heart come evil thoughts, murder, adultery, sexual immorality, theft, false testimony, slander. These are what make a man 'unclean'" (Matthew 15:18–20). The teachings of the Bible, especially those of Jesus, make it clear that sin is a pervasive and irremediable problem. The solution must be radical, coming through divine initiative, not human effort. Once again, when Muslims see this fact, the gospel becomes a beautiful message of reconciliation, drawing them into the loving arms of a heavenly Father.

Muslim apologists have complained that the Christian doctrine of original sin amounts to sin being passed on to us by our forebears through DNA! I have explained it to Muslims this way: If you put me beside my biological father, you would see very clear similarities. Our noses look alike; our ears look alike; we are about the same height. Adam is not my physical father but my spiritual father. I look like him in a spiritual sense. Just as Adam and Eve did not trust God to provide what was best for them but took it on themselves to better their station, so do I. Adam is not responsible for my rebellion against God; I am. In Christ I have been adopted. I now have a new spiritual father. Although many of my habits still look like my old father, Adam, I am beginning to look more and more like Christ. One day I will resemble him perfectly.

Atonement: How to Be Right with Allah

If Islam's view of God is that of a transcendent other and if Islam's view of humanity is that we are fallible but not fallen, it would naturally follow that Islam's view of the solution to the human dilemma would be of a different nature than what Christianity proposes. If you start out with different ingredients, you get a different stew. Islam's proposed solution for the plight of humanity, as we've discussed, is not redemption but guidance. There is no need for a radical remaking of human beings such as Jesus spoke of when he said, "You must be born again" (John 3:7). Instead, human beings must submit and embrace the guidance offered to them.

While doing my master's thesis in Arabic at the American University in Cairo, I read an Islamic theologian named Muhammad Abduh, who lived in the early part of the last century. Abduh interacted with Christian thinking to some degree largely because Egypt was under the British Protectorate, which allowed quite a number of Protestant missionaries to come into Egypt. Abduh's critical mind recognized that the difference between his faith and that of the British missionaries was not inconsequential; in fact, it touched the defining characteristic of Islam and Christianity. It went right to the heart of how man is put in right relation with his Creator.

Abduh quoted a Qur'anic verse that, at the time, I found difficult to understand. In Abduh's understanding this verse succinctly summarized the essence of Islam. Translated simply, the verse states that "no burden bearer can bear the burden of another" (6:164; 17:15; 39:7). While Islam calls on its people to live as one united nation, emphasizing the corporate nature of the faith, it also reminds all Muslims that each one must stand before Allah with his own good or evil deeds. No father is able to bear responsibility for his son. No mother can stand in the stead of her daughter. No prophet or holy man is able to take anyone else's place on the day of judgment. All persons stand or fall on their own merit.

We have to be careful in evaluating this doctrine. I have heard some well-meaning Christians refer to Islam as a religion devoid of grace or a religion that relies on crass works of righteousness. Actually both of those statements betray a failure to grasp the breadth of Islamic faith. First, we have to remember that righteousness in the Christian sense of moral purity before a holy God is not the preeminent value in the Islamic worldview. It seems Muslims are not so much asking, "How can I have a righteous standing before God?"

Their concern is not perfection that, in the Christian view, must be imputed to the believer as an alien righteousness (a righteousness originating from outside oneself). Rather, their hope is that their conduct will demonstrate them to be a Muslim (one submitted to Allah), and thereby they will escape his wrath and displeasure.

Admittedly, the concept of grace as God's favor bestowed on undeserving people does not figure large in the Qur'an. But the idea that God gives more favor than his slaves deserve is not unknown in Islam. Muslims have related to me how Allah rewards them with ten times their earned merit for each good deed. Many also hope for the intercession of the Prophet on their day of judgment.

What then is the solution for man's weakness and failure? *Islam.* The word means "to submit." The submission in view is to Allah's revelation for mankind. Man is perfectly able to submit. He is required to do so by Allah and will be held responsible for his failure to do so on the day of judgment.

I've been told that Islam is a man's religion, meaning it is not the religion of weaklings—those who depend on others. In other words, it requires that one be willing to own up to one's own mistakes and accept correction—accept to do the things that Islam prescribes. For many Muslims the claim that someone else took the punishment of God for their transgressions is hardly conscionable. How could they expect God to hold a prophet accountable for their actions? Even if Christ could pay for their sin, why would he be required to die? After all, the sin was theirs, not his. Why was the solution so radical as to claim the life of one of Allah's prophets? Of what value was Christ's death for their sin?

In my opinion, these questions that are uppermost in the minds of Muslims bode well for the future of Christ's kingdom in that part of the world. I much prefer to examine these questions honestly with a Muslim than to try to broach the same subjects with a Westerner whose materialist proclivity may not allow him to even consider them. By understanding why a Muslim thinks the way he does about these questions, you will be better able to address them in everyday interactions.

As an example, Muslims are astute students of world events. They are acutely aware that wars and rumors of wars are ever on the increase. In casual conversation I might make reference to this fact and draw ready consent from my Muslim friend. I then suggest that we often see the same enmity and desire for revenge among neighbors and friends. "Yes," my friend says and shakes his head, acknowledging the truth of the proposition. One more assertion commends itself to any thinking person: this same enmity has a way of creeping into the most sacred and honorable of our relationships. For instance, we see sons who rebel against their fathers (unthinkable in an Islamic context, but too true to deny) and men who insult their wives and at times even resort to abusing them physically. Unable to remain true to their wives, they divorce them. Muslims would not deny any element of what I've just said—assertions that are true in East and West, in all societies. By painting this realistic picture of the degree of incursion of enmity into relationships where it simply should not exist, the obvious question is, Where do you think this enmity came from? In the Qur'an, Allah tells Adam and Eve to "go down, each of you to the other an enemy."

The enmity is there because it originated in our alienation from a loving God. The Muslim explanation that this is due to human weakness is hardly satisfying. Something deeper is taking place here.

◆ SEEKING FRESH VISION ◆

These issues—God, how God communicates to humanity, the problem with humanity, and the solution to that problem—are not minor points of Islamic doctrine. Together, they actually constitute the Islamic worldview. When we begin to see the world, God, and humanity as Muslims do, it makes sense why they are not eager to embrace the Christian faith. Their preconceived ideas about these and other issues leave them at a distinct disadvantage when trying to decipher what on earth Christians are talking about. Realizing this theological polarity may cause us to despair at the enormity of the task.

You may be asking what the solution is. What is the stone that we can place in David's sling to quickly and easily bring down the giant? The analogy is unhelpful. First of all, Islam is not our enemy, and we are not fighting Muslims with tangible weapons. But there is an application here. David did not instantly slay the giant. His deadeye with a slingshot was developed, I suppose, through years of practice in the Judean hillside while tending his father's sheep. He perfected his shot, taking aim again and again, moving the target just a bit farther out until he could hit it a perfect ten out of ten times.

Now the analogy is helpful. Effectiveness in doing God's work comes by perseverance and practice. The practice of prayer, thorough study of Scripture, awareness of Islam and its doctrines—all these and more must be diligently attended to. There is no quick fix, no golden key that will magically unlock the door of the Muslim world to the gospel. After all, the Muslim worldview has been a little over thirteen hundred years in the making.

The hope that is driving me to write this book is that we all will accept the call to live out the gospel in the world and among

Muslims. Are you ready, like David, to practice and prepare with all diligence, waiting on the anointing of God's Spirit to effect the delivery of what you've developed at the right moment?

The astounding truth of the New Testament is that the ministry of reconciliation has been committed to us (2 Corinthians 5:18–19). Jesus makes clear to his disciples that he fully expects them to carry on his ministry in the power of the Holy Spirit. "'As the Father has sent me, I am sending you.' And with that he breathed on them and said, 'Receive the Holy Spirit'" (John 20:21–22). The solution for the human predicament is the gospel of Jesus Christ, committed first to his apostles and by extension to the universal church. This ministry of reconciliation between God and Muslims is committed to us—Jesus-followers. It cannot be done by military might, persuasive philosophical arguments, or governmental prestige and influence. It is the gospel that must go out in human form through people like you and me—incarnation!

Additional Resources for Chapter 5

Campbell, William. *The Qur'an and the Bible in the Light of History and Science.* Upper Darb, PA: Middle East Resources, 1992.

Geisler, Norman L,. and Abdul Saleeb. *Answering Islam: The Crescent in the Light of the Cross.* Grand Rapids: Baker Books, 1993.

Gilchrist, John. *The Codification of the Qur'an.* Warley, UK: T.M.F.M.T., 1989.

Moucarry, Chawkat. *The Prophet and the Messiah.* Downers Grove, IL: InterVarsity Press, 2001.

CHAPTER 6

JESUS' KINGDOM IN THE MUSLIM WORLD TODAY

New births are a bundle of contradictions: the unadulterated joy of welcoming a new child into the world and the tremendous agony of labor and delivery; the delicate skin of the newborn and the shedding of blood that brought that newborn to life; the satisfied sleep of a child who just fed at her mother's breast and the restless nights tending to a child with colic or other pains we are helpless to discern. Suffice it to say that any new life is accompanied by a multitude of new challenges. The joy of the new birth and the distant hope of a maturing child give parents the staying power to cope with the challenges.

New life is springing up all through the Muslim world. Muslims from Iraq to Indonesia and from Mauritania to Manila are discovering Jesus! Not unlike the birth of a baby, this new life can be a source of joy and inspiration while it produces heartbreak and consternation at the same time. Many books depict the struggles and victories of those who, having grown up as Muslims, now are following Christ. We have applauded the courage of these people and have been challenged by their willingness to endure hardship.

In this chapter we take a look at the miracle of new birth that is moving through the Muslim world with great force. No doubt, Muslims who opt to follow Christ will be a great encouragement to us in our pursuit of fresh vision for the Muslim world. (But before we get too excited, we need to recall that God loves the world with its good, its bad, and its ugly. He loves those Muslims who choose to follow his Son, and he also loves their brothers, sisters, fathers, mothers, uncles, and aunts who may never make such a choice.)

What follows is simply a series of vignettes—scenes from the lives of real people I have known over the years. Hopefully, you will get a sense of the elation of their faith as well as see some of the authentic struggles that accompany this new birth. What better place to start than with one of my favorite little girls. The names are changed, by the way.

Farah

Farah lives on the outskirts of a major Middle Eastern city. She attends a school that probably doesn't challenge her active mind adequately, but it's the best her mom and dad can afford. She's in the fourth grade now.

Farah's dad has quite a story himself.[1] Like many lower-class men, he came up through the ranks of a fundamentalist Islamic group where he was trained in a worldview of hatred and intolerance. As a result of his crimes and those of his group, he was forced to flee his country. He remained outside his homeland several years, plotting to overthrow the government so that a truly Islamic state could be established. After he returned to his country, he was assigned the task of reading "the Christians' book" and writing a response that would prove it to be corrupted. You can probably guess the rest of the story. This man's reading of the Bible was the beginning of a pilgrimage that led him to faith.

Farah's story is little known. Consider the plight of a young girl whose father and mother are both Christ-followers from Islamic background. There are no believing uncles and aunts. The grandparents are staunch Muslims. The family holidays are not Christmas and Easter but Ramadan and *Eid al-Adha* (the Feast of the Sacrifice). In school Farah will attend a compulsory religion class, yet she understands that she is a follower of Jesus and desires to be nothing else. She attends a church not far from her home; she knows all the songs and memorizes Bible verses.

Yet her name tells a different story. She takes her father's name, immediately recognizable to all Arabic speakers as a Muslim name. All her government papers identify her as a Muslim in a country where no Muslim has yet to convert to Christianity with legal recognition by the state. In her religion class Farah will learn the mandatory prayers of Islam and memorize the Qur'an. She will be expected to recite the creed, "There is no God but Allah, and Muhammad is his prophet." Farah's cousins and friends at school are Muslims. She is already under pressure to fast during the month of Ramadan. Her friends at school are already donning the Muslim veil. Will she? I do not know.

Farah is unusually bright and articulate. She's a little chatterbox who speaks to us foreigners in her rapid-fire Arabic and looks puzzled when we don't seem to get all she's saying! Her physical features match her precocious personality. Her dark complexion showcases a bright, inquisitive smile and curious, deep brown eyes. She's the kind of girl you might look at and wonder how far she will go in life. I wonder how one so young will navigate the confusing religious waters in her society. Her desire to follow Jesus will be increasingly difficult to reconcile with her Islamic family and society. Yes, the new birth was hilariously joyful, but what comes after that? Who will stand with her? Who will guide her?

Farag

"Yes, Mom. Do pray for me, won't you? Enjoy your trip, and come back to us safely!"

I was an eavesdropper on this telephone conversation that concluded as I made my way to the sofa. Knowing something of Farag's history and his past relationship with his mother, I was slightly mystified by his request that she pray for him. I noted that he used the word Muslims typically use for prayer rather than the word commonly used by Christians. As I was to learn later, Farag's mother was on yet another of her yearly pilgrimages to Mecca and had called her wayward son, extolling the virtues of the hajj and assuring him that her prayers for him would not go unanswered in the holy sanctuary of Mecca.

Farag's coming to faith had produced quite a scandal for this conservative family that hailed from the birthplace of the Muslim Brotherhood, a fundamentalist Islamic organization. He was intelligent and outgoing and identified as a leader in his school. The family agonized over his conversion (or, as the family viewed it, his shameful defection from Islam). Was it his wide reading that led him into these divergent views? Was it a classmate who had enticed him away from his conservative Islamic upbringing? Farag's mother was a pious woman who played hostess to weekly gatherings in her middle-class home for prayer and exposition of the Qur'an. His father, shortly after Farag's dangerous defection, had mysteriously passed away while still a relatively young man.

"It is because of you, Farag. You killed your father." This was the scathing accusation of Farag's mother, who linked her husband's death to the shock and shame of their son's defection. Her intercessory prayer for him while on pilgrimage was a testimony of her abiding love for him and her desire that he return to the fold of Islam. Rather gracious of him, I thought, to accept his mother's prayer and trust that God would bless him through her intercession.

Jasmine

Although strange for a single woman to live alone in Cairo, there seemed to be no option. Jasmine had experienced such difficulties while trying to live with her conservative Muslim family that all had agreed the best thing for her was to move to the capital and try to live anonymously among its masses.

No one knew where she was. But family ties run deep. She could not resist making contact with cousins, aunts, and others in the family circle. Perhaps it was through that contact that her uncles located her and picked her up from the street near her apartment. Now her day of reckoning had come. Her strange odyssey of faith had begun when she accepted employment from a Christian businessman. But now her liberty had exceeded all reasonable limits. She was to be taught a lesson. She was taken to a deserted apartment building on the north coast, where her interrogation began. For days, she was fed meagerly, questioned incessantly, beaten and tortured intermittently. Her uncles carefully explained to her that they would rather see her suffer here than to suffer the eternal punishment of hell.

She escaped as her captors stepped out for a meal. She managed to unlock the apartment door and ran for her life. Her return to the capital city has been painful. Will they find her again? What tactics will they employ next time?[2]

Ali and Bahija

Marriage is always a monumental challenge for those from Muslim background who seek to follow Christ. For young women, marriages are usually arranged. The women are usually consulted, but final arrangements are left up to the family. According to Islamic law, Muslim men may marry non-Muslim women with the understanding that the children will be raised as Muslims. Muslim women, however, are not allowed to marry non-Muslim men. In this way, the progeny is ensured to be Muslim. For this reason, no self-respecting Christian family will allow its daughter to marry a Muslim man.

For a Christian woman from Islamic background, the odds of finding a husband with similar beliefs are exceedingly small. Christians in the minority community often fear that the male Muslim-background believer will abandon his faith, leaving their daughter in a precarious position—married to a Muslim. Even if he remains true to his faith, the children will be regarded as Muslims by the state. This is a difficult pill to swallow for most Christian families.

Ali had made attempts to marry into the minority Christian community. He had high hopes that at least one set of in-laws would be sympathetic with his new faith. That would have been an immense benefit in raising the children as Christians. However, he was rejected by the family of his proposed fiancée. The risk was too great. Ali had no choice but to seek a girl from Islamic background who, like him, had decided to follow Christ. The network of Muslim-background believers is small but constantly growing. Soon a young woman was located who had grown up in the Arabian Peninsula. A hasty meeting was arranged, and the two accepted the marriage proposal.

Ali desired that his family—the family of faith—be around him on the occasion of his marriage. It happened that a conference had been planned for a number of Muslim-background believers from various countries. This was to be the occasion of Ali and Bahija's wedding. What an event! It stands out in my memory as one of those rare moments of pure joy that one experiences in this short life. We danced, sang, and celebrated late into the night as Ali and Bahija were joined in the covenant of marriage. It was fitting that the officiating pastor was also a believer from Muslim background. Today, Ali and Bahija make their home in a large Middle Eastern city. They have a young child. No doubt, this child will grow up facing the same pressures as Farah.

Yasiin

"You must honor me by coming to my house!" Yasiin's hospitable offer reflected the welcoming beauty and simplicity of the town he had been raised in. Nestled in the hills of North Africa, the buildings of the town were a pristine white, set against the azure waters of the Mediterranean. As my eyes drank in the sights along our tour route, Yasiin constantly greeted his friends, cousins, neighbors. "How's the wife? Any news from your brother in France? Give my greetings to your father." In a strange way, it reminded me of the small town where I had grown up in the mountains of North Carolina.

For pennies we bought a paper cone of sunflower seeds. I tried unsuccessfully to match Yasiin's technique of separating out the seed from the shell using only teeth and tongue—a skill I never quite mastered but one that Arabs seem to be born with! Munching as we ambled along, we greeted old friends of Yasiin, new acquaintances for me. Everything seemed as it should be. Kids kicked plastic balls and erupted into a celebration befitting Renaldo or Beckham after releasing the perfect shot between the two rocks that formed a make-shift goal. We strolled past the centerpiece of the town—the mosque prominently situated near the town square. Its ornate calligraphy and arabesque decor belied the modest station of the townspeople. Peering through its massive wooden doors, I felt the attraction of its cool shaded courtyard, open spaces, and peaceful allure. There was no church in the town. There were no Christians in the town. At least that would have been the common assumption.

But Yasiin was a Christ-follower. He had given up attending the local mosque when he sensed the prayers and confessions made there were at odds with his new faith. While still very young in his faith, he proposed marriage to one of the local girls. Now they lived in a small apartment. Yasiin was able to pay the bills through a meager salary as a functionary of the government. Their attempts to have children had proved unsuccessful. His bride remained a Muslim, and although she knew of his rather strange faith, she urged him not to discuss it in front of her family. She showed no interest in his repeated attempts at engaging her in conversation on the subject.

Yasiin occasionally met with some of the brothers, as he called them, in town. One had moved from a neighboring port city. Another had secretly listened to Christian radio broadcasts for years. Together they formed a small cell. They kept in touch with a larger group based in the capital and exchanged visits whenever they could. To his surprise, Yasiin had discovered a gift: he could sing. His beautiful baritone voice landed him an invitation to record indigenous worship music with some of the brothers and sisters from other cities. Back at his home, he proudly played a few selections for me, making no attempt to cover his glee as he expressed clearly that this was "his music, music from his country."

We shared long conversation that night and a generous breakfast the next morning before Yasiin accompanied me to the train station. He requested prayer for his wife. He confessed to me that he loved her deeply, but her refusal to listen to his explanations of his faith had caused deep conflict between them. In some ways their failure to have children had been a relief for him. He knew that if children came they would quickly be indoctrinated and whisked away to the mosque by doting grandparents.

For Yasiin's wife and for her family, Yasiin's conversion was a defection and a source of shame. In this town manliness and integrity are intimately bound up in one's religion. To be a good man is to be a good Muslim. Conversely, to be a non-Muslim is to be a traitor. I could understand that, as "good men" in my hometown were often referred to as "good Christian men."

Yet Yasiin defied the stereotype. His faith, though not widely known, was slowly being discovered by his friends and peers. He was faithful in his job and a good provider for his wife. How will the presence of Yasiin and a handful of other believers affect that town? Hard to say, but I venture that the impact will be a good one and that Yasiin will discover a few more brothers and sisters in his town as the years roll by.

Abdu Latif

"I'm the one Joe told you about—Abdu Latif—Joe told you about me." I immediately knew two things about the person on the other end of the line: he was from one of the countries of the Arabian Peninsula (I could tell from his dialect), and I was supposed to know him, although I didn't. Abdu Latif kept firing away, assuring me that my friend Joe in a country of the Arabian Peninsula had told me about him.

OK. Now I had Joe placed, but who was this Abdu Latif? I drove to the rendezvous, concerned that this might be a setup because I hadn't heard from Joe in over a year.

From the moment I laid eyes on Abdu Latif, he never ceased to amuse, amaze, and befuddle me. He climbed into my car, and I greeted him with the traditional Arabic formality *kayf al-haal* (How is your condition?). Abdu Latif punctuated his reply with sighs of deep satisfaction and expletives of what a uniquely blessed man he was.

I kept trying to figure this guy out. He looked pretty average—about fifty, but vigorous as a thirty-year-old. He was a talking machine. He just kept talking and talking, but what he had to say was as interesting as it was entertaining—tales of his family, his business, how he came to know the Lord (through a Sudanese Christian in India!)—and he had a magnetic belly laugh that exuded joy and even coaxed some chuckles from this melancholy American.

Oh, there was much to discover in Abdu Latif! Finding believers from his country was a rarity in itself and begged for an explanation. Gradually, I heard his story of leaving his home country in search of employment in India. While there he made the acquaintance of a Sudanese man who thoroughly turned Abdu Latif's world upside down as day after day they discussed the merits of Islam and

Christianity. While working in India, Abdu Latif had met numerous Christ-followers and continually compared their morality, language, work ethic, and faith to the exemplars of piety from his country. He read the Bible for the first time and decided to become a follower of Christ. After returning to his home country, life was not easy; he was the lone Christ-follower in his family and in his town. Now he had made his way to Egypt, desiring to expand the family business but also eager to connect with Egyptian Christians.

After learning that the family business was primarily a muffler repair shop, I was confused. What possible benefit could Abdu Latif derive from visiting the hole-in-the-wall muffler repair shops I was familiar with in Egypt? Nevertheless, Abdu Latif came home with me and ended up staying in our home for a few weeks. He left early in the morning to make his way around Cairo on foot! (Later I learned that a Cairo taxi driver had taken advantage of him and that he vowed never to let that happen again.) Each day he came back with tales of his accomplishments and new ideas for his family business.

Eventually he ran out of money. He asked to borrow . . . not money, but my wife's sewing machine. In a flash he was working away, producing stuffed dolls, each with its own handmade cos-tume—pharaoh, upper-Egyptian farmer, Muslim sheikh. Abdu Latif was a real artisan. He painted portraits, made clothing, produced beautiful designs in metal. He was also a gifted sculptor. I will never forget the day I came home to find Abdu Latif beaming with pride. "You won't believe it," he said. "You just won't believe it!" He led me to another room, and there sitting on my desk was a sculpted bust—of me! I really couldn't believe it. Abdu Latif had sculpted my head from memory and had achieved a very good likeness (for better or worse!). Now I understood why he had been scrutinizing my face for the past three days. He was an artist on a mission.

Abdu Latif spent part of his time in Egypt, making connections with the local Arab church (Egyptians born to Christian families). He was excited to learn of a small group of believers from Islamic background—people just like him—and he made the rounds getting to know them as well. For Abdu Latif, Egypt presented a rare opportunity—an Arab environment where one could get to know other Christians and be taught in the faith. He returned home with a purpose—that he would work to come back to Egypt with various members of his family. He wanted to replicate his experience in India for some of his family members.

Over the years that I was in Egypt, Abdu Latif made three trips there. On one he brought along his wife, son, and another family member. During that visit his wife placed her faith in Christ. Abdu Latif's son, who inherited his father's skills as an artisan, came to the faith later, back in their home country. As it happened, some Egyptian friends moved to Abdu Latif's town in the Arabian Peninsula. There his family became the nucleus of a new church, and it remains faithful to the Lord there to this day.

I haven't seen Abdu Latif in a few years, but his memory remains engraved in my mind. Whether telling me the latest joke about an Arab politician or recounting the latest heated interaction with his fundamentalist friends, Abdu Latif loved life. The memory of his antics still brings a smile to my face. He had tasted grace, been forgiven, and lived life as though each day really mattered. In all the places I've traveled and lived, I don't think I've ever met a more entertaining and engaging personality than Abdu Latif. I thank God for that phone call.

Abu Kathiir

Survival of the fittest—that phrase could describe the educational system in this Middle Eastern country. If you pass your secondary school exams with the highest marks, you are allowed to apply to the college of medicine. Those with the second-highest marks apply to the college of engineering, and so on down the line. Abu Kathiir had hoped and worked for a place in the college of foreign languages. He wanted to study English. However, his marks were just a bit shy of that standard, and that's how it happened that he was consigned to the college of Semitic languages—read "Hebrew."

Hebrew is quite an important language in Middle Eastern countries. Similar to the prevailing sentiment in the United States concerning the Soviet Union during the Cold War, Israel is viewed with a great deal of suspicion, and those who master Hebrew are called upon to advise and occasionally spy on their Semitic neighbor. It was through his Hebrew classes that Abu Kathiir was first introduced to the Scriptures of the Old Testament. Along with his readings, he made the acquaintance of a colleague whose investigations into the truth of the Hebrew Scriptures had led him to faith in Christ.

By the time I encountered him, Abu Kathiir had already made a long journey of faith. He had been under the tutelage of a number of expatriate Christians. Because he was a thinker and a linguist, we enjoyed some common interests. I recall reading through the Old Testament book of Ruth with him in Hebrew. Not only was his grasp of Hebrew grammar and morphology impressive, but he also had an intuitive understanding of the culture of the book and could easily draw applications for believers like himself—believers from Islamic background. Sensing his potential as a scholar and teacher, I tried to encourage him to keep up his studies. He appreciated that, I believe, as very few in his context aspire to a thorough-going study of the Word of God. Computers and English hold more promise for a profitable career path and the study of Islam more potential for prestige.

Abu Kathiir came from a middle-class Muslim family. His older brother had gone into the fundamentalist camp. His father was largely absent, so he continued to live with his mother—a loving and gentle Muslim woman. He continues to update me on the state of his mother and brother. In our most recent phone conversation, he was pleased to report that his brother, rather than threatening him, which was the norm, had now begun to ask him sincere questions about his faith. His mother, in Abu Kathiir's estimation, is now a believer. She is a simple woman who has no use for doctrinal comparisons of Islam and Christianity. However, she knows what she sees in her son, and inasmuch as she has understood the truth of Christ from him, she has believed.

One of my best memories was meeting weekly with Abu Kathiir and another friend for an intensive study of the book of Romans. Together we grappled with the implications of Paul's doctrine. There were heated disagreements while together we built a deepening conviction of the truth and authority of God's Word. I am still amazed when I consider the faithfulness and commitment of these two men who regularly took a full morning out of their week to come to my office and hammer away at Romans.

While studying at a seminary here in the United States, I began to appreciate this kind of commitment more fully. My seminary colleagues were motivated by their sincere desire to serve Christ, no doubt, but also by the real possibility that they would be able to earn their living teaching and preaching God's Word. Abu Kathiir, living in a Muslim context, has no such hope. Is his penchant for study foolishness? I think not. Rather, in searching out God's Word, he is storing up treasure for all of life—the treasure the psalmist extolled, saying its worth is more than fine gold.

Abu Kathiir has recently been summoned by the police and continues to be subjected to occasional interrogation. He has suffered humiliation and physical abuse at the hands of cruel men. His only crime—trusting Christ. For this book, I have chosen to call him Abu Kathiir—the name of an ancient Islamic scholar meaning "father of many." I trust that this dear friend, as he dwells in his own land, cultivating faithfulness to God, will become the father of many.

◆ SEEKING FRESH VISION ◆

It would be wrong to assume, as many Christians do, that these believers from Islamic background are the "real heroes" of the faith. In actual fact, they are flesh and blood—men and women made of dust just like you and me. However, their situation has placed them under some unique strains and stresses. Despite their best efforts to avoid it, they are often ostracized or at least misunderstood by family members. If they express their faith overtly, severe persecution may follow. Some have been imprisoned and tortured. Many have lost jobs. Many have been denied their first choice in seeking a life partner.

Many Christians in the West have asked me, "What can we do to help?" Our first recourse is usually to give money. Although that may be necessary in some circumstances, the real gift we can give these brothers and sisters is our solidarity. They want to know they are not alone. They want to know they are remembered by their Christian brothers and sisters around the world. When three of my friends were imprisoned in Egypt in 1991, Christians in many

Western countries embarked on a letter-writing campaign. The deluge of letters perplexed the prison authorities, who thought this was a routine investigation of some youths from a town on the Suez Canal. They began to think differently when the letters came in by the thousands. As the young men discovered that believers around the world were with them, they took courage despite being tortured and held in solitary confinement.

The body of Christ around the world had another occasion to stand with the church in the Muslim world recently, as two Turkish believers and one German man were martyred in Malatya, Turkey, on April 18, 2007. Ugur, Necati, and Tilmann were meeting to study the Bible with some others who had responded to an invitation. Unknown to them, the five men who joined them for the Bible study intended to attack the perpetrators of the "false religion" as an act of service to their faith. The massacre was brutal and left behind mourning widows and fatherless children. Still, it served as a rallying point for the emerging Turkish church and made many Christians in the West aware of their brothers and sisters in the Muslim world.

Sometimes these brothers and sisters will make headlines, but most often they will continue to live a quiet life, working as yeast and salt in their own societies. Even then they must not be forgotten, but upheld in our prayers and uppermost in our minds as an integral part of the fabric of God's work in the Muslim world.

The story of these believers is probably the "tip of the iceberg." Because of the kinds of pressures believers in Jesus face in Muslim societies, it is probable that there is a vast number of believers whose faith is rarely expressed in any visible way. Those whom I have been privileged to know are the elite few. There are probably many, many others hovering just below the surface whose names and stories may never be told. As we open our eyes to the Muslim world, we can celebrate the reality that Jesus is drawing many people to himself.

New life in the Muslim world will bring the pain of separation and the labor of new birth. As an expectant mother clings to the hope of her newborn child, we also cling to the fact proclaimed by the angelic herald over the hills of Bethlehem: "I bring you good news of great joy that will be for all the people" (Luke 2:10). Jesus is the source of reconciliation. His kingdom, rightly understood and lived, will bring great blessing to the Muslim world.

Additional Resources for Chapter 6

The following two books are the personal stories of two who have come to Christ from an Islamic context. Both are personal friends, and I can vouch for the accuracy of their stories and the reality of their faith.

Hawatmeh, Abdalla with Roland Muller. *Man from Jabalawi*. See www. rmuller.com.

Zeidan, David. *The Fifth Pillar: A Spiritual Pilgrimmage*. Carlisle, UK: Piquant, 2000.

For more stories of Muslims who are turning to Christ, see www.answering-islam.de/Main/Testimonies/index.html.

CHAPTER 7

THE ISRAEL OF GOD

I suppose it is my favorite story of all times and places. I've already referred to it, but let's revisit the story of the shepherd turned giant slayer.

David became one of my boyhood heroes. A ruddy shepherd boy is sent by his doting father to take roasted grain and bread to three valiant brothers serving as soldiers in the army of Yahweh. He had grown up in the countryside, taking the sheep out early in the day to graze and then bringing them home at night. Wide spaces and silent hours perfected him in the art of worship. He sought a voice for his pondering of the ineffable God who sculpted the hills and sky around him and found that voice in a lyre, an ancient guitar. He mastered the instrument—a skill that would eventually land him in the presence of a king.

Life was not all music and worship. Yahweh's world held good and evil, predator and prey. The sheep David led were in a state of constant vulnerability to the ravenous hunger of lions and bears, which, with one swipe of a giant paw, could transform David's meditative watchfulness into soldierlike readiness. The simplicity of his weapons belied their deadliness. Again, David had perfected his skill in their use in long hours of solitude and perpetual practice. His targets got farther and farther away. The slightest miss meant tenfold repetition until perfection was attained. Eventually, David never missed. He was a sharpshooter—yet another skill that destined him for greatness.

But skill alone fails to explain what possessed him on the day of that first visit to the battlefield. Did he realize by soldier's intuition that the field of battle would be his new home? Heart of the worshipper and skill of the warrior wed on this day, launching this young shepherd to the pinnacles of leadership in the ancient world. "Who is this uncircumcised Philistine that he should defy the armies of the living God?" David asked (1 Samuel 17:26).

"Impudent upstart! Go back to the sheep!"

Were there other shepherd boys who had killed lions and bears? Where were they this day? David's boast of past victories might have seemed like ramblings of a braggart in any other circumstance. The ruddy shepherd boy was resolute and fearless, even as Goliath's taunt echoed through the troops: "This day I defy the ranks of Israel! Give me a man and let us fight each other" (1 Samuel 17:10).

David's attempt to use Saul's armor is laughable. David could fight only with his own weapons; he knew that. This war would not be won conventionally. Neither his fleetness of foot nor his mobility could be sacrificed. Five smooth stones and a well-worn sling—that's all the armament David took into this battle:

"Am I a dog, that you come at me with sticks?" And the Philistine cursed David by his gods. "Come here," he said, "and I'll give your flesh to the birds of the air and the beasts of the field!"

David said to the Philistine, "You come against me with sword and spear and javelin, but I come against you in the name of the Lord Almighty, the God of the armies of Israel, whom you have defied. This day the Lord will hand you over to me, and I'll strike you down and cut off your head. Today I will give the carcasses of the Philistine army to the birds of the air and the beasts of the earth, and the whole world will know that there is a God in Israel. All those gathered here will know that it is not by sword or spear that the Lord saves; for the battle is the Lord's, and he will give all of you into our hands."

As the Philistine moved closer to attack him, David ran quickly toward the battle line to meet him. (1 Samuel 17:43–48)

The story grabs me. I shout yes in allegiance to the shepherd underdog and fall in behind David's charge as the giant's bloody head is hoisted in the air! But what does this story of my boyhood hero have to do with today's Muslim world?

Everything.

Like many who read these lines, I was schooled in the battles of ancient Israel. I memorized their battle songs and pored over their prophecies. I became an avid student of their exiles and watched as they fell away from the law of Yahweh and were renewed. I knew little of the geography of other ancient civilizations, but I could place many of the towns and cities of Israel on a map. I knew the basic layout of the Sea of Galilee, the Jordan River, and the Dead Sea. I was discipled in the stately Shema: "Hear, O Israel: The Lord our God, the Lord is one. Love the Lord your God with all your heart and with all your soul and with all your strength" (Deuteronomy 6:4–5). Old Testament Israel was the seedbed of my understanding of God and his purposes in the world.

My Sunday school upbringing inculcated another dimension of my views relative to the contemporary Middle East. I learned that Israel had enemies, evil enemies. First there was Ishmael, Abraham's other son: "He will be a wild donkey of a man; his hand will be against everyone and everyone's hand against him, and he will live in hostility toward all his brothers" (Genesis 16:12). I immediately associated Ishmael with the Arabs (a false association, by the way). Then there were the Edomites, the Moabites, and various other Canaanite peoples, all of whom stood in stark contrast to God's chosen people, the Israelites.

One particular people group constantly plagued the Israelites— the Philistines. Their name in Arabic, *filistiin*, is precisely the term used in contemporary media to designate the residents of the land of Israel prior to 1948—Palestine. It appears the ancient enmities live on between God's chosen people Israel and the surrounding nations.

Not all who read these pages will share my fondness for Israel's ancient history. No doubt some will see in the Old Testament stories the relics of a vengeful God and an exclusivist religion. Defending the Old Testament against such assertions is beyond the scope of this book. Others have excelled at that task.[1] Rather, my purpose is to reexamine our affection for Israel in the hope of refining it (removing the impurities).

I suspect that statement raised an immediate red flag in your mind: *Wait a minute! God will bless those who bless the seed of Abraham and curse those who curse them. I don't want to be reading anything that leads me away from what I know to be God's purpose.* Neither do I.

Talking about Israel and the Arabs is a minefield among evangelicals. There is probably no quicker way to be labeled *anti* this or *pro* that. Jesus himself spoke words that caused the Jews to take up stones to put him to death, labeling him "a Samaritan and demon-possessed" (John 8:48). He challenged the synagogue worshippers in his hometown to get a new understanding of their Scriptures as he pointed to Naaman (a Syrian army officer) and a widow of Zeraphath in Sidon (also a non-Jew) as sterling examples of faith. Some of the ideas in this chapter might make my readers want to throw stones. A better alternative is that we all learn to drop our stones (and our labels) and take a fresh look at God's Word and his purposes for our world.

I invite you to think with me through some basic questions. Were the Old Testament prophecies of the return from exile fulfilled in the Old Testament, or were they fulfilled when Israel was reconstituted as a state in 1948? Is it conceivable that both events are a fulfillment of prophecy? Could the 1948 establishment of Israel be a preliminary fulfillment that awaits a final fulfillment in the millennial kingdom? How do the prophecies of the Old Testament interrelate with the teaching of Christ and the apostles in the New Testament? What implications do these things have for our view of the modern-day state of Israel?

Granted, my treatment of these subjects will be cursory at best. For those wanting a more detailed discussion, refer to the additional resources at the end of the chapter. A subsequent chapter will delve into our understanding of the end-times—eschatology. In this chapter we are seeking perspective on the question of precisely who is "the Israel of God" (Galatians 6:16).

First, let's take a look back at the Old Testament.

Old Testament Israel

The Old Testament is rather anticlimactic. The end of the story is not very exciting or encouraging. If we were to try to tell the story of the Old Testament in a few lines, it might look something like this: God created human beings as an act of love. Human beings rebelled against this loving God. God established a covenant with a family that became a nation. This family was the channel of God's blessing to the nations. This nation/family repeatedly failed to walk in holiness and faithfulness to God. God warned them through the prophets to change their ways, but they did not. Consequently, the people were uprooted from the land in which God settled them. They suffered reproach at the hands of other nations and were carried away into exile. But God promised through the prophets that they would return to the land and that he would bless them yet again. They did return and rebuild their temple and their society. However, even their return and reestablishment in the land left much to be desired. The Old Testament ends with stories of new disobedience and unfaithfulness to God, and the prophets stopped speaking.

I suppose a Hollywood scriptwriter would need a better ending. Since we know the New Testament, we know there is a better ending. But before we rush ahead to that ending, let's pause a moment to look at some of the prophetic promises of a return of the people of Israel to their land after the exile.

Ancient Promises, New Realities

It is clear that Jeremiah prophesied at the risk of his own life that Judah (southern Israel) would be carried away into captivity. "This whole country will become a desolate wasteland, and these nations will serve the king of Babylon seventy years" (Jeremiah 25:11). After the seventy-year exile, Judah would return to its own land. "This is what the LORD says: 'When seventy years are completed for Babylon, I will come to you and fulfill my gracious promise to bring you back to this place'" (Jeremiah 29:10).

The renowned Daniel, who was carried off into exile, corroborated this prophecy as he pored over Jeremiah's writings and realized the time of return from exile was approaching. Daniel began to confess the sins of his people and plead for God's mercy. In response to this prayer, found in Daniel 9, Daniel saw a vision, the meaning of which is still debated by Bible scholars. We will look more closely at Daniel's vision in the next chapter. Suffice it to say that the basis for Daniel's prayer was Jeremiah's prophecy of a seventy-year exile.

Daniel relates that a decree would be issued to rebuild Jerusalem. In fact, more than one decree was issued. We read about one of these in 2 Chronicles 36:23: "This is what Cyrus king of Persia says: 'The LORD, the God of heaven, has given me all the kingdoms of the earth and he has appointed me to build a temple for him at Jerusalem in Judah. Anyone of his people among you— may the LORD his God be with him, and let him go up.'" Ezra and Nehemiah are the primary Old Testament characters who relate to us the circumstances of this rebuilding.

So far, so good. We have a neat picture of prophesied exile and prophesied return from exile seventy years later. Both the exile and the return are well documented in the pages of the Old Testament.

However, history didn't stop after the Old Testament. The picture is clouded in our day by several realities:

Reality #1. Israel was scattered yet again at the end of the New Testament era. The nation suffered unmentionable atrocities throughout history.

Reality #2. Israel has again been regathered and constitutes a nation in our day. Furthermore, it has reclaimed the land of its ancient heritage in the face of considerable opposition from surrounding Arab nations.

Reality #3. The Old Testament makes it crystal clear that God's covenant with Israel is an everlasting covenant. He will never forsake his people. "But Zion said, 'The LORD has forsaken me, the Lord has forgotten me.' Can a mother forget the baby at her breast and have no compassion on the child she has borne? Though she may forget, I will not forget you! See, I have engraved you on the palms of my hands; your walls are ever before me" (Isaiah 49:14–16).

Is it not right and proper, therefore, that you and I, when we read the great promises of God of bringing back the people of Israel to their land understand them to be speaking of our day? Don't we look at the reestablishment of Israel in 1948 as an amazing act of God in which he revived his ancient promises to bring his people back to their land after scattering them among the nations of the world? It is even more glorious when we begin to think of the atrocities that the Jews suffered in their diaspora and especially at the hands of the Nazis in the twentieth century. Surely we must understand the ancient prophecies of the Bible in the light of modern-day events. God has vindicated his Word and reestablished his people.[2]

Many Christian teachers have interpreted the events precisely this way. Books and historical fiction have been written around these realities, and some have topped the best-seller lists of religious and nonreligious titles. In fact the reestablishment of Israel has evoked an end-times enthusiasm. Could it be that the events in today's Middle East are the mere ticking of a prophetic clock? Are we watching a reenactment of the ancient enmity of Israel with the surrounding nations just prior to God's ultimate vindication of his people?

Tiny Israel has been ruthlessly subjected to wars of aggression against her. Just as the young shepherd boy whose star now emblazons the banners of the state of Israel overcame all odds to defeat a giant, so Israel stands today in defiance of its enemies—the enemies of God. For many Bible-believing Christians, other nations will be blessed in proportion to their support of the state of Israel, and the United States owes much of its economic and military prosperity to its staunch support of Israel. Christians, therefore, should throw their support behind candidates who uphold Israel against its aggressors. Any hesitation to endorse Israeli policies can be seen as tacit approval of the radical Islamists who call for Israel's destruction. The presence of Hamas activists and a radical Iranian regime set against Israel paint the issue clearly in black-and-white. Surely Israel is a tiny persecuted minority, while the Islamists are radically devoted to killing innocent civilians in addition to taking their own lives through suicide bombings. Fidelity to God's Word, not to mention common human decency, leaves no alternative to an unqualified endorsement of Israel over against the Islamists.

The State of Israel in the Light of Prophecy

Is the modern-day state of Israel a fulfillment of the Old Testament prophecies of a return to Israel's ancient land? When we look at the prophecies, we find an Israel that returns to the land in belief and covenant faithfulness to its God, who said:

> I will surely gather them from all the lands where I banish them in my furious anger and great wrath; I will bring them back to this place and let them live in safety. They will be my people, and I will be their God. I will give them singleness of heart and action, so that they will always fear me for their own good and the good of their children after them. I will make an everlasting covenant with them: I will never stop doing good to them, and I will inspire them to fear me, so that they will never turn away from me. I will rejoice in doing them good and will assuredly plant them in this land with all my heart and soul. (Jeremiah 32:37–41)

While it is clear that God intends to bless Israel in its land, it is equally clear that the Israel he has in mind will be a faithful people, a consecrated kingdom, a holy nation. The contemporary state of Israel simply does not fit this description.

Two options, perhaps more, emerge. The first is that the contemporary state of Israel is a fulfillment of these prophecies, although it has yet to become a holy nation. I believe many Christians in the United States embrace this option and look upon the state of Israel as uniquely favored by God and await a coming turning to God in that nation—a revival. The second option is that God has fulfilled and is fulfilling that promise as people of all nations are becoming the expanded Israel—the church.

We will discuss these two options in more detail further on. For now, let's look at the New Testament.

A New Testament Perspective

Jesus showed not the slightest hesitation to provide his authoritative interpretation of the Old Testament. Jesus declared himself to be superior to the temple (Matthew 12:6). He proclaimed that the Law, the Psalms, and the Prophets revolved around one supreme topic—himself (Luke 24:27, 44)! He showed no reservation about adjusting the Pharisees' understanding of the Sabbath (Mark 2:27). His ingenious use of Old Testament themes such as the shepherd and the vine linked him inextricably to the eternal purposes of God that Israel's prophets had proclaimed. He even took on the sensitive subject of the temple and said that his own body was the temple that would never be destroyed and would, in fact, be resurrected three days after an attempted destruction. As for Herod's temple in Jerusalem, Jesus proclaimed that not one stone would be left on another! To the heated debates of his day, Jesus gave ready answers. When he was challenged, "Our fathers worshiped on this mountain, but you Jews claim that the place where we must worship is in Jerusalem," he responded, "Neither in Jerusalem nor on this mountain, for God is spirit, and those who worship him must do so in spirit and in truth" (see John. 4:20–24).

When we look at the Old Testament, we do so through the filtering lens of the teaching of Jesus and his apostles. This is not to say that Jesus trumps the Old Testament or that the apostolic teaching replaces or amends the Old Testament. Rather, we hold that Jesus provided the authoritative interpretation of the Old Testament. In order to understand the Old Testament, its history and its prophecies, we must view it in the light of Jesus' teaching. He is the supreme interpreter.

So what assistance does Jesus offer us in this thorny issue of Israel? We'll look at Jesus' teaching first, then the apostles'.

The People of Jesus

Jesus' identification of his people was not based on ethnicity.³ When his mother and brothers came to seek him, he declared, "Whoever does the will of my Father in heaven is my brother and sister and mother" (Matthew 12:50). Jesus elevated non-Jews—much to the irritation of the Jewish leaders—as paragons of faith: the Roman centurion (a commander of one hundred Roman soldiers) of whom he said, "I have not found anyone in Israel with such great faith" (Matthew 8:10), and a Canaanite woman who humbly implored Jesus to free her daughter from demon oppression (Matthew 15:21–28).

The Jews of Jesus' day were hardly in a place of world dominance. They were under the protection of the Romans, and their repeated maneuvers to displace the heavy hand of Rome went unrewarded. On his way to Jerusalem, Jesus got into a heated showdown with the gatekeepers of Jewish orthodoxy, the Pharisees. He told a parable of two sons. One willingly agreed to do what his father asked him, but it was only lip service; he didn't obey. The other son at first refused to obey his father but later went and did as requested. Just to make sure the Pharisees didn't miss the point, Jesus told them that the tax collectors (servants of the Roman occupation) and prostitutes were making their way into God's kingdom while the Pharisees stayed outside (Matthew 21:31–32)—hardly the way to make friends and influence people! Then he put all his cards on the table with another little story (vv. 33–39).

It's about a landowner who owned a vineyard and went to great lengths to make sure it was well cared for. After that he went on a journey, leaving his vineyard in the care of tenants. Time passed, and the landowner sent some representatives to bring the produce of his vineyard to him. They never made it back. They were seized, beaten up, and even killed by the tenants. The patient landowner tried again, sending more emissaries to gather his vineyard's proceeds. Again the wretched tenants beat and killed the owner's representatives. Incredibly, the landowner then decided to send someone who was sure to command the respect of the tenants—his very son! When the tenants saw the son, they consulted together and decided that this is the heir of the vineyard; if they killed him, they could possess it. Although the tenants' response stretches the imagination, they did, in fact, kill the son of the owner!

Jesus asked the Pharisees what the landowner would do to the tenants when he returned to the vineyard himself. "Why, of course, he will bring those wretched tenants to a wretched end and give the vineyard to other tenants," they replied. Bull's-eye. "Therefore I tell you that the kingdom of God will be taken away from you and given to a people who will produce its fruit" (Matthew 21:43). Jesus told the Jewish religious leaders of his day in no uncertain terms that they would no longer be the gatekeepers of his vineyard.

I do not wish to suggest that this parable teaches the ultimate rejection of the Jews. It does teach, however, that persistent and arrogant rejection of Christ and his works leads to estrangement from the kingdom of God. That estrangement takes place with absolutely no regard for ethnicity or religious pedigree; it is based solely on the response given to Jesus Christ. It is striking that Jesus seemed to place no importance on which political entity is sovereign over the land of Israel. In his own day, it was Rome. Jesus, however, never denounced Rome or promised that Rome would be cast out of the land, which would have been a very popular theme in Israel. Ironically, the Jews accused Jesus of assuming kingship. They pointed out to Pilate that this was in opposition to Caesar, hoping to seal Jesus' fate. Jesus, on the other hand, was mystifyingly silent in reference to Rome but outspoken in his scathing rebuke of the spiritual leaders of his people. It could not be more obvious that his preoccupation was with another kingdom—the kingdom of heaven.

The healing of the centurion's servant also casts light on Jesus' understanding of the relationship of ethnic Israel to his kingdom. This Roman commander came to Jesus with a request for him to heal his servant. Calling himself unworthy for Jesus to enter his home, the centurion asked that Jesus merely say the words so that his servant would be healed. "For I myself am a man under authority, with soldiers under me. I tell this one, 'Go,' and he goes; and that one, 'Come,' and he comes. I say to my servant, 'Do this,' and he does it" (Matthew 8:9). Jesus, elated at this demonstration of faith by the non-Jewish centurion, not only healed his servant but also made this startling declaration: "I tell you the truth, I have not found anyone in Israel with such great faith. I say to you that many will come from the east and the west, and will take their places at the feast with Abraham, Isaac and Jacob in the kingdom of heaven. But the subjects of the kingdom will be thrown outside, into the darkness, where there will be weeping and gnashing of teeth" (vv. 10–12). Jesus made it explicit: non-Jews will be recognized by Abraham as part of the family.

Jesus was a very insightful prophet, was he not? He told Peter that he would deny him and that when he was restored he should strengthen his brothers. He perceived clearly that Judas was to betray him, and he even gave the command that initiated Judas' treachery. He prophesied his own death and resurrection, citing where his murder would take place and the number of days that would elapse between his death and resurrection.

Jesus also prophesied clearly and precisely about Jerusalem shortly before his death, when he was making his way to that city to be nailed to rough-hewn beams outside the city walls. He had just finished his sevenfold declaration of woes against the Pharisees. He then cried, "O Jerusalem, Jerusalem, you who kill the prophets and stone those sent to you, how often I have longed to gather your children together, as a hen gathers her chicks under her wings, but you were not willing. Look, your house is left to you desolate. For I tell you, you will not see me again until you say, 'Blessed is he who comes in the name of the Lord'" (Matthew 23:37–39). The Jewish leaders' rejection of Jesus meant the plundering of their house. It is left desolate until such time as they respond to him who comes in the name of the Lord by declaring him to be blessed.

It seems the disciples didn't get it. After Jesus' diatribe against the Pharisees, the disciples came to Jesus remarking about the beautiful stones of the temple. Jesus then clearly told them that not one stone would be left on another. He indicated the total destruction of the Jerusalem temple, which was the pride of the Jewish people of that day. That destruction did take place as prophesied in 70 CE, and the temple has not been rebuilt to this day.

Did Jesus prophesy the return of the Jews to their land and the rebuilding of their temple? Two passages are sometimes interpreted in this way. The first is Matthew 23:39, which we just looked at: "I tell you, you will not see me again until you say, 'Blessed is he who comes in the name of the Lord.'" The second is Jesus' prophecy in Luke 21:24 that "Jerusalem will be trampled on by the Gentiles until the times of the Gentiles are fulfilled."

In the first instance, Jesus indicated that a historic opportunity for the Jewish nation to acknowledge its Messiah had passed. There will come a day when they will declare, "Blessed is he who comes in the name of the Lord." I believe Jesus to be referring to his second coming. Whatever the case, if this prophetic word were fulfilled with the 1948 reestablishment of the state of Israel, why has the nation persisted in its refusal to bless Christ? In the second instance, the fulfillment of the times of the Gentiles may well refer to the Gentile occupation of Israel. However, the passage is silent as to a return of Israel to its land. In the verses that follow each of these passages, Christ turns his attention to his second coming.

How are we to understand Jesus' silence about a reestablished state of Israel? I suggest his silence is perfectly consistent with his lack of interest in the geopolitical state of Israel during his earthly ministry. His concern is with his kingdom—the kingdom of heaven.

Those who see the 1948 reconstitution of Israel as a fulfillment of biblical prophecy normally draw their conclusions from Old Testament prophecies that relate to the Jewish return to the land after exile. This is done for the simple reason that Jesus' teaching gives very little indication that there will ever be a return to the land or a rebuilding of the temple. If our guiding principle holds true—that Jesus is the supreme interpreter of the Old Testament—where does this leave us? Before attempting to answer that question, let's look further at the teaching of the apostles to see what light they have for us on the reestablishment of Israel and the return to its ancient land.

Abraham's Descendants through the Eyes of the Apostles

We have minimal knowledge of what transpired between Jesus' resurrection and his ascension. We're dependent on inference from the apostles' words and writings to know exactly what was talked about. Luke informs us that the disciples asked Jesus, "Lord, are you at this time going to restore the kingdom to Israel?" (Acts 1:6). I find it ironic that this sincere question from the Jewish disciples was recorded by Luke, a Gentile doctor.

The advance of God's kingdom to the nations of the earth is the theme of the book of Acts. The restoration of the kingdom to Israel that so dominated the minds of the disciples was not Jesus' issue at all. He explicitly told them that his agenda began with their being anointed with power from heaven in the near future. From that point on, the disciples would be involved in worldwide conquest, bringing men and women into the kingdom of Christ through their proclamation of his Word.

Once this Pentecost anointing took place, we find that Jesus' values and objectives were reaffirmed and further developed by the apostles. When the Samaritans received the gospel through the preaching of Philip, Peter and John were sent to Samaria to verify what was taking place. They witnessed the outpouring of the Holy Spirit on the Samaritans, similar to what had taken place with the Jews at Pentecost. Peter's reticence to eat unclean foods was reprimanded by a vision in which he learned to call no one unclean. The result is that a Roman God-fearer found Christ, and his home became an outpost of Jesus' kingdom. This story is recounted twice in the book of Acts (10–11) in abundant detail. The story line turns to Paul in Acts 13, where we find the Antioch church led by a multicultural team. Small wonder that Paul's ministry sees the church established beyond the boundaries of the Jewish world as both Jews and Gentiles embrace the gospel.

Colin Chapman has pointed out[4] that the book of Acts in many ways parallels the book of Joshua in the Old Testament. Joshua was commissioned to take possession of the land by military conquest. The apostles, in Acts 1, are commissioned to take the gospel into the entire world, using not military arms but the proclamation of the Word of God—the "sword of the Spirit" (Ephesians 6:17). Acts recounts the progressive spread of Jesus' kingdom beginning from Jerusalem, then to Judea, Samaria, and the uttermost parts of the world.

Paul distills his apostolic experience of establishing the church among the nations of the Mediterranean basin in Romans 2. Abraham is portrayed not as the father of an ethnic group or a geopolitical state but as the father of those who have faith. Those who are children of Abraham are those who are of a similar faith. Those who are of the bloodline of Abraham are demonstrated *not* to be of his line by their lack of such faith:

> A man is not a Jew if he is only one outwardly, nor is circumcision merely outward and physical. No, a man is a Jew if he is one inwardly; and circumcision is circumcision of the heart, by the Spirit, not by the written code. Such a man's praise is not from men, but from God. (Romans 2:28–29)

> Understand, then, that those who believe are children of Abraham. The Scripture foresaw that God would justify the Gentiles by faith, and announced the gospel in advance to Abraham: "All nations will be blessed through you." So those who have faith are blessed along with Abraham, the man of faith. (Galatians 3:7–9)

The New Testament indicates clearly that God has removed once and for all the ethnic boundaries of his people. All are welcome—both Jews and Gentiles—regardless of race or background.

Paul refers to Israel as the native olive tree into which we Gentile Christians have been grafted. We do well not to forget our debt to the Jewish people in terms of our spiritual heritage. However, this debt is best discharged by honoring the purposes of him who was the embodiment of the longing of Israel, the fulfillment of Yahweh's covenant promise "I will dwell among them" (Exodus 25:8)—Immanuel.

Peter refers to the *inheritance* of believers in 1 Peter 1:3–5. This word would have normally been used for the land that was the inheritance of the Jews. Peter, living during the time of Nero's ruthless persecution of the Jews, encourages Christ-followers that they have "an inheritance that can never perish, spoil or fade—kept in heaven for you." What a contrast to the earthly inheritance of a land occupied by a foreign power! Furthermore, Peter associated Christ-followers with the Israel of the Old Testament in a way that well-read Jews would find indisputable. He drew from the imagery used by Moses in the prologue to the Ten Commandments and applied this imagery to the New Testament people of God, consisting of both Jews and Gentiles: "But you are a chosen people, a royal priesthood, a holy nation, a people belonging to God, that you may declare the praises of him who called you out of darkness into his wonderful light" (1 Peter 2:9–10; see also Exodus 19:6).

The writings of the apostle John are not commonly associated with teaching on the state of the Jews and their relation to the apostolic church. However, in the book of Revelation there is a significant mention of those Jews who continued to worship in the synagogue. Jesus spoke through John to the church in Philadelphia: "I will make those who are of the synagogue of Satan, who claim to be Jews though they are not, but are liars—I will make them come and fall down at your feet and acknowledge that I have loved you."

(Revelation 3:9). You might be led to believe there was some kind of satanic cult in Philadelphia, but in fact John is more likely referring to the local Jewish synagogue. Did the lie of these synagogue Jews consist in their not being ethnically related to Abraham or religiously the descendants of the Mosaic faith? I think not. It would seem their lie consisted in their refusal to recognize the seed of Abraham—Jesus Christ. Jesus declares that these people are not Jews. How revealing!

The expansion of God's people that began in the Old Testament is greatly increased in the New Testament. Jesus, who rejoiced to receive the Samaritans into the fold of his kingdom, is yet rejoicing as people of all tribes and tongues flock to his leadership. He himself declared with a note of urgency, "I have other sheep that are not of this sheep pen [presumably, not of the Jewish fold]. I must bring them also" (John 10:16).

What Do We Make of This?

In our attempt to foster fresh vision for the Muslim world, we are trying to see that part of the world as Jesus sees it. In order to do so, we have to return to his teaching, elaborated by his apostles. First, we'll need to admit that our own vision may have become skewed by our predispositions and our constant exposure to various teachings and views. If we are willing to make that admission, we can come to the New Testament expecting that our understanding may need to be corrected. It is perhaps overly optimistic to hope that such a correction can take place in reading a short chapter like this. My modest hope is that this chapter might be the first step in a long journey of change.

I am not seeking to deconstruct our affection for the state of Israel but merely to refine it. I hope that we can strip our affection for the state of Israel of all that is unbiblical and embrace Israel with new awareness and compassion. (In much the same way, we will need to strip our view of the Arab and Muslim peoples of the world of all that is unbiblical and embrace the Arab peoples with new awareness and compassion.)

Earlier in this chapter I discussed two main options related to our thinking about the present-day state of Israel. The first is that this nation is a fulfillment of biblical prophecies, but we await a full return of the Jewish people to their covenant God through Christ. For those who embrace this option, it is necessary to remember how God has, in the past, addressed the people of Israel; he often expressed his love to that people through the dire warnings and stern rebukes of his prophets. Some of these exhortations remain so poignant that it makes our hair stand on end. Think of Hosea, Jeremiah, Ezekiel. Does it not stand to reason, if we await a revived state of Israel, that the role of Christ-followers in relation to the state of Israel would be a prophetic voice, exhorting Israel to faith in Christ and challenging that people to walk humbly with their God?

The second option is that in Jesus Christ the Israel of the Old Testament has been radically expanded to include people of all nations and languages. The Israel of God is not a geopolitical entity at all but the kingdom ruled by the Messiah, descended from David, who ascended to the throne of power at the right hand of Yahweh. Thus the modern-day state of Israel is a geopolitical entity and not synonymous with the Israel of God. Within this view are those who expect many ethnic Jews to embrace Christ as their Messiah. Romans 11 forms the foundation for this hope, as Paul teaches that God is able to graft these "natural [olive] branches" back into "their own olive tree."

Thus both options have an empathy and a concern for ethnic Israel. The first option identifies the state of Israel as an important element in the unfolding of God's plan. The second option views the state of Israel as incidental and emphasizes the necessity that ethnic Jews be restored to a right relationship with their God through their Messiah, Jesus Christ.

I will tip my hand to say that I believe the second option fits best with the biblical evidence. At the same time, I realize that many Christians in the United States will continue to hold to the first option. That being the case, my plea is that we continue to think of and pray for the state of Israel not as the final fulfillment of biblical prophecy but as a preliminary to a future fulfillment. Because Israel has yet to embrace its Messiah, we should not view the state of Israel as a uniquely blessed geopolitical entity. Our support of that state should be according to God's standards of truth and righteousness, as would be the case with any other political state.

While we may not settle long-standing differences over the identity of Abraham's descendants, we can and should adopt the attitude of Christ and his apostles. This attitude can be summed up in three propositions:

First, Jesus himself is the great deliverer of Israel. By following Christ, his people are delivered from bondage and set free to become the sons and daughters of God. Jesus himself is the lawgiver and the fulfillment of the longing of Israel—Immanuel, God with us.

Second, Jesus lovingly warns Israel that should it persist in its rejection of him, the people will reap the bitter consequences of that rejection. Thus modern-day Israelis need to hear and understand the gospel of Christ.

Third, the Israel of God includes both Old Testament Jews and New Testament people of faith who have embraced the Messiah. These, like Abraham, have placed their faith in God and are following him in obedience.

Then Who Are the Arabs?

A friend recently asked me, "Aren't these all secondary matters? Do we not all agree on the basic issues of Scripture, which are clear to all?"

Our view of Israel necessarily implicates us in a life-and-death struggle currently being waged in the Middle East. The simple fact is that most of us see the opposite poles of the Arab-Israeli conflict and immediately take a side, that of Israel. To our way of thinking, to do anything less would be to oppose God's people. So our bias in favor of Israel is equally a bias against Arabs and Muslims. We hear the news and read the media with this kind of attitude, such that our predisposition is confirmed over and over again. The result is that we misread the purposes of God for all peoples, including Jews and Arabs.

This misreading is largely due to a misreading of the Bible. For instance, God's declaration that Ishmael will be a wild donkey of a man is perceived as a final sentencing on all Arab and Muslim people, eternally consigning them as the staunch antagonists of Israel. We fail to question our association of Ishmael with all Arabs (while some Arabs may be ethnically linked to Ishmael, many are not). An unpublished article by M. Harlan[5] points out that a fuller appreciation of the biblical evidence will lead to a shift in our opinions:

> Recent evangelical scholarship[35] reveals how astonishingly mistaken is this stereotype that misses the prevailing positive

picture of Ishmael and his descendents in Scripture. In summary, God promised to *bless* Ishmael (Gen. 17:20), whom He so named because He heard Hagar's affliction. To comfort her and encourage her to return to her mistress, the Lord promised to reverse her subjection, helplessness and flight by making her son free as a nomad who would not be subjugated and who would live in the Arabian desert next to his brothers (Gen. 16:12). God was "with" Ishmael and remained uniquely present in his land of Paran and made him a great nation (Gen. 21:17–21; 25:12–17; Hab. 3:3). Ishmael's descendants were known as the "sons of the east" renowned for their godly wisdom (as portrayed in the book of Job). Proverbs 30 and 31 were written by the Arab sages, Agur and Lemuel, and included in the Old Testament canon. Prophecies of the restoration of Israel (cf. Isaiah 42 and 60) mention Arab tribes as the first nations to bring tribute to the Lord—an event in which Matthew finds initial fulfillment with the coming of the magi who have been convincingly shown to have been Arabs. Moreover, the myth of hostility between Israel and Ishmael has been dispelled; rather biblical history has evidenced a theological cause-effect relationship where Ishmael's spiritual fortunes have closely followed the ups and downs of Israel's.[36]

35. See the impressive work by Tony Maalouf, *Ishmael in Biblical History,* Dallas Theological Seminary doctoral dissertation, May 1998 (as well as John Culver's dissertation at Fuller Theological Seminary, 2001).

36. Ibid., 252. Evangelical prejudice against the Arabs is even more ironic if, as Dr. Maalouf argues, this remnant of Jewish believers that will be persecuted during the great tribulation (Revelation 12) will be sheltered by Arabs living in the desert.

While Muhammad traced his lineage to Ishmael, it is not true that all Arabs (and certainly not all Muslims) can be linked directly to Ishmael. Much like the nation of Israel, which has enfolded many proselytes who have no ethic connection to Abraham, so the Arabs are a composite of many nations and peoples. The original Arabs descended from Shem, the son of Noah. Genesis 10 records that Shem had a descendant named Eber who had two sons: Peleg and Joktan. It was Joktan's descendants who populated the Arabian Peninsula, whereas Peleg was the forebear of Abraham and the Jewish people.

In essence, Christians need to understand that a clear ethnic association of Muslim people (and particularly the Arab people) with Ishmael is inaccurate. Intermarriage, warfare, and migrations mean that these ethnic lines are blurred at best. Therefore, we will need to be wary of transferring our reading of the ancient Scriptures of the Old Testament to today's enmities in the Middle East. It is unfortunate that the ancient enemies of Israel are identified with the contemporary residents of the Arab world. I would even go so far as to say that Christians may need to repent of this misapplication of the Old Testament to modern-day realities.

◆ SEEKING FRESH VISION ◆

I cannot overemphasize the importance of such a change of orientation in our thinking in regard to our vision for the Muslim world. If we arrive at our positions based on principles of justice and equity, Muslims will recognize that fact and appreciate it. They are mystified and enraged when Christians appear biased in their political positions. Furthermore, we must exercise great caution not to generalize in these discussions. Just as all Americans are not alike in their political views, all Arabs do not wish the destruction of Israel. A large number merely wish to live at peace.

You may feel that your opinion will have little impact on such a complex and involved conflict. Before we close this chapter, may I point out that views adopted by Christians on social and political issues have helped shape world events both for good and for evil. Imagine my shock and surprise to learn that some of my forebears in the faith, theologians whom I studied in seminary, defended slavery as an institution consistent with biblical revelation, the evils of which should be limited.[6] A similar point could be made about the complicity of Christians in Nazi Germany with Hitler's Third Reich. Those who stood up to oppose Hitler's oppression and persecution of Jews were the blessed exceptions rather than the rule. As a result the Holocaust went forward unabated while the church's deafening silence remains as a haunting reminder that the enmeshment of the church with the political establishment leads inevitably to a loss of the salty savor.

Evangelical Christians have a long history of support for the state of Israel. The existence of fundamentalist Islamic groups that oppose Israel by instigating suicide bombing, murdering noncombatants, and producing instability in far-flung reaches of the world make this support appear to be the only rational option. In our reaction to both the fundamentalists and the state of Israel, we must return to the teachings of Christ for light and wisdom. Uncritical empathy with the Arab-Muslim side of the conflict could lead to a resurrection of anti-Semitism—an evil that continues to inflict torment on the Jewish people. On the other hand, an uncritical empathy with the Jewish people will lead to a deprivation of the legitimate human rights of the Arab people. Failure to reexamine our positions may lead to perpetration of excesses and oppression of the innocent. The stakes are high. Wars are being fought even as I write.

Additional Resources for Chapter 7

These two books add important dimensions to the line of argument being pursued in this chapter.

Burge, Gary. *Whose Land? Whose Promise?* Cleveland: The Pilgrim Press, 2003.

Chapman, Colin. *Whose Promised Land?: The Continuing Crisis over Israel and Palestine.* Oxford: Lion, 2002.

This article is by a friend and fellow minister of the gospel. His views deserve careful attention especially by those who hail from the dispensational camp.

Harlan, M. "Between Iraq and a Hard Place." *Christian Witness in Pluralistic Contexts in the Twenty-first Century.* Enoch Wan, ed. Evangelical Missiological Society Series, 11. Pasadena, CA: William Carey Library, 2004.

The last resource is an open letter composed by the faculty of Knox Theological Seminary relative to the contemporary state of Israel.

"An Open Letter to Evangelicals and Other Interested Parties: The People of God, the Land of Israel, and the Impartiality of the Gospel," www. originaldissent.com/forums/archive/index.php?t-3694.html.

CHAPTER 8

WHAT'S NEXT
OR WHAT'S NOW?

In the 1960s at the height of the Cold War, missiles carrying enough explosive firepower to destroy the earth many times over were said to be pointed at American cities. (Of course, the sentiment and preparedness for conflict were mutual.) Americans recounted in hushed tones their vivid memories of the world wars. Korea had come and gone, and our nation was heavily engaged in the newest front of Communist expansionism—Vietnam. To my young mind it all made for a terrifying expectation of looming war on our own soil.

Where do you turn for illumination in such confusing times? Because I grew up in a home that honored Christ, and with his church as our primary, if not solitary, source of loyalty, the local preacher greatly shaped my vision of the times. My impression almost forty years later is that I have never met a man older than this village holy man. Short of frame, with penetrating eyes and gray hair combed straight back, he accompanied his preaching by persistently pointing a crooked index finger, which reinforced the earnest conviction of a man of much study and contemplation. I cannot claim to recall much of the substance of his preaching. No doubt he was a faithful shepherd of his flock and much loved by his congregation. Yet one aspect of his proclamation remains etched on my memory and demonstrates that this venerable old sage was also a product of his era: We learned, as countless generations of faithful have, that the end of time was upon us.

Large charts synthesized the complexity of world events into a comprehensive view of prophetic fulfillment. The Soviet Union figured large in this interpretive scheme. Its military prowess was indisputable, and its expansionist thirst made it a prime candidate for igniting the feared battle of Armageddon. Our preacher adeptly expounded the number of the beast, 666. The 144,000 of the twelve tribes of Israel found their proper place in this description. The "time, times and half a time" of John's Revelation was nailed down with penetrating accuracy. I remember being mystified that the United States seemed to receive so little attention in this depiction of events yet to come; everything focused on events that would transpire in and around the country of Israel.

I don't recall anyone seriously questioning the teaching we received in that tiny church. In fact, we were all comforted by the fact that God had a plan for his church, his chosen people (us!)—the *rapture*, an odd word and one I heard used only in this context. Followers of Jesus, we learned, would be removed from the earth before the great and awful devastation began to take place. The preacher exhorted us to examine ourselves regarding our preparedness for this great event, and he warned us to be vigilant because the return of Christ to take his children home was imminent.

The whole scheme seemed inherently reasonable. After all, the miracle-like reestablishment of Israel in 1948 certainly meant the prophetic vision soon would be enacted. The year 1967 brought a further miraculous event—the city of Jerusalem united again under Israeli rule. Surely we were witnessing the beginning of the end of time! After all, many Old Testament passages referenced the return of the Jews to their Promised Land.

A wealth of books by evangelical leaders corroborated and further developed the theory. Noteworthy among these were Hal Lindsey's *The Late Great Planet Earth* and the Left Behind series by Tim LaHaye and Jerry Jenkins. The latter has been developed into a film series that graphically portrays a modern-day interpretation of many of the events foreseen in the biblical book of Revelation.

I remember crossing the Allenby Bridge in a taxi on my way to Jerusalem from Amman, Jordan. I found myself sharing the ride with a middle-aged woman from Great Britain. Like me, she was a committed follower of Christ and his teachings. Unlike me, she had committed several years of her life to living in Israel to assist the Jewish people in resettling their ancient land.

This woman related exciting stories of new kibbutzim and territories Israel was developing in order to settle Jewish emigrants from all over the world. I sensed she was genuinely excited at the prospect of playing a part in the outworking of this great prophetic plan. Like the churchgoers I grew up around, she possessed a solid confidence that the time was near when God would remove the church from the world scene and resume his Old Testament program for the Jews, preserving 144,000 faithful followers of Christ from among them—the survivors of the great tribulation. They would come through the most horrid devastation the world has ever known and be rewarded by Christ himself for their faithfulness. My new friend saw herself as preparing the way for God's revisitation of his ancient people, Israel.

Many well-intentioned Christians share this woman's zeal to prepare the way for the Lord's return by lending their support (financial, spiritual, political) to the state of Israel. My intention in this chapter is not so much to advocate a particular view of the end-times as it is to point out possible implications of such views for what we are trying to develop—fresh vision for the Muslim world. I will focus on two contentious issues about which the church lacks consensus: the identity of the people of God and the Old Testament promises of specific land to Israel.

Who Are the People of God?

One of my good friends in Cairo was thrilled to meet a Jewish Messianic Jesus-follower. My friend had come through quite an ordeal to make his decision to follow Christ, enduring ostracism from his family, lost educational and professional opportunities, police brutality, isolation, and a host of other troubles. In Europe he made the acquaintance of a Jewish man who had endured very similar challenges in order to follow Jesus. Both men had to leap over some cultural and linguistic barriers to communicate, and I imagine they might have initially looked at each other with some suspicion. As they became acquainted, however, they discovered a kinship through their mutual faith in Christ and the common bond of their shared sufferings. They embraced physically and emotionally and declared the cross of Christ to be the source of their unity.

I suspect that any sincere Christian would rejoice at the prospect of the cross overcoming a long-standing ethnic and religious animosity to reconcile the two men. But what we affirm in practice—the unity and brotherhood of these two men—do we deny in our theology? In other words, do we truly hold that the cross of Jesus Christ unifies us in himself and destroys the "dividing wall," as Paul says in Ephesians 2:14?

One of the building blocks of the vision of the end-times that I heard from my pastor as a child and that continues to be propagated through popular books and films posits a distinction between the Jews as the Old Testament people of God and the church as his New Testament people. In the previous chapter I discussed two options for thinking about Israel: First, that the state of Israel, although not walking in faithfulness to God at the present time, may be considered a precursor to a coming return of Israel to faithfulness to God. The second option sees Israel, the Old Testament people of God, now radically expanded to include people of all nations.

Let's turn our attention first to the practical outworking of the first option.

A Theology of Two Distinct Peoples

If we insist on the fulfillment of God's promises to ethnic Israel, we must in effect recognize a fork in the river of God's people: God works out different and distinct purposes for his people Israel and his people the church. In fact, the seventy weeks of Daniel, according to this scheme, applies not to the church but to Israel only. That is why expositors of this view say that Jesus' life completed the sixty-ninth week of Daniel's seventy weeks when he was offered to Israel as its king and Messiah on Palm Sunday. Each week is a period of seven years. The seventieth week was deferred—held in abeyance—by the Jews' rejection of Christ. Why? The seventieth week will recommence when the church is raptured out of this world.[1] The conversion of many Jews will take place in the seventieth week (again, a period of seven years), which will be followed by Christ's return and kingly reign on earth for a thousand years—a golden age of peace and tranquility referred to as the millennium.

Further evidence is marshaled for this view by the lack of reference to the church as such in the Apocalypse (the book of Revelation), beginning with chapter 4. For most proponents of this school of thought, this fact corroborates their position that the church is not present in the world during the time of tribulation described in John's Revelation. While the tribulation is taking place on earth, Christians will be in the presence of Christ in heaven at the marriage supper of the Lamb.

Proponents of this viewpoint hold that God's covenant with Abraham was eternal and irrevocable and was reiterated at various points during Old Testament history. They cannot accept that the church (New Testament followers of Christ) replaces Israel (sometimes referred to as *replacement theology*). God's purpose during this period of time is to bring people of all nations to faith in Christ; however, the covenant with Israel made with Abraham stands and will be fulfilled through Abraham's biological descendants, the Jews. Many see the reestablishment of the state of Israel as a key component in the final and ultimate fulfillment of God's covenant with Israel.

One element of that covenant was God's promise to Abraham of the land that is now modern-day Israel. Present-day Jews, therefore, as Abraham's descendants, have an unassailable divine right to the land of Israel. In fact, some proponents of this understanding of

Scripture would go so far as to say the Jews have the right to much more land than they currently occupy, as God promised that Israel would occupy land from the Euphrates River to the great river of Egypt, the Nile (Genesis 15:18). Therefore, those who hold this position are sympathetic with Israel in its quest to possess the land of its God-given heritage. Furthermore, they are averse to human contrivances such as United Nations resolutions that require Israel to return land confiscated during its successive wars with surrounding Arab nations. Indeed, any such ceding of territory runs counter to the purposes of God and should be resisted by Christians. This view was echoed in the words of a friend who recently referred to the Israeli withdrawal from Gaza as "giving the land back to the enemy."

I'll refer more to the land later in the chapter, but now let's consider the viewpoint that there is only one people of God, not two.

A Radically Expanded People from All Nations

Early in the story of the Bible, God seeks his erring people. His voice in Eden calls, "Adam, where are you?" God's covenant with Abraham reflects that same seeking nature. God chooses Abraham to be a repository of his blessing and a dispensary of it as well. Abraham will be blessed, and in him, in his seed, all the nations of the earth will be blessed also. Theologian and missionary Lesslie Newbigin pointed out in *The Gospel in a Pluralist Society* that God elects not to a place of superiority or privilege but to a purpose—expressing God's continual love and long-suffering in seeking people of all nations. "Israel is called to embody in her own life God's agony over his disobedient world."[2]

This purpose echoes throughout the Old Testament. God displays his greatness to the Egyptians, accomplishing the exodus "so that you [the Egyptians as well as the Israelites] may know that there is no one like the LORD our God" (Exodus 8:10). The law is given by Moses so that Israel will be a "kingdom of priests" (Exodus 19:6; see also 1 Peter 2:9, where "a royal priesthood" is applied to the universal people of God, the church). What is the function of a priest if not that of mediation? Stories about people such as Ruth, Esther, Daniel, and Jonah clearly illustrate the mission of God among the peoples of the nations.

By the way, the nation of Israel was not exclusively made up of descendants of Abraham. Although the people of Israel were reminded again and again of their distinctiveness from the nations surrounding them, Exodus 12:48–49 makes provision for foreigners who wished to join them. By being circumcised, non-Jews were allowed to partake in the Passover meal celebrating God's redemption of his people. Even in Old Testament times, the promises of God were not based merely on biological descent but on faith expressing itself in obedience.

My point is this: the distinction of Israel in Old Testament times was for a purpose—to reveal the glory and holiness of God to the other nations of the world. In much the same way, the people of God in the New Testament are called to "come out" (2 Corinthians 6:17) from among the world and be holy. The missional purposes of Yahweh in the Old Testament are carried on by the people of God in the New Testament, the church. Clearly, the covenant of God with Abraham is irrevocable. The critical question, however, is, Who are Abraham's descendants?

The New Testament explicitly teaches that the seed of Abraham referred to in God's covenant with Abraham is none other than Christ (Galatians 3:16). Those who are in Christ, the apostles teach us, are in this covenant (Galatians 3:29). The covenant remains intact (Romans 11:1–2), but by the grace of God it includes all—both Jew and Gentile—who believe, love, and obey Jesus Christ. That's why Paul can refer to those who follow Christ as "the Israel of God" (Galatians 6:16).

I am not suggesting the church replaces Israel; I am suggesting that Israel is inclusive, not exclusive. Many Jews have found Christ to be the fulfillment of the Old Testament promises. They are, as Paul taught, the original olive tree. Many Gentiles also have embraced Christ as the fulfillment of God's covenant. These non-Jews can be understood as wild olive branches grafted into the original olive tree. The wild branches are supported by the cultivated olive tree; one tree now supports diverse branches.[3] There are not two! This is the beauty of the gospel. God's promises are for all peoples and nations and tongues. There is no exclusivity. The dividing wall has been destroyed! In a world racked by racism and prejudice based on skin color, language, and ethnicity, this is good news!

The position that there is only one people of God is not anti-Jewish (anti-Semitic). I see it as honoring the immense heritage that the Jewish people have bequeathed to the world. It gives me incentive to pray earnestly for the Jews. It gives a great sense of affinity with their religious history as well as with their struggle for nationhood in today's world. It also equips me with a built-in aversion to associating God's kingdom with a political entity, whether that entity is in Washington, Tel Aviv, or Mecca. The kingdom of God is under the rule and reign of God's appointed Messiah, Christ. His kingdom comes into the hearts of his people, where he rules and continues to pursue the mission of God in this world among all peoples and nations.

No doubt some who read these lines will recoil at the suggestion that there is no distinction between Jew and Gentile. Didn't Jesus say salvation was from the Jews? Paul, as well, indicated that the Jews were the source of the Law and the covenants. By positing a theology of just one people of God, are we not destroying this distinction?

In the gospel the distinction is not destroyed but the *barrier of separation* is. In other words, we Gentiles still recall with gratitude our debt to the Jewish people, who bequeathed to us the Law, the prophets, the covenants, and finally Christ himself. Needless to say, there is no room here for anti-Semitism. The glorious truth is that we are made full participants in Christ. The distinction is one of heritage and gratitude. We, nonnative olive branches, are grafted into the native olive tree.

What Does This Have to Do with the Muslim World?

A significant aspect of the gospel is that Christ-followers are to be agents of his reconciliation—peacemakers—in a world of enmity and conflict. But if Christians see the contemporary geopolitical state of Israel and ethnic Jews as the special repository of God's blessing—his unique people—we will inevitably be predisposed to biased political and social views in favor of Israel. How tragic that our theological positions can work against our call to be agents of the mission of God in this world to bring all people to a right relationship with him.

I am fully aware that not every reader will buy into my thesis that there is only one people of God. Many will continue to hold to a distinct role for the ethnic Jew. If you are one of those, may I suggest a few important considerations relative to Israel?

First, beware of adopting an Israel-right-or-wrong position. God himself gave Israel repeated warnings and punished the nation severely for breaking his covenant. The role of the Old Testament prophets was to warn Israel of God's impending judgment.

Second, we should exercise great care not to make a one-to-one association between Israel's enemies and those people who made war with Israel in the Old Testament.

Third, Israel was granted its land on condition of covenant faithfulness. It would stand to reason, therefore, that Israel's right to occupy the land is not an inalienable, divine right. It has attached conditions.

Fourth, the state of Israel is not the millennial kingdom ruled by Christ. Even for those who believe Israel will become that, the evidence compels us to declare that not to be reality at this time. Israel is a modern state with its fair share of both good and evil, justice and equity, as well as crime, injustice, and oppression. While many hope that the establishment of the nation of Israel is a precursor to Christ's return and the establishment of his millennial reign, this hope remains unfulfilled until Israel has declared, "Blessed is he who comes in the name of the Lord" (Matthew 23:39).

Finally, whether we see a distinction of two peoples of God (the church and Israel) or one unified people of God (Israel expanded to include people of all nations), we have a mandate to fulfill toward both Jews and Gentiles—the Great Commission of Jesus. We are to carry his gospel and teach all that he taught to the nations of the world. Many Jews in our day are acknowledging Christ as the Messiah and Savior. Might I suggest that our enthusiasm for the establishment of the secular state of Israel should be considerably less than our enthusiasm for the establishment of Christ's reign among people of all nations of the world—both Jew and Gentile?

I have a friend who is not from the United States but was educated in one of the leading Christian colleges here. Having grown
up in the Middle East, he felt the pain of the crises that continually
shook the region. While he was in the United States studying, he
struggled to understand American Christianity, which surrounded
him on all sides. When Israel pulled out of the Gaza Strip, I remember hearing American Christians denounce Israel for returning its
God-given land to Muslims. Few took the time to investigate what
this development would mean for the people of the region—both
Jews and Arabs. My friend's reaction contrasted greatly with that of
American Christians. He went to the Gaza Strip. He's living there
now as I write these words; I receive e-mails from him just about
every week.

The situation there is horrific. When Israel pulled out, it also
sealed the borders and virtually sealed the ocean ports as well, halt-
ing the fishing industry that was one of the few thriving industries
among Palestinians of Gaza. Rather than becoming a free and inde-
pendent country, the Gaza Strip became a prison. A desperately poor
and overcrowded Gaza looked to a powerless Palestinian Authority
to provide some sustenance. There are no jobs. People are starving.
Militants recruit young men with absolutely nothing productive to
do to further stoke the flames of rage and warmongering. Yet my
friend is there helping a few other like-minded disciples of Jesus
distribute food and provide basic medical care. He's an example to
me, challenging me deeply. Like the Good Samaritan, who found
his enemy battered and bleeding on the side of the road, my friend
is busy tending the wounds and feeding the starving people of Gaza.
If I may be blunt, while many seem confused about just who are the
people of God, this friend of mine demonstrates what the people of

God look like by his actions. I suspect Jesus smiles on him, and I hope his tribe increases.

A Radical New Vision for Inheriting the Land

But God promised land! What are we to make of the promises of God given to Abraham unconditionally with clearly defined boundaries of land? Admittedly, this is a complex issue, made more difficult by the fact that we search in vain for some explicit New Testament teaching on this issue that is so vital to our understanding of contemporary events.

If the Bible forever gives the land of Israel to the biological descendants of Abraham, then it is only reasonable for Christians to support the Jews in their quest to repossess the entire land, and many do. Also, the struggle for the land pits Jews against Arabs, many of whom are stringent in their fundamentalist Islamic views, which also fuels Christian support of the Jewish claim to the land. The situation seems clear: God gave the land to the Jews, and it is our duty to uphold that. But is the situation really as clean and clear cut as it seems?

In the previous section I argued that there is only one people of God; the Old Testament people of God, never intended to be exclusive, now has been greatly expanded to include both Jews and Gentiles. If this is an accurate reading of Scripture, it bears heavily on the whole dilemma of the land and who should own the land; it would not make sense to argue that the land promises are only for those of a particular DNA or genetic chain.

The land belongs to the descendants of Abraham; that much is clear. I have argued that those descendants are those with faith similar to Abraham's—faith in the promises of God through Christ. This may seem like a leap of logic for some who are unaccustomed to this kind of thinking. Perhaps it will be helpful to consider three issues relative to the question of who inherits the land.

First, we must consider if there is built-in conditionality in the promise of the land as given in the Old Testament. Second, did Jesus give us any indication about what would happen with this land? Third, the New Testament teaches that Old Testament worship was but a shadow of the reality that is revealed in Christ in the New Testament. What does that imply for the Old Testament promise of land? We can draw these issues together in how Jesus talks about inheriting the land.

Remember, our purpose is to gain fresh vision for the Muslim world. Stay with me, and you'll see that these questions are important.

Conditionality

God's promise to Abraham that his descendants would possess the land contains no inherent conditions (Genesis 15:18). This was God's covenant with Abraham, and we must assume it was to be fulfilled. Later, the promise of God to the people of Israel was that they would inherit the land. This promise was given in the form of a covenant with clear terms and conditions: the condition on which the descendants of Abraham would continue to possess the land was their faithfulness to God expressed primarily through obedience to the Ten Commandments. Listen to Moses' warning in a solemn ceremony of covenant renewal, should the people of Israel fail to abide by the terms of the covenant:

> The whole land will be a burning waste of salt and sul-
> fur—nothing planted, nothing sprouting, no vegetation
> growing on it. It will be like the destruction of Sodom
> and Gomorrah, Admah and Zeboiim, which the LORD

overthrew in fierce anger. All the nations will ask: "Why has the LORD done this to this land? Why this fierce, burning anger?"

And the answer will be: "It is because this people abandoned the covenant of the LORD, the God of their fathers, the covenant he made with them when he brought them out of Egypt." (Deuteronomy 29:23–25)

The sad lament of the author of the Chronicles is a repeated refrain of the Old Testament:

The LORD, the God of their fathers, sent word to them through his messengers again and again, because he had pity on his people and on his dwelling place. But they mocked God's messengers, despised his words and scoffed at his prophets until the wrath of the LORD was aroused against his people and there was no remedy. He brought up against them the king of the Babylonians, who killed their young men with the sword in the sanctuary, and spared neither young man nor young woman, old man or aged. God handed all of them over to Nebuchadnezzar. He carried to Babylon all the articles from the temple of God, both large and small, and the treasures of the LORD's temple and the treasures of the king and his officials. They set fire to God's temple and broke down the wall of Jerusalem; they burned all the palaces and destroyed everything of value there.

He carried into exile to Babylon the remnant, who escaped from the sword, and they became servants to

him and his sons until the kingdom of Persia came to
power. (2 Chronicles 36:15–20)

The period of the exile saw the Jews removed from the land. The
prophets Isaiah, Jeremiah, Ezekiel, and others clearly taught that this
exile was due to the people's unfaithfulness to the covenant of their
God. The Jews were promised a territory with very clearly defined
boundaries; however, the promise of that territory was conditional
upon their adherence to a covenant. They were to be a people of justice
who walked humbly before their God. In so doing, they were ensured
enjoyment of the land and its blessings throughout their posterity.
One element of many in this covenant is that the Israelites were told
to remember that they had once been aliens in a foreign land and
therefore they were to treat the aliens among them with equity and
justice (Deuteronomy 24:14–22). The story of Ruth relates how one
alien received sustenance by the kind favor of Boaz. Ruth, ethnically of
the hated Moabites, became the ancestress of King David.

The promise of the land to the descendants of Abraham is an
abiding covenant. Deuteronomy 30:1–9 assures that even after
disobedience, by obeying the Lord's voice, God's people could anticipate being regathered from the nations and reassembled in their
land. The conditions for occupancy of the land still apply. Israel is
under obligation to walk before God in faithfulness to him, exercising justice and equity and upholding his law in the land. The Old
Testament never promised the Jews that they would live in the land
regardless of their behavior.

I believe you can see how this element of conditionality casts a new
light on our thinking about Israel in the land. If we understand Christ
to be the fulfillment of the Old Testament promises, and that man, by
virtue of his descent from Adam, is unable to uphold the Law apart from

new birth in Christ and renewing of the Holy Spirit, we have a dilemma. Is modern-day Israel fulfilling its covenant obligations? Some statistics suggest that the majority of Jews in Israel are functional atheists. There are, of course, Jews who are zealous for the Law and wish to uphold it as their national standard. In both cases, we have a problem. Jesus remains the fulfillment of the Law. Neither those Jews who totally disregard the Law nor those who cling to it as the basis for national justice can claim to live in covenant faithfulness to God.

Jesus' Teaching concerning the Land

Jesus told a Samaritan woman who was eager to worship God on her own holy mountain that "a time is coming when you will worship the Father neither on this mountain nor in Jerusalem" (John 4:21). Jesus was not here affirming Samaritan worship. In fact, he told the Samaritan woman clearly that the Samaritans were worshipping a God they did not know. He pointed out that salvation is from the Jews. However, if Jesus saw this salvation tied to an earthly center of worship in Jerusalem, his response is baffling. He continued, "Yet a time is coming and has now come when the true worshipers will worship the Father in spirit and truth, for they are the kind of worshipers the Father seeks. God is spirit, and his worshipers must worship in spirit and in truth" (vv. 23–24). Jesus emphasized not locale but attitude and quality of worship. He derived his view of worship from the nature of God as spirit. Since God is spirit (nonmaterial, omnipresent), his worship must not be contained in one locale. Solomon recognized this when he dedicated the original Old Testament temple: "But will God really dwell on earth? The heavens, even the highest heaven, cannot contain you. How much less this temple I have built!" (1 Kings 8:27).

The temple was the place where God dwelt among his people. It symbolized a people firmly planted in their land and their God dwelling in their midst to bless and protect them. You remember that when David proposed to build a temple in the City of Jerusalem, God responded that he had never asked for a house to dwell in all the years of the wandering of the children of Israel. He had dwelt in a tent (the tabernacle), and that was sufficient. The tabernacle was mobile; it moved with the people of God wherever they went. However, the Lord also revealed that David's son would be the builder of a house.

Through the teaching of Jesus, we grasp new realities about the temple that are consonant with the old realities and yet broader. First, Jesus spoke of his own body as the temple. It was, in effect, to be destroyed through death on the cross. But it would not remain so. It would be raised up in three days (John 2:19–21). The apostles developed this imagery further. All followers of Christ who are baptized into his death become one with him—part of his body (see Ephesians 1:23; 4:13; 1 Corinthians 12:27). This body of Christ becomes the new temple made up of the people of God themselves as his Spirit indwells, forming them into a holy temple with Christ as the cornerstone. "You are no longer foreigners and aliens, but fellow citizens with God's people and members of God's household, built on the foundation of the apostles and prophets, with Christ Jesus himself as the chief cornerstone. In him the whole building is joined together and rises to become a holy temple in the Lord. And in him you too are being built together to become a dwelling in which God lives by his Spirit" (Ephesians 2:19–22). Jesus promised his disciples that he would come to them and that he and his Father would dwell with them. The Old Testament spoke of a covenant in which God would dwell among his people. The temple was the Old Testament representation of a coming reality—the dwelling of God among his people.

In fact, the only prophecy Jesus gave about the temple of his day was that it would be completely and utterly destroyed—a prophecy that was fulfilled when the Roman army sacked Jerusalem in 70 CE, less than one generation after the crucifixion. We might notice a little of our own fascination with the Holy Land and Holy Land artifacts as we read of the disciples pointing out the massive stones of the temple of their day, but their admiration failed to impress Jesus: "I tell you the truth, not one stone here will be left on another; every one will be thrown down" (Matthew 24:2).

How are we to understand these teachings of Jesus? Do we anticipate that after the outpouring of God's Spirit on people of all nations and his dwelling with them in the Spirit, we are now to go back to a piece of real estate in the Middle East to receive the "real promises"? No, it's the other way around! The reality of the promise was in Christ. In him God comes to dwell among us, making us a holy temple.

As mentioned earlier, we find precious little explicit teaching about the land in the New Testament. One reason for this might be that the Jews were in the Promised Land at that time. The return from exile had taken place several hundred years earlier, and little thought needed to be directed to this question that, for us, looms large in the light of contemporary events. However, it is instructive to note the absence of any indication that Jewish sovereignty over the land was somehow related to the mission and ministry of Jesus. For instance, Jesus never overtly condemned the Roman occupation of the land. He never explicitly tied his mission to the geographic boundaries or the political aspirations of a Jewish state. This is certainly not because it was a mute issue in Jesus' day—far from it! So the silence of the New Testament about specific land promises may be a significant silence—an indicator that new realities have dawned as the old order passed away. The testimony of the New Testament, while not always explicit, is remarkably consistent on issues related to the land and the temple that sat upon it.

Even if the evidence offered here fails to convince you that the land promises need to be understood and applied differently, perhaps it will at least cause you to ask serious questions. If a future return to the land of Israel was central to the plan of God for later ages, it would stand to reason that Jesus Christ would have given us a strong indication of that fact.

Doubtless some will counter, "Oh, but he did! The book of Revelation speaks at length about the restoration of Jerusalem." There is much disagreement over the interpretation of this apocalyptic book. Jerusalem is mentioned three times in the book—once in chapter 3 and twice in chapter 21. In both appearances, Jerusalem is a city that comes down from heaven to the earth. It is clearly not the same city found in today's Middle East. Its dimensions are astounding—a city built like a cube, the length, height, and depth of which are each approximately fourteen hundred miles (about half the distance across the United States!).

We must not forget our former discussion about the identity of the Israel of God. If, as I have suggested, Israel has been radically expanded to include people of all nations, then it would be reasonable to assume that the promise of inheritance of land would be expanded in parallel. The promise of land for the seed of Abraham was never abrogated; on the contrary, it has been expanded. Remember that God did not promise Abraham he would become the father of *a* nation but the father of *many* nations (Genesis 17:4).

My point is simply this: although Israel as a people has yet to acknowledge her Lord and Messiah, God is actively bringing the nations (both Jews and Gentiles) into the kingdom of Jesus. God is building a temple that spans the entire earth. His Spirit's presence among his people carries on his purpose of displaying his glory to all nations that he began in Old Testament Israel. Is it possible that our persistent focus on Israel as the Holy Land could in fact divert our attention from lands and peoples that our Lord is visiting today?

There is no denying, of course, that the incarnation was a unique event and that Jesus' earthly ministry in the land of Israel will continue to bequeath to it the fascination of the Christian world. However, many well-meaning Christians take their fascination with Jerusalem to an extreme, supposing that God is uniquely present and active in the Holy Land. I find this to be disturbing in the light of the book of Hebrews, which describes a new Holy of Holies—the place where Jesus is right now. He has entered into that place with his own blood as a sufficient plea for our redemption.

Resurrection of Shadows

When the apostles met in Jerusalem to determine if the Gentile believers would need to be circumcised, they lit a fire that is still going strong in our day and will not be extinguished. They opened a floodgate for peoples of other cultures to enter the flock of Jesus. They removed the old Jewish standards, casting away much of the Old Testament law, by establishing a few clearly recognizable principles of conduct that would sufficiently demonstrate a godly life to the watching world.

Modern-day missions has coined the term *contextualization*. It's a hotly debated umbrella word that asks what cultural and religious forms (dress, chanting, worship styles, etc.) can be borrowed from other cultures such that the Christian faith is not perceived as a foreign entity? What is at stake is removing the garb of our own culture from the faith so that it is embraced on its own terms through vehicles of expression understood and accepted in the local setting.

Peter, James, and the others were essentially approving of Paul's and Barnabas's contextualization of the gospel to the Gentiles. They made a tough decision with plenty of dissenters on the other side. Still, the apostles made the ruling and set the standard for the church for the coming centuries.

The book of Hebrews was written, it seems, to a group of Hebrew Christians on the brink of apostasy—leaving their faith in Christ and returning to Judaism. The writer of Hebrews gives some instructive insight pertinent to the whole question of what we anticipate will take place in the end-times. He begins by pointing to Christ as the radiance of the glory of the invisible God and the exact representation of his person. This Christ entered a tabernacle, not on earth, but in heaven. The priests of the Old Testament entered the earthly tabernacle with the blood of bulls and goats, which could never atone for sin (see Hebrews 10:4). The blood of Jesus Christ, on the other hand, is of infinite value and sufficient to accomplish atonement for sins. The priests of the Old Testament constructed a tent made after a pattern shown to Moses on the mountain. It was a replica, an imitation. In the new covenant we do not come to a physical mountain that shook and smoked like Mount Sinai; rather, we come to Mount Zion, the place of Christ's dwelling.

The argument of the book of Hebrews is that the vast superiority of Christ to the old covenant renders its forms and worship of no use. That is not to say that they were not worthy types and figures of what was to come. But the advent of Christ's kingdom rendered them obsolete. The Old Testament tabernacle was but a shadow of the reality that is in Christ.

Christian scholars who advocate that the temple will be rebuilt after the rapture of the church do not see in it an alternative means of salvation. They caution against a reestablishment of temple worship as a way of reconciliation to God. However, much of their theological nuancing is lost on contemporary temple enthusiasts, who would be happy for the reconstruction of the temple in our day as it would, in their estimation, necessarily point to the impending return of Christ. While it is easy to see that the temple could, in fact, be rebuilt because Israel holds control over the temple mount, what would be the implications for a watching world? What message about the gospel would be conveyed if Christians fell in line to support such a project? What biblical foundations might we be betraying?

At the very least, the book of Hebrews suggests to us that Christ has entered a heavenly Holy of Holies while the temple on earth is made up of his people, with Christ himself as the cornerstone. His worship has no earthly center or ethnic base, but all peoples and tribes and tongues worship with equal validity. Is popular enthusiasm among Christians for the rebuilding of the temple sending a message that is anti-Christian? Are temple enthusiasts grappling with the implications of a rebuilt temple and a reinstituted sacrificial system for the Jews and for a watching world?

The Jerusalem council depicted in Acts 15 and the book of Hebrews have much in common: they both recognize that the Old Testament forms served to point forward to Christ. Now that Christ has come, an insistence on the worship forms of the Old Testament (as some in Acts 15 desired) or a return to them (as in Hebrews) is out of the question. It just does not line up with what we know of Christ.

FRESH VISION for the MUSLIM WORLD

I remember walking with a friend in the beautiful mountains of northern Morocco. We strolled past a village mosque where, he told me, he used to pray. I asked him if he ever had the desire to return to the mosque. He smiled at me in disbelief. "How could I go back?" he said. "There's nothing there." In fact, my friend had left much of his former identity when he embraced Christ. A return to the mosque for him would be tantamount to a return to his former life, apart from Christ. I suspect that for many, a return to Jewish worship is not in any way parallel to returning to the mosque. After all, the temple worship was originally given by God and points to the reality of Christ. Unlike the prayers in a mosque, the worship in the tabernacle and temple was a pattern that pointed forward to a coming reality. Now that the reality has come, the pattern has simply lost its usefulness.

When a seamstress sews an article of clothing, the pattern she uses is of great value. It is that pattern that gives shape to the garment. However, once the article of clothing is complete, the pattern is of no further use. The pattern has fulfilled its purpose and lost its purpose at the same time—the garment is complete, ready to be worn. Jesus Christ is the garment of which the Old Testament worship was the pattern. Now that the reality has come, the pattern can safely be discarded.

Jesus on Inheriting the Land

The Sermon on the Mount has been likened to Jesus' giving of his law—the constitution of his kingdom. Much like Moses ascended a mountain and heard from God, Jesus ascended a mount and spoke from his own authority. It remains the most poignant of all sermons, and its meaning and depth have yet to be plumbed.

In one phrase of that sermon Jesus made the simple assertion, "Blessed are the meek, for they will inherit the earth." Some commentators have pointed out that the language bears a similarity to Psalm 37:11, "But the meek will inherit the land and enjoy great peace." The word used in this Old Testament passage for "the land" is *ha-eretz,* the common word associated with the land of Israel. The peace these meek ones are said to enjoy is *shalom,* an all-encompassing peace with God that results in peace with one's acquaintances and environment.

Is Jesus asserting in this passage that the inheritance of the land is for the meek, for those who live with an awareness of their fallibility and imperfections? Could it be that he is teaching his listeners, "You have heard that you will inherit the land because you are of Abraham's seed, but I say unto you that those who are meek will inherit the land"? Many assert that Jesus' words cannot be taken so explicitly, that the beatitude is not intended to enlarge on the covenant with Abraham in this way. Perhaps they are right, but I find this reading of the beatitude to be consonant with the tenor of the entire New Testament.

The Old Testament promised the land of Israel to the seed of Abraham; in the New Testament we are told explicitly that the seed of Abraham is Jesus Christ. By faith you and I unite ourselves with Christ and become adopted daughters and sons of Abraham with full rights to his inheritance. The land is for the meek—for Christ and for his people. His promise to his disciples was that he would go away and prepare a place for them and then come again and receive them to himself. Only the meek will inherit this land—the New Jerusalem being prepared for Christ and his people. The criterion for receiving this inheritance is not genealogical, biological, or ethnic. It is our being "in Christ" by faith, whether Jew or Gentile.

◆ SEEKING FRESH VISION ◆

In this chapter we have sought answers to two critical questions. First, what is the identity of the people of God—one people or two? The second question concerns the promise of specific land to Abraham. I have said that the people of God are one people, including both Jews and Gentiles, and argued that, by extension, the promise of land to Abraham has expanded parallel with the identity of Abraham's descendants. The land is no longer bound by geographical borders but is such that God's presence can be seen clearly in many places on the earth—wherever his people dwell.

These issues grow out of our reading of Scripture, but they are intimately related to very contemporary concerns. Today the battle rages over the possession of land in the Middle East. If we are prepared to think clearly and biblically about these issues, we will be much better suited to discern the conflicting claims to the land in the Middle East. Hopefully, this broadening of our understanding of God's purposes in the land of the Bible will help us gain fresh vision for all the peoples of the Middle East, all of whom need peace and security. Let us not forget that the pressing need of the entire world is to see the manifestation of the kingdom of Jesus in his people.

Additional Resources for Chapter 8

Burge, Gary. *Whose Land? Whose Promise?* Cleveland: The Pilgrim Press, 2003.

Chapman, Colin. *Whose Promised Land?: The Continuing Crisis over Israel and Palestine.* Oxford: Lion, 2002.

Grenz, Stanley J. *The Millennial Maze.* Downers Grove, IL: InterVarsity Press, 1992.

CHAPTER 9

PERSPECTIVE MAKES ALL
THE DIFFERENCE

After I addressed a men's group in a U. S. church about the issue of the Israel of God and our end-times expectations, one of my listeners raised his hand and commented, "But these are all secondary issues. They have little to do with the primary issues of salvation and discipleship." Yes. It is certainly true that we can hold various views on these issues, as they are not foundational to the Christian faith. Nevertheless, the stakes are incredibly high.

Take one example from a recent conflict in the Middle East.

Late in 2006, Hezbollah militants managed to seize two Israeli soldiers. The Israeli reprisal came swiftly and vigorously. Hezbollah insisted on a prisoner exchange. Israel wasn't taking that bait and launched a ferocious air attack over Lebanon, bombing the country from head to toe. Meanwhile, Hezbollah flexed its rather anemic muscles by launching rockets into Israel. Rockets reached Haifa, an Israeli town on the Mediterranean coast about thirty miles south of the Lebanese border. Some Israelis died. Europeans and other nationalities were clamoring to be repatriated, and a general sense of panic hovered over the entire region.

While some secular commentators criticized Israel for what they termed its "disproportionate response," most of the evangelical community in the West firmly supported Israel's right to retaliate in the manner it chose. During the conflict I attended a prayer meeting in which a well-meaning believer suggested we pray for Israel because its very life was being threatened. I did pray for Israel, but I could not shake off the irony of at least a dozen e-mails from friends in Lebanon stating that hundreds of Lebanese who had nothing to do with Hezbollah were dying because of Israeli bombs.

I think some thoughtful questions are in order. First, if the evangelical community persists in its unconditional support of Israel, what message are we sending to a watching world, increasingly networked by the Internet and satellite communication? Do Christians care most about military victory for their political allies or the containment of the evils of war? Second, what message are we sending to the church? Lebanon has the highest percentage of Christians of all countries in the Middle East. We would do well to consider how those brothers and sisters in Christ come to terms with our enthusiasm for Israeli bombs falling on their heads.

That is not to suggest for a moment any solidarity with Hezbollah. My point is this: there are missional implications to the political affinities of evangelicals. The stakes are high because the church is commissioned to make disciples of the nations. Although issues such as Israel and the end-times are secondary, they affect our ability to carry on the mission of Jesus Christ in our world. They are secondary in terms of doctrinal importance but primary in terms of missional impact. That's why a fresh examination of these questions is critical to our pursuit of fresh vision for the Muslim world.

In this chapter we look at the historical and political process that gave rebirth to the nation of Israel. Once again, I am asking you to attempt to see the world from a perspective that may seem strange and unnatural; I appeal to you to read with an open mind and heart.

Beginnings

Rome ruled the land of Israel after the destruction of the temple in 70 CE. Constantine's conversion to Christianity brought the land of Palestine under the rule of a Christian Roman emperor. The emperor moved his capital to Constantinople, and the land became a province of the Byzantine Empire (the eastern half of the Roman Empire) until 632 CE.[1]

In 637, only five years after the death of the prophet Muhammad, Arab armies overtook Jerusalem. For the next 450 years, Palestine was part of the Islamic empire. Although Arabic became the most widely spoken language, the people of the area were allowed to retain their religious views, whether Jewish or Christian. The Islamic capital moved from Mecca to Damascus (661, the Umayyads) to Baghdad (750, the Abassids), but the land of Palestine remained under Islamic rule until 1099. The Catholic Crusaders invaded Palestine and overtook Jerusalem, massacring the Jewish and Christian populations of that city. They held power in Jerusalem for less than one hundred years, as the Muslim army of Saladin retook the city in 1187. The final Crusader stronghold—the port of Acre—fell to the Muslims in 1291. The Muslim Ottoman Turks overtook Palestine in 1516 and held power until 1918, which brings us up to World War I. In summary, the land that constitutes modern-day Israel has been under Muslim rule for approximately twelve of the past thirteen centuries.

Two Perspectives

The history of the formation of the state of Israel is a sore point among Muslims of the Arab world. In my estimation it is the focal point of the conflict in our day and is likely to remain so for some time. We want to peer into the typical Muslim impression about the establishment of Israel. However, before we do that, it will be instructive to identify our own impression of the formation of that state. What is our reading of the historical conditions that brought the state of Israel into being?

In my attempt to describe our reading of history, I will generalize, of necessity. You may not agree with every aspect of this description, although I think you will recognize at least the broad contours of this reading of the events. In presenting the following two views of events, my intention is not to sanction or approve either of them. I merely wish to help us recognize that two vastly different readings of history are being promoted. Let's consider first what we may recognize as a Western Christian perspective.

A Western Christian Perspective

The modern-day establishment of the state of Israel came about as a fulfillment of divine destiny, bequeathed to the people of Israel by God through their father Abraham. Although the Jews had been dispersed and regathered to their own land numerous times throughout history, the final regathering of the Jews in our day is perhaps the most remarkable of all.

Their land had lain desolate for centuries after many wars had brought about great destruction in Israel. The Jews themselves had been subject to recurrent persecutions in the lands to which they had been scattered in the Diaspora. They were a people without a homeland, struggling to maintain their own religious identity in a world often bent on their destruction. But their homeland awaited them. After the atrocities of World War II and the infamous concentration camps that ruthlessly exterminated six million Jews, it was clear that the Jews needed their own homeland. This was recognized by the leaders of Europe, and a homeland was proclaimed in the historic habitation of the Jews—the land of Israel.

The reestablishment of the Israeli state brought an immediate reaction from the enemies of Israel. Rather than allow Israel to return to its God-given heritage, Arab Islamic states surrounding Israel proclaimed an immediate war on the new nation. Surely the newly established state would fall to its enemies, which so vastly outnumbered it. Would this be the end of the dream of the Jews to return to the land of Zion? Amazingly, the Arab states did not prevail. Israel won its first war against its foes, the Arabs. The signs were clear to all who were willing to read them: Israel was being reestablished by direct favor of God.

Some of the original occupants sold their land to the new Jewish arrivals. Others left voluntarily when Arab regimes informed them that a war was about to take place. They fled in order to save their lives from the aggression of Arab armies. Rather than choose to live peaceably under the Israeli government, the Palestinian Arabs began to mobilize acts of war against Israel, amassing around her borders to attack her villages and towns.

The enemies of Israel were not about to lose face. These guerrilla warriors had foregone the scruples of military conscience. They attacked innocent people and killed unarmed civilians. Calling themselves *fedayeen* (redeemers), they were obsessed with the destruction of Israel. These warriors adopted a mind-set of terror. Gradually they collected funding and recruits from outside of Israel. They organized themselves, over the years, into militant Islamic groups such as Hamas, Fatah, and Hezbollah. These groups continue to be a thorn in Israel's side and must be resisted steadfastly if Israel is to offer peace and security to its new and old settlements in the land.

In 1967 the enemies of Israel were again strategizing against it. Egypt, Syria, and Jordan conspired to attack; however, Israel preempted their attack, destroying their air power before it ever got off the ground. Amazingly, this war was won in one day. A few ground battles ensued, which Israel won handily within the span of a week. This amazing turn of events has come to be known as the Six-Day War. In it Israel demonstrated its complete military mastery over its Arab enemies. For those willing to admit it, the Six-Day War was proof positive of a divine seal of approval on the state of Israel.

During this war Israel made tremendous progress in reclaiming its ancient territory. It annexed the West Bank, including the City of Jerusalem, and took over the Golan Heights, creating a security buffer zone between Israel and Syria. Finally, Israel took the Gaza Strip and the Sinai Peninsula as well. Not only were the Arab armies defeated soundly, but Israel was well on its way to inheriting the entire land given to it by God as part of a solemn covenant.

In 1973, under the leadership of Anwar Sadat, Egypt once again attacked Israel. Although caught off guard, the Israeli army regrouped and fended off the Egyptian advance. The Camp David

Accords brought together Shimon Peres and Anwar Sadat and gave the Sinai Peninsula back to Egypt. In exchange Egypt recognized Israel as a country. Egypt was the first Arab nation to recognize Israel and begin a formal diplomatic relationship. The reaction of the rest of the Arab world was swift and predictable. They ousted Egypt from the Arab League! No country that recognized Israel would be allowed. Egypt would have to go it alone!

Since the Camp David Summit, Israel continues to be plagued by militant Muslim groups. Yasser Arafat led the Palestine Liberation Organization until his death. His implication in terrorist activities is obvious even to the most casual observer. The *Intifada* (often translated "uprising" but closer in meaning to "shaking off") of Palestinians within the state of Israel underlines just how intransigent Arabs can be. Palestinian youths resort to throwing stones to irritate the Israeli military and upset the delicate balance of power in Israel. In recent years a new phenomenon of suicide bombing has come to the fore. Buses, restaurants, and other public venues have become the targets of desperate killers who are willing to die themselves for the gratification of killing a few Jews.

Resistance from the outside continues through armed militant groups like Hamas and Hezbollah. These groups have significant arms stashes and receive funding from like-minded states such as Iran and Syria, which would like nothing better than to wipe Israel off the map. Their proclivity toward terror-inspiring attacks against Israel is not unlike the Scud missiles launched by Saddam Hussein in his desperation to inflict some harm on Israel during Gulf War I. Muslim nations are fixated on Israel's destruction.

The only acceptable response to such unrestrained aggression against Israel is to support Israel in its God-given destiny of occupying its ancient land. Western powers must stand firmly behind their ally, refusing to allow Israel to be eliminated by its enemies. In fact, God's ancient promise still stands: "For whoever touches you touches the apple of his eye—I will surely raise my hand against them" (Zechariah 2:8–9).

A Muslim Perspective

If the last section contained very few surprises for you, be prepared to be shocked as you read what follows. If you find this perspective distressing, keep reading, and remember—I am not out to condone this view but to listen carefully to what Arab Muslims are saying. Readers who are sympathetic with this view may be uncomfortable with some of the generalizations. Remember that I am attempting to present the broad lines of how the establishment of the state of Israel is viewed in the Arab world. It is impossible to agree on every detail.

The Western world wasted no time in its attempts to overrun Islamic territory. In the aftermath of World War II, when the Islamic countries were being carved up and placed under the care of Western powers, a blow was struck right to the heart of Islamic heritage. They cut out a portion of the Muslim heartland and gave it to Jews from Europe in order to assuage their guilty conscience of their own war crimes against them. They all said this was a "land without a people for a people without a land."

Nothing could possibly be further from the truth. The Arab peoples of Palestine had cared for the land and passed it down from generation to generation for hundreds of years. The Palestinians were a hardworking agricultural people with ancient traditions that bound them in tight family and tribal units. They worked the land, becoming expert farmers who raised figs, olives, and many other kinds of produce. Many also kept livestock. In this ancient land, Christians, Jews, and Muslims lived side by side, sharing their farm produce and caring for one another in times of distress. Church, mosque, and synagogue existed together in Palestinian villages. To be sure, they had never developed an industrial economy like their new Zionist invaders. They were left helpless in the face of their invaders.

For whole villages and towns of Palestinians, there was very little warning. They were simply told by the occupying power to leave their homelands temporarily in order to protect their families and loved ones. They were also assured that those lands would be returned to them in the following weeks. They left their farms and villages in the hands of the European invaders bearing machine guns, and many have not returned to this day. Although they have appealed numerous times within Israel and outside Israel, their villages have been destroyed by the hundreds. They made their way into the surrounding Arab countries—Lebanon, Syria, Jordan, and the Gaza Strip, where many continue to live in refugee camps. Their numbers have swelled through successive wars until today there are 5.5 million Palestinian refugees inside and outside Israel. Despite United Nations resolutions declaring that Israel should give back the land it occupied after the 1967 war, Israel remains resolute in confiscating land through military occupation.

But the pride of the Palestinians would not die so easily. If the world would take no notice of their plight, they would raise their own resistance. Many of their young men began to volunteer as freedom fighters. They would no longer allow the Zionist occupier to destroy their farms and villages. Rather, they would fight, to the death if need be. Armed with an Islamic heritage of jihad, Palestinians slowly began to effect damage on those who had cast them out of their homeland. Forces outside Israel joined with those Palestinians who remained inside, many of whom were forced to take menial jobs caring for lands that had passed from the hands of their fathers into the powerful hands of the Zionists. The Intifada and the Palestinian resistance from outside the country made common cause of reasserting the identity of a proud people, despite its near decimation at the hands of the Zionists.

The world sat by and watched while Israeli tanks, helicopters, and planes continued to annihilate the Palestinians. When Palestinians threw stones, Israelis brought in tanks. Israel still denies the Palestinians—the original occupants of the land—the right to return. Not only that, Israel has had a hand in massacring Palestinians inside their camps, such as happened at Shabra and Shatilla in the early 1980s in Lebanon. It was all done in a very calculated way such that Israel could claim it was not responsible, but it was Israeli guards who stood guard at the camp while the massacre took place. Furthermore, if Palestinians attack their occupiers, Israel merely finds some Palestinian town or village and starts bombing its houses. All of this is portrayed in the West as Israel's self-defense against the terrorist Palestinians. Of course, Jews control the media and use them as a vehicle of Zionist propaganda.

Each successive armed conflict with the Jews has allowed them to expand their occupation. How is it that the United Nations passed resolutions calling Israel to withdraw to its borders before the 1967 war, and yet the world sits idly while Israel continually grabs more and more land away from the Palestinians? The gigantic eight-meter-high wall that they have built through the land splits orchards in two, separates towns, drives a wedge between family members, and makes jobs and lands inaccessible. The border around the West Bank is about 350 miles. However, Israel, in its attempt to confiscate the land of the West Bank, has built a wall over 600 miles long, taking in huge tracts of West Bank land and making much of the West Bank inaccessible to Palestinians. Can't anyone see that this is a perversion of justice? Can't the Palestinian people at least work on their farms and visit uncles, aunts, and cousins who live in various towns throughout the land?

The West applauded Israel for returning the Gaza Strip. What a farce! They imprisoned the Palestinian people! They sealed the borders and hold control of the seaports, effectively terminating the only viable industry the Gazans had—fishing. There are no jobs. Gaza is hopelessly overcrowded. The people are starving. The babies are dying of diseases. Men have lost their dignity. Of course, Palestinians struck back with missiles and detained two Israeli soldiers. But what about the hundreds of Palestinian young men who sit in Israeli prisons? Won't someone listen?

Why does the world continue to turn a blind eye as powerful Israel builds its settlements in areas that belong to Palestinians according to international law and specific United Nations resolutions? The Fourth Geneva Convention, Article 49 (1949) declares: "The occupying Power shall not deport or transfer parts of its own civilian population into the territory it occupies."[2] Also, UN Resolution 452 "calls upon the Government and people of Israel to cease, on an urgent basis, the establishment, construction and planning of settlements in the Arab territories occupied since 1967, including Jerusalem."[3] But the occupied West Bank is dotted with Israeli settlements and crisscrossed by roads that serve those settlements.

The only superpower in the world, the United States, continues to provide unqualified support to Israel in its crimes against the Palestinians. If the UN passes a resolution against Israel, the United States is sure to veto it. They think that Israel was given to the Jews by God. How can the United States seriously believe that Israelis should own this land because they lived on it thousands of years ago? We, the Muslim people, have been the recent occupants of this land. We have a right to this land. Although we don't have America on our side, Allah is on our side, and right will prevail!

A Fresh Look at Reality

Both of the perspectives above are precisely that—*perspectives* on the events. While living in the Middle East, I was constantly amazed at the chasm between the Middle Eastern Muslim perspective and the Western perspective on contemporary events. Obviously, the perspectives flow out of the worldview and presuppositions of each side.

I am not an advocate of relativism. I do not believe that both sides are right. I believe that Jesus Christ, who described himself by saying, "I am the truth," will be the ultimate arbiter of right and wrong. His truth is not merely a personal truth that effects piety; his truth is also a societal truth that effects justice and righteousness. Christ's truth will restore the downtrodden and mend the broken. He will supply justice to the oppressed and provide security for those who are threatened. I believe that as Christ-followers our perspective on the Muslim world and particularly on the issue of Palestine and Israel should be reflective of Christ's truth. His truth will separate the wheat from the chaff—penetrating contradictory truth claims and exposing false elements.

Christ-followers must take a fresh look at the facts as best we can ascertain them. We should listen to both sides. Both perspectives (as well as the whole spectrum of perspectives between the two) will need to be run through a grid well informed by Scripture and the teaching of Christ in order to discern the right course of action. Obviously, there are certain givens in the discussion—points of agreement that are nonnegotiables. The killing of innocent civilian noncombatants cannot be tolerated. The suicide bombings of militant groups can be viewed only as abhorrent and must be condemned in the strongest possible way; it is self-destruction that is also "other-destruction" (murder) and can never reflect the high purposes of God for his creation. The senseless taking of Palestinian lives must be decried and rejected. An informed Christian worldview insists on the sacredness of life, whether Palestinian or Israeli.

Beyond these givens, as we examine the historical events more closely, we may be forced to acknowledge that some of our conclusions have been in error. That is a welcome process and one we should not fear. Changing some of our views may not, in the end, entail a complete reversal of position. It will, I believe, allow us to become more impartial judges and thereby more helpful peacemakers in a situation in desperate need of peacemaking. Ultimately, this process is absolutely essential to preserving the missional nature of evangelicalism among the Muslim and Jewish peoples of the world.

Consider some areas that have not received adequate attention in our Western understanding of the Israeli-Palestinian conflict.

The Problem of Palestinian Displacement

Granted, Jews have suffered unspeakable atrocities due to anti-Semitism. Nazism was the climactic expression of hostility toward the Jews, but other forms existed throughout the Western world. Even in our own day, neo-Nazi movements are proclaiming the superiority of the Aryan race and the necessity of ridding our society of the Semitic scourge. Such a despicable evil must be recognized for what it is. The formation of the state of Israel was an attempt to redress some of these injustices. Nevertheless, the attempt to resettle a Jewish people in their ancient homeland has been accompanied by a displacement of its long-term occupants, the Palestinian people.

My father-in-law was the proud owner of a thirty-acre farm on the outskirts of a rapidly growing city in the southern United States. After marrying his daughter, I became privy to his perpetual struggle to keep the land he owned. As his thirty acres were annexed by the city, taxes tripled in one year. The political maneuvering that took place in order for the city to annex the outlying farm communities left landowners like my father-in-law in a vulnerable position. He could not afford to pay the taxes. The farm would have to be sold, which was, of course, the intention of the city planners.

A wealthy land developer purchased the property and built as many as four or five houses on each acre of land. The whole process had the feel of injustice, but it was an unstoppable process—one that my father-in-law accepted, albeit unwillingly. At least he received some compensation for his land.

In our suburban society we may have forgotten the immense value farmers attach to land. Palestinians relied heavily on their land for their livelihood—their crops, their flocks, housing for their families, etc. Their primary currency was their land. Elias Chacour, a Palestinian Christian and archbishop of Galilee of the Melkite Greek Catholic Church, recounts the story of how his family and his entire village of Biram were forced from their land in northern Israel. In the

1940s, shortly after World War II, the residents of Biram were told they would need to host a group of European Jewish soldiers who were coming through their area. Although they were anxious about hosting soldiers in their village, they prepared for their arrival and expected that the ordeal would quickly pass.

In a short time, the villagers were informed that they would need to leave their village in the care of the soldiers for a few weeks. The villagers made their way into the fields and groves surrounding Biram. Their exile continued for many weeks as protests and requests to return to their homes were denied again and again. The citizens of Biram finally received word from the central Israeli government that they could return to their village. As they strode across the Galilean hills in festive procession on Christmas Day to reoccupy their village, they were stunned by what they saw. Biram was surrounded by tanks and bulldozers. The soldiers opened fire, not on the former residents of Biram, but on their buildings. Their churches, school, and homes were destroyed and left in shambles, never again to be occupied.[4]

Some would dare to assert that the story of Palestinian displacement from homes, jobs, schools, mosques, and churches is an effort of anti-Semite propaganda. Admittedly, it is difficult to find a fair court of appeal, for the facts and statistics can be manipulated. Gary Burge, noted Wheaton College professor of New Testament, asserts: "Since 1948, 531 Arab villages have been either destroyed by bulldozers or occupied by Israeli residents despite UN resolutions calling for the rightful return of these homes and lands to their Arab owners. According to UN records in June 1999, about 3.6 million Palestinian refugees are the victims of Israel's nationhood."[5]

In 1947 a decision of the UN to partition the land into two parts awarded 55 percent of the land to Israeli Jews, who had owned only

7 percent of the land until that time and composed approximately 30 percent of the population. By the end of the war in 1948, Israel occupied 78 percent of the land, far more than the original UN partition mandated. The renaming of towns, villages, and landmarks added insult to injury. To Palestinians, it seemed that their very culture was being negated.

The Palestinian displacement that began with a massive upheaval in 1948 has continued since that time. The 1967 war (the Six-Day War) enabled Israel to occupy the remaining 22 percent of the land. The continual establishment of Israeli settlements in Palestinian territories has been an irritant to Arabs inside and outside of Israel:

> On January 26, 1999, more than a hundred Israeli soldiers accompanied by bulldozers arrived at the village of Isawiyeh on the outskirts of East Jerusalem. In this village the fourteen-member Awais family had outgrown their home and had built a four-room house on their own property. They were refused a building permit by Israel—as so often happens in these villages—so that the family would leave. But on this Tuesday, bulldozers arrived and began demolishing their new home. About a hundred local people gathered and started to throw stones. Soon the army used batons to suppress them. Next the troops shot rubber-coated metal bullets at close range and killed Zaki Ubayd, the twenty-eight-year-old father. The troops then left quickly, leaving the children in shock and tears, standing in the midst of rubble and death."[6]

A report of Amnesty International states that 16,700 Palestinians (including 7,300 children) in East Jerusalem and the West Bank were displaced as over 2,650 homes were demolished. In East Jerusalem

over 10,000 Palestinian homes, fully one-third of the Arab population of the city, are threatened by demolition orders.[7]

One of the issues standing in the way of any settlement between the Palestinians and Israelis is the Palestinian insistence on
the right of refugees to return to their homes. Israel refused to allow
such a return, insisting that it would be a demographic suicide on
its part. Palestinians, on the other hand, insist that they should be
allowed to return to their homeland and occupy the homes that are
legitimately theirs.

The original Balfour Declaration issued in 1917 by Lord Balfour
of the British government declares: "His majesty's Government view
with favour the establishment in Palestine of a national home for the
Jewish people, . . . it being clearly understood that nothing shall be
done which may prejudice the civil and religious rights of existing
non-Jewish communities in Palestine, or the rights and political
status enjoyed by Jews in any other country."[8] Unfortunately, such
apparent goodwill toward other ethnic and religious groups has
not always been apparent in the Zionist agenda. Menachem Begin
and his Likud party's ascent to power gave further impetus to the
annexation of Palestinian land. Begin advocated an "iron wall" of
Israeli domination, while strengthening ties with leaders of American
evangelicals.[9] It is still too early to claim that historians have reached
a consensus, but some historians are pointing out a disturbing trend
to purge the land of Israel of its original occupants.[10]

In recent months, the construction of a security wall has further
hardened resentment among Palestinians. The wall is an impenetrable
barrier prohibiting the free flow of traffic between Palestinian areas.
In certain areas the wall separates family members. Brothers and
sisters find themselves with no hope of seeing each other, separated

by an eight-meter-high edifice running between their homes. Many Palestinians have lost their jobs by the construction of the wall. Teachers cannot get to their schools. Students are fenced out of their universities. Towns are divided. Perhaps the worst effect of the wall is that it annexes more Palestinian land. Vineyards, orchards, and grazing lands formerly belonging to Palestinians are now behind the wall and under Israeli control. In desperation, Palestinians watch. Hatred and revenge grow to a fever pitch. The result is the intractable situation we see today in Israel and Palestine.

In no way do I wish to validate or justify terrorist activities and the slaying of innocent Israelis by enraged Palestinians. My concern is simply that both sides of the story be told. Aggression against innocent Israeli civilians cannot be tolerated, but neither can aggression against innocent Palestinians. Proverbs 18:17 urges us to hear both sides of a story before making a judgment.

Abuse of the Innocent

The undeniable reality is that war creates an environment where oppression and abuse are likely to proliferate. In the chaos of Israel's conflict with Palestinian Arabs, there has been much abuse of power. Its effects cannot be erased overnight, nor can its presence be canceled out by the murderous attempts of Palestinians to take Israeli lives. The evil must be exposed. The balm must be applied for healing to take place.

Perhaps no other media image has received such wide publicity as the killing of Muhammad al-Dura and his father, Jamaal, during a battle between Palestinian militants and the Israeli forces. The video graphically portrayed a father frantically begging the combatants to stop shooting so that he and his son could pass through to safety.

There was no cessation of fire. The father tried valiantly to cover his son's frail body so as to protect him from the rain of bullets, but to no avail. The father took the first hit while his little boy looked on in horror. It wasn't long until his little life ebbed away as a result of a gunshot wound.

In an amazing show of insensitivity, both sides have sought to prove their innocence. Israelis have defended their role in the incident by saying that Palestinian fire killed the pair. Palestinians have pointed the accusing finger at Israelis. The Arab world was enraged by the graphic photos that depicted a scene painfully commonplace in the conflict—the death of the innocent.

Elias Chacour relates how he stumbled on a mass grave in Gish after his family had relocated there from his original village. As was the habit of the young men of Palestine, Elias played soccer with his companions. While chasing a stray ball beyond their dustbin field, Elias caught a glance of a rather strange looking "twig" protruding from the ground. As he pulled it up, he found it to be a human finger, attached to a human hand, arm, and body. Two dozen residents of Gish had been shot and buried in a shallow grave. The discovery of the bodies would be a constant reminder to young Elias to work for peace in his homeland.[11]

The death toll in the two Intifadas and continued conflict between Israel and the Palestinians has risen to over four thousand. Hundreds of thousands of Palestinian refugees have never been allowed to return to their towns and villages. By order of Israeli courts, 4,170 Palestinian homes have been demolished, while no Israeli homes have been demolished; one Israeli prisoner is being held, while 9,599 Palestinian prisoners are held; 4,126 Palestinians have lost their lives, as opposed to 1,084 Israelis; over 30,000 Palestinians injured and 7,000 Israelis. The U.S. government gives $15,139,178 per day to the Israeli government and military, while Palestinian nongovernmental organizations receive $232,290.[12] U.S. aid to Israel totals over five billion dollars per year.[13]

Statistics like these can be abused. However, it is doubtful that members of the highly touted Israeli military would skew the facts in favor of the Palestinian aggressors. The following is a letter submitted by reserve combat officers of the Israeli Defense Forces:

> **We, reserve combat officers and soldiers of the Israel Defense Forces,** who were raised upon the principles of Zionism, self-sacrifice and giving to the people of Israel and to the State of Israel, who have always served in the front lines, and who were the first to carry out any mission in order to protect the State of Israel and strengthen it.
>
> We, combat officers and soldiers who have served the State of Israel for long weeks every year, in spite of the dear cost to our personal lives, have been on reserve duty in the Occupied Territories, and were issued commands and directives that had nothing to do with the security of our country, and that had the sole purpose of perpetuating our control over the Palestinian people.
>
> We, whose eyes have seen the bloody toll this Occupation exacts from both sides,
>
> We, who sensed how the commands issued to us in the Occupied Territories destroy all the values that we were raised upon,
>
> We, who understand now that the price of Occupation is the loss of IDF's human character and the corruption of the entire Israeli society,

We, who know that the Territories are not a part of Israel, and that all settlements are bound to be evacuated,

We hereby declare that we shall not continue to fight this War of the Settlements.

We shall not continue to fight beyond the 1967 borders in order to dominate, expel, starve and humiliate an entire people.

We hereby declare that we shall continue serving the Israel Defense Force in any mission that serves Israel's defense.

The missions of occupation and oppression do not serve this purpose—and we shall take no part in them.[14]

I have been accosted many times in the Arab world and interrogated as to why my country persistently vetoes UN resolutions that uphold the Palestinian cause. Frankly, I was surprised to discover this reality. Between 1972 and 2002, the United States vetoed approximately forty UN resolutions upholding the rights of Palestinians.[15] It is not difficult to detect the pattern. But one must ask why.

There was a time in Israel's history when injustice was rife. The oppressed were not given just judgments. Aliens and foreigners in the land were not meted out justice. Merchants abused consumers by using false weights and balances. Others based their injustices on false visions and dreams. When these things took place, God raised up prophets who warned his people to abandon their abuses and to walk humbly with their God. He used other nations to discipline his people and even used the Israelites to be a testimony of his grace to the nations where he carried them into exile.

I am, to be honest, baffled. The more I investigate the injustices that have led to a perpetual cycle of violence in the Muslim world, the more I find my own people are implicated. It is not difficult to trace the direct link between American evangelicals and Israel.

Admittedly, it is not only evangelical Christians who strongly support Israeli policies; there is also a strong Jewish lobby in our land that wields great power. Nevertheless, the presence of evangelicals exerts its influence on every decision and every policy. Though we might decry the affiliation of American Christianity with injustices perpetrated throughout the world, it can no longer be denied.

◆ SEEKING FRESH VISION ◆

You and I are part of a global village. Our decisions and our ballots have implications in this increasingly interconnected world. If we close our eyes to the plight of the oppressed, we become guilty. If we ignore the pleas of the bleeding victim of violence, how can we claim to follow a crucified Messiah? Should not Christians, of all people, be listening intently to the suffering people of the world? Has our doctrine of the end-times upended Christian compassion? Are we so obsessed with the borders of a Middle East state that we have done away with the kingdom of God?

One missiologist I know has stated emphatically that the Palestinian issue is a "missiological emergency." Does unequivocal support of Israel's actions uphold the teachings of Christ and his apostles, or is it merely a reflection of an immature end-times frenzy? Have Christians become so eager for the comfort of heaven that we no longer hear the cries of Lazarus outside our gate? Are we right to infer from passages in the Old Testament that we must uphold the policies of the Israeli state no matter what? Should not these policies be examined in the light of solid biblical criteria such as justice, equality, charity, and the sanctity of human life? Is there no fresh vision for a displaced people?

Some will, no doubt, respond, "Yes, but Islamic militancy cannot be tolerated." The objection is a fair one. That's why we must look at the phenomenon of Islamic fundamentalism in the next chapter.

Additional Resources for Chapter 9

Alatar, Muhammad. *The Iron Wall.* Palestinian Agricultural Relief Committees: 2006. This is a documentary concerning the effects of the Israeli security fence on Palestinians.

Ruether, Rosemary Radford, and Herman J. Ruether. *The Wrath of Jonah: The Crisis of Religious Nationalism in the Israeli-Palestinian Conflict.* Minneapolis: Fortress Press, 2002.

PART IV
A REALITY CHECK

The Bible presents to us a complex worldview. While human beings bear the image of God, they are nonetheless radically alienated from him. We humans are capable of great acts marked by nobility and dignity, and at the same time we are capable of destroying ourselves and others with unimaginable ferocity. This ironic complexity holds true of all human beings everywhere. When encountering the Muslim world, we should not be surprised to find a world marked by the good qualities of hospitality and magnanimity as well as the evil qualities of religious fanaticism and despotism, as is true in the Western world. Fresh vision for the Muslim world must not naively assume that it is welcome in all quarters of that world. In fact, it will encounter great resistance, as Jesus himself predicted of his servants.

CHAPTER 10

REFORMATION À LA ISLAM

In the aftermath of 9/11, political and religious leaders expended much effort to absorb the massive anger being unleashed toward radical Islam.

Political leaders in the United States and Britain went to great pains to state that Islam is a "religion of peace." Moderate Islamic clerics were called upon to explain the mysterious actions of the 9/11 hijackers. When asked why young Muslims engaged in blatant terrorist activity against innocent people, some clerics resorted to denying that the perpetrators were Muslims. Even if the terrorists were Muslims, some clerics maintained, they were sorely deceived, as Islam is a religion that respects all beliefs and does not force others to embrace its tenets.

A famous Qur'anic injunction, "There is no compulsion in religion" (2:256), constantly came to the attention of the Western world. Many were led to believe that the word *Islam* means "peace."

It does not, although it is derived from the same root as the Arabic word for *peace*. The word means "submission." A Muslim, therefore, is a "submitted one."

In an attempt to provide a frame of reference for the actions of the radicals, Westerners were reminded that there are radical fringes of Christianity as well. As an example, the actions of the Ku Klux Klan in the early twentieth century are abhorrent to Christians today. Yet the KKK adopted the cross as its symbol and invoked many Christian principles in the propagation of its philosophy. Were not the young radicals of Islam a parallel to the KKK? Although they invoked religion as the cause of their violence, they were, in fact, estranged from the true practice of Islam. It would follow that just as Christians are incensed by the actions of racial bigots, so Muslims were outraged by the actions of these radical fringes of their religion.

In the minds of most thinking people, the analogy rang hollow. First, there was the fact that many Muslims throughout the world affirmed the religious sincerity of the 9/11 hijackers and even embraced their mission as Allah's divine retribution on the United States. I have already made reference to this fact and tried to come to terms with it as a stumbling attempt to resurrect a power-deprived Islamic empire. Nevertheless, the muffled celebrations expressed around the Muslim world betrayed the lie that the work of the young hijackers was merely a radical fringe element of Islam.

Second, the confession of the 9/11 hijackers confirmed their complete loyalty to Islam as the primary motivation for their action. Their association with al Qaeda and Usama bin Laden's relentless appeal to the Qur'an sealed the verdict. The young men were convinced they were giving their lives in jihad in the way of Allah. Their sacrifice would be rewarded in paradise!

Whether the young men who carried out the attacks represented the beliefs of Islam is a question that remains open. What is clear is that they perceived themselves to be following the tenets of Islam in attacking one of the most tenacious enemies of their religion—the United States of America.

In this chapter we continue to pursue fresh vision for the Muslim world. This vision, if we are to find it, must be based on reality. We dare not sugarcoat the bitter pill of Islamic fundamentalism (*Islamism*) in an attempt to lure ourselves into a misplaced vision; the results would be disastrous. Better to pursue an analysis built on reality while at the same time not dismissing our own culpability in our failure to disciple the nations as we have been commanded.

The preceding chapters have laid necessary groundwork for examining Islamism. The phenomenon cannot be reduced to mere Western provocation, nor can the blame be laid entirely at the feet of Islamic beliefs. It is a complex movement drawing from many streams, some of which come from outside the Islamic world and some of which come from within.

I hope that you will bear in mind that typical Muslims the world over expend very little energy each day in considering these questions. The primary concerns of most Muslims are similar to ours—raising their children, providing for their children's education, saving for that new car or outfit. While Islamism is a phenomenon we must come to terms with, we must exercise care not to be monofocal in our understanding of Islam. It is an unfortunate fact that radical Islamists have monopolized the media coverage of Islam such that most of what we see and read related to the Muslim world concerns a small percentage of the population. It reminds me of a funny conversation I once had with a Middle Easterner who asked me how many

Americans owned jets. In astonishment I asked the reason for his question. It seems he had been watching the television series *Dallas* and was convinced that most Americans lived a lifestyle similar to JR's. We will do well to remember that Muslims are human beings with the same real-life issues that we face.

The remainder of this chapter will look briefly at philosophies that have devalued human life. My hope is to show that Islamic fundamentalism is not the first such philosophy and will not be the last. Next we'll observe the historic roots of Islamic fundamentalism, beginning with the Qur'an and Hadiith, framing our discussion around the concept of jihad. Then we will look at how this vision of struggle for the establishment of power was practiced by the prophet of Islam, Muhammad.

Worldviews of Violence

What an amazing book is Genesis! The splendor of the garden of Eden with man and woman having fruitful labor, loving relationships with each other and their environment, and walking in the presence of God, their Creator. From this majestic and pristine view of man's unassailable dignity, the book then moves into the tragedy that becomes the theme of the remainder of the Bible. Adam and Eve choose another way. Although you would expect a subtle and slow infusion of the poison of this broken relationship with God into the perfect world, that is not the case. The shocking reality is that humankind quickly degenerates to self-destruction. In the first generation following Adam and Eve, Cain takes his brother's life. It is most intriguing that the motivation for the crime falls under the rubric of religion; Cain envies his brother's acceptable offering to God.

Murder takes up its abode in the descendants of Cain as well. We are told in Genesis 4 that one of the descendants of Cain, named Lamech, murders a young man. Lamech sings his own praise to his two wives and boastfully asserts that God will take revenge on whoever kills him. Thus, within the first four chapters of the Bible we have two murders. Already we find religious man boasting in his murderous exploits and declaring that God will vindicate him in his killing. The wonder and mystery of Genesis is that it is such an accurate mirror of life's realities.

History has borne out the truth of the early chapters of Genesis. It is replete with examples of philosophies and worldviews that devalue the sacred nature of life and then permit the taking of life, asserting divine approbation for murderous acts. A quick historical survey could demonstrate that human civilizations have repeatedly taken life not only in warfare, but even in worship and entertainment! Those who practiced ancient Canaanite religions offered their sons and daughters as offerings to their gods. The Israelites were corrupted by these religious practices (1 Kings 11:7; Jeremiah 32:35). The Romans made sport of bloodletting in the Coliseum. Convicted criminals (including those convicted of worshipping Jesus Christ) were released into the Coliseum to be devoured by ravenous animals. This was the sport of the day!

As a philosophy, Nazism upheld ethnic cleansing. As a result six million Jews went to the gas chambers in an attempt to purify the Aryan race. The perplexing genocide in Rwanda in the mid-to-late 1990s claimed the lives of 500,000 to one million of the Tutsi and Hutu population of that country.[1] In southern India, female infanticide is still being practiced today. In the district of Salem, India, it is estimated that over forty-five hundred female children have been killed in recent years simply because it is an economic liability to have a baby girl.[2] The media recently focused our attention on the war crimes tribunal in The Hague that brought Slobodan Milosevic to trial for genocidal crimes in former Yugoslavia.

The widespread nature of genocidal killing and religiously motivated murder may help us gain a more realistic picture of Islamist warlike activities. Western European societies and cultures cannot claim immunity in the devaluing of human life. In 2002 the Netherlands moved to the cutting edge of the slippery slope by prescribing a set policy of euthanasia. Patients can be euthanized by the medical establishment in order to avoid pain or to flee from a life that is deemed not worth living.

The devaluing of human life extends to our own society as well. Recent events such as the Columbine and Virginia Tech mass murders are forcing Americans to grapple with a culture that glorifies murderous exploits in much of its entertainment media. America is also deeply divided on the issue of abortion. Approximately 1.5 million abortions take place each year. Can we not surmise that the freedom to end life in the womb is part of the global devaluation of life in our society?

The point is simply this: the widespread attempt to displace and dispose of life, while abhorrent, is nothing new in human societies and cultures. It is prevalent in both East and West. It often has religious underpinnings and is carried out with great fervor by its practitioners. This repetitive refrain in human history arises from a complex philosophy asserting that the taking of life is a necessity. Human beings become convinced of the justice of their cause through a complex matrix of motivations and justifications. This is not a new phenomenon that arose with Islamism. That does not resolve the issue, of course. But it will, I believe, help us deal with the phenomenon if we are equipped with a broad historical and theological awareness such that we are not taken unawares by the gruesome nature of life devaluation and murder.

One more example of the devaluing and usurping of sacred life deserves mention. Jesus Christ was led before a Roman governor to determine his fate. His co-religionists accused him of blasphemy and political treason. Though Pilate washed his hands of the affair, he implicitly granted the Jews their request—death by crucifixion. Jesus was neither alarmed nor incredulous at the verdict. His prophecies show that he fully expected it and yet recognized it as an expression of the reigning powers of darkness. Death for Christ was an extreme agony, yet one he endured with a sure knowledge of his destiny. He made no attempt to redress the injustice through popular uprising. He did not instruct his followers to vindicate his death by exacting their vengeance on his murderers. He faced the evil intent of his killers with the sure conviction of the nobility and superiority of the divine purpose: "Not my will, but yours" (Luke 22:42).

We claim to be his disciples.

Now the explosive zeal of Islamic radicals is directed not toward a far-off African tribe or some Asian ethnic extraction deserving of our pity. It is taking the lives of our own family members and friends. It is aimed at us. How do we deal with this?

Historic Roots of Islamic Fundamentalism

When the Reformers of Europe were gripped with the deplorable state of the Christian church in the 1500s, they developed a methodology of reform that advocated a return to the original sources of the faith. These original sources were, of course, the Scriptures of the Old and New Testaments. Returning to these texts effected a purification of the doctrine of the church. One of the watchwords of the Reformation was *sola scriptura*—Scripture alone as the source of the church's authority.

Similar to medieval Europe, the Muslim world of our day is riddled with strife and confusion. The economic and military downfall of Islamic nations begs for some explanation. Those who wish to effect reform in the Islamic community will doubtless look to the sources of Islam—the Qur'an and the Hadiith.[3] These documents brought about the flowering of Islamic civilizations such as the Umayyad, Abbasid, and Ottoman empires. Surely, Islamic reformers reason, if Islamic civilization is to return to its place of preeminence, it will be under the guiding aegis of the Qur'an and the traditions of the Prophet.

So what does the Qur'an say? Ideally we would look for an authoritative position on the subject from some Islamic court or council with weight throughout the Muslim world. Unfortunately, there seems to be a great deal of confusion about the issue. Part of the difficulty in determining just what the Qur'an says stems from the fact that many common people view the *ulema* (religious scholars) as having been co-opted by their corrupt governments and leaders. Thus many Muslims are no longer looking to the *ulema* as their source of authoritative information. Generally the religious scholars hold to interpretations that uphold the status quo within their countries. Although there are variations in the opinions of the *ulema*, they would generally eschew the use of violence on noncombatants and people of other faiths, except in cases where Muslim lands are being occupied by foreign powers. In no case of which I am aware do they uphold the validity of suicide bombings.

The Islamists, on the other hand, have a different opinion. They find in the life of Muhammad and the Qur'anic revelation a clear call to jihad. *Jihad* is the noun form of the Arabic verb *jaahid*, which can mean "to strive or to fight." Most Muslims are aware that Muhammad engaged in military conquests (jihad) to suppress the infidels and establish the superiority of Islam. Muslims hold that Muhammad, unlike Jesus Christ, was a role model in every conceivable area of human life. Many have told me, for instance, "Jesus never fought in a war. Muhammad did. Jesus never married. Muhammad did. Jesus never had children. Muhammad did." They refer to him as a model of courage and valor while also presenting him as an example of mercy and tolerance. Thus, for Muslims, Muhammad was a worthy example in every area of human life, including war.

There are many verses in the Qur'an that strongly uphold a tolerant and pluralistic approach to other faiths. Some of these include the following:

> 2:256 Let there be no compulsion in religion. Truth stands out clear from error: whoever rejects Evil and believes in Allah has grasped the most trustworthy handhold, that never breaks. And Allah hears and knows all things. (Yusuf Ali translation)

> 29:46 And argue not with the People of the Scripture [those who received Scripture prior to Islam] unless it be in a way that is better, save with such of them as do wrong; and say: We believe in that which hath been revealed unto us and revealed unto you; our God and your God is One, and unto Him we surrender.

> 5:48 For each We have appointed a divine law and a traced-out way. Had Allah willed He could have made you one community. But that He may try you by that which He hath given you (He hath made you as ye are). So vie one with another in good works. Unto Allah ye will all return, and He will then inform you of that wherein ye differ.

The Qur'an was revealed over a period of approximately twenty-two years, during which Muhammad faced situations of war and peace, political prominence and flight for his life. Therefore, one might expect to find variance in the way in which he dealt with people of other faiths. Islamic scholars have noted this variation and even found justification for it within the Qur'an. That justification is explicit in this verse: "Nothing of our revelation (even a single verse) do we abrogate or cause be [sic] forgotten, but we bring (in place) one better or the like thereof. Knowest thou not that Allah is Able to do all things?" (2:106).[4]

The following verse cites critics of Muhammad's practice of abrogating former revelations with later ones: "And when We put a revelation in place of (another) revelation,—and Allah knoweth best what He revealeth—they say: Lo! thou art but inventing. Most of them know not" (16:101).

Drawing upon these verses, Qur'anic commentators and experts in Islamic law have defined the *doctrine of abrogation*.[5] According to this doctrine, when there is some variation in the Qur'an, the latter revelation is said to abrogate the former. Therefore, in the case of variance or conflict, some verses of the Qur'an—those revealed earliest—are abrogated by the later verses.

You may reasonably ask if all Muslims believe in this doctrine of abrogation. Many Muslims simply are not aware of it. However, it is a widely accepted tenet of Islam taught at Al-Azhar University and upheld by Muslim commentators both Sunni and Shia. Exactly which verses are abrogated and which remain in effect is a matter of debate within Islam. But the principle of abrogation is widely accepted in exegesis of the Qur'an.

This is the challenge facing moderate and tolerant Muslims (yes, there are many): it is the latter verses of the Qur'an that abrogate the former. In his early years (in Mecca), Muhammad was a persecuted prophet, calling polytheist Arabs to the monotheistic faith of Islam. In the latter years of his life, Muhammad had formed an extensive army and was engaged in military conquest. The revelations that came to Muhammad in those years speak of displacing all other faiths so that Islam would become the one and only religion in the Arabian Peninsula. Islamists, following the principle of abrogation, hold that the verses that advocate tolerance and pluralism are abrogated by the later revelations.

These later revelations are noticeably more antagonistic in their treatment of those of other faiths. Here is a smattering of such verses:

> 9:5 Then, when the sacred months have passed, slay the idolaters wherever ye find them, and take them (captive), and besiege them, and prepare for them each ambush. But if they repent and establish worship and pay the poor-due, then leave their way free. Lo! Allah is Forgiving, Merciful.

> 9:12–14 And if they break their pledges after their treaty (hath been made with you) and assail your religion,

then fight the heads of disbelief—Lo! they have no binding oaths—in order that they may desist. Will ye not fight a folk who broke their solemn pledges, and purposed to drive out the messenger and did attack you first? What! Fear ye them? Now Allah hath more right that ye should fear Him, if ye are believers. Fight them! Allah will chastise them at your hands, and He will lay them low and give you victory over them, and He will heal the breasts of folk who are believers.

8:39 And fight them until persecution is no more, and religion is all for Allah. But if they cease, then lo! Allah is Seer of what they do.

2:190–193 Fight in the way of Allah against those who fight against you, but begin not hostilities. Lo! Allah loveth not aggressors. And slay them wherever ye find them, and drive them out of the places whence they drove you out, for persecution is worse than slaughter. And fight not with them at the Inviolable Place of Worship until they first attack you there, but if they attack you (there) then slay them. Such is the reward of disbelievers. But if they desist, then lo! Allah is Forgiving, Merciful. And fight them until persecution is no more, and religion is for Allah. But if they desist, then let there be no hostility except against wrong-doers.

4:74–76 Let those fight in the way of Allah who sell the life of this world for the other. Whoso fighteth in the way of Allah, be he slain or be he victorious, on him We shall bestow a vast reward. How should ye not fight for the cause of Allah and of the feeble among men and of the women and the children who are crying: Our Lord! Bring us forth from out this town of which the people are oppressors! Oh, give us from thy presence some protecting friend! Oh, give us from Thy presence some defender! Those who believe do battle for the cause of Allah; and those who disbelieve do battle for the cause of idols. So fight the minions of the devil. Lo! the devil's strategy is ever weak.

2:216 Warfare is ordained for you, though it is hateful unto you; but it may happen that ye hate a thing which is good for you, and it may happen that ye love a thing which is bad for you. Allah knoweth, ye know not.

61:10–12 O ye who believe! Shall I show you a commerce that will save you from a painful doom? Ye should believe in Allah and His messenger, and should strive (*tujaahiduuna* from the verb form of jihad) for the cause of Allah with your wealth and your lives. That is better for you, if ye did but know. He will forgive you your sins and bring you into gardens underneath which rivers flow, and pleasant dwellings in Gardens of Eden. That is the supreme triumph.

The following passages are taken from the Hadiith (these selections are taken from the al-Bukhari collection, whose recorded traditions are deemed accurate by all Muslim scholars):

Hadiith 48 Paradise has one-hundred grades which Allah has reserved for the Mujahidun who fight in His cause, and the distance between each of two grades is like the distance between the Heaven and the Earth. So, when you ask Allah (for something), ask for Al-firdaus (the Paradise) which is the best and highest part.

Hadiith 53 Nobody who dies and finds good from Allah (in the here-after) would wish to come back to this world even if he were given the whole world and whatever is in it, except the martyr who, on seeing the superiority of martyrdom, would like to come back to the world and get killed again.

Hadiith 72 "Whoever amongst us is killed will go to Paradise." Umar asked the prophet, "Is it not true that our men who are killed will go to Paradise and theirs (i.e. those of the Pagans) will go to the (Hell) fire?" The prophet said, "Yes."

Hadiith 78 You who believe! What is the matter with that when you are asked to go forth in the Way of Allah (i.e. jihad), you cling heavily to the earth? Do you prefer the life of this world to the Hereafter? If you go not forth we will punish you with a painful torment and will replace you by another people and you cannot harm Him at all, Allah is able to do all things (quoted from Qur'an 9:38–39).

As you can imagine, the fundamentalists have been accused of choosing verses capriciously to uphold their own vision of jihad. This accusation has caused them to seek support of *ulema* (Islamic scholars) for their opinions.

Jihad, sometimes translated "holy war," is a divine institution of war to extend Islam into the *dar al-harb* (the non-Islamic territories, described as the "abode of war," or of disbelief) or to defend Islam from danger.[6] For the original followers of Muhammad, jihad meant striving against the polytheists of the Arabian Peninsula as well as those of other faiths who resisted Muhammad. In subsequent generations Muslims have spiritualized these commands to refer to the *greater jihad*, which is the jihad of the soul. This stands in contrast to the *lesser jihad*, the jihad of warfare. Other novel attempts to modernize the call to jihad have referred to the *jihad of the pen*—the attempt to convince unbelievers of the rightness of Islam through debate and persuasion.

The root definition of the word *jihad* does not necessarily imply armed combat. The word can be used in a general way to denote "striving" or "taking pains." Therefore it is not difficult to see that a contemporary and less militant understanding of jihad is indeed possible. Moderate Muslims repudiate the insistence of Islamists on embracing the literal acts of the early Muslim mujahideen. Jihad can be recast into a modern mold. As Western non-Muslims, we must be careful not to prescribe a particular bias in interpreting these texts.

Despite the attempts to harmonize jihad with the contemporary world, the example of Muhammad and his followers remains as a constant call to Muslims to strive for the defense of the Islamic nation and to press into submission those who challenge it. Yet many Muslims advocate that Islam must live as one religion in a world of many religions. Many also try to propagate their faith through peaceful means and dispute the legitimacy of the Islamist reading of these Qur'anic passages.

By examining these texts, we can see something of the predicament Islam is facing today. Because of these texts and a literalist hermeneutic, radical Islamic fundamentalism enjoys broad support among Islamic peoples today. Whether this reading of the Qur'an is correct, it does, in my opinion, enable Islamists to mobilize for militant action. Although I think Western Christians would do well to examine the Muslim perspective of the West's aggression against Muslim nations, I also view the foundational building blocks of Islamic militancy to be found in the texts of the Qur'an and Hadiith. Thus, if moderate Muslims are to succeed in recasting the concept of jihad, they will need to do it through a reformed Qur'anic hermeneutic. In other words, they need to explain jihad in the Qur'an and in the life of Muhammad in such a way that it does not leave the door open for religious war in our day. Furthermore, they will need to win the argument within the Islamic community. Until that happens, Islamic militancy may be around for quite some time.

Muhammad's Practice of Jihad

As a guest in Islamic culture, I often asked questions about cultural things that I did not understand. Why did the men grow their beards but shave their mustaches? Why did they have a bruise on their forehead? Why did they hold their hands up to their ears before bowing in prayer? Why were there green lights on the mosque? The list went on and on. The surprise for me was how often the answer to these questions was *sunna rasuul Allah* (the custom of Allah's apostle).

For Muslims, Muhammad is much more than a prophet or teacher. He is the epitome of manhood, the moral role model for all people and all times. Al-Ghazzali (eleventh century), the famous Muslim philosopher and theologian said: "Know that the key to happiness is to follow the Sunna [the custom of the prophet] and to imitate the messenger of God in all his coming and going, his movements, his rest, in his way of eating, his attitude, his sleep and his talk. 'What the messenger of God has brought—accept it and what he has prohibited—refrain from it'" (Sura 59:7).

The question of Muhammad's involvement in warfare is a well-traveled road. Muslims are generally offended when this is referred to and uphold Muhammad's activities as a necessary measure taken for the good of mankind in establishing Islam. The Islamic consensus is that Islam brought a reign of peace and prosperity to the tribes of Arabia and the surrounding nations. One Islamic website summarizes well the Muslim consensus about Muhammad's initial invitation to the surrounding tribes to become Muslims. It is interesting to note how the ancient clash is portrayed in modern terms as the pursuit of religious freedom:

> To this effect, Mohammed sent his delegates to eight neighboring rulers with messages calling them to embrace Islam. The appeal was rejected. Some of them even killed the Prophet's delegates, and some tore the message and threatened the delegates who had brought it. The rulers of the time were a clear obstacle in front of the individuals' freedom and their right to live in justice and to choose their religion freely. Islam was the civilized step in the development of humankind that the despots of the time were a barrier to. Islam declared war against an obsolete form of

tyrannical governing. If Islam used force, then [*sic*] only to enforce justice that resulted in fascinating civilizations in every area where Islam entered.[7]

Once again, I cannot claim to offer an authoritative Islamic interpretation of these events. My only contention is that Muhammad's practice of warfare is embraced by Islamic militants (whether rightly or wrongly) to promote their vision of reform. If Muhammad practiced military raids with divine sanction, then to fail to act in a similar way in the modern world would be a failure to submit to the *sunna rasuul Allah*. While Muslims do not all agree on the issue, the force of the Islamist argument is demonstrated by the often-noted failure of Islamic moderates to mobilize the masses in demonstration against terrorist attacks. Muslims know that imitation of the Prophet is the path of virtue. They also know he (and his successors) established the Islamic nation through military prowess.

While this section will hardly do justice to the history of the Islamic prophet's jihad, I do hope to scratch the surface of an area quite unfamiliar to many Western readers. Bear in mind that Muslim reflection on these events is of a vastly different nature from that of Westerners. All of Muhammad's actions were done under the approbation and direction of Allah. Thus, it is incumbent on Muslims to examine Muhammad's action for their own moral and ethical principles.

Muhammad's early years after his prophetic call were spent in the City of Mecca. During this time, Muhammad was part of the well-established Quraysh tribe and enjoyed the protection of his powerful uncle. When his uncle passed away, Muhammad no longer had clan protection. His call to the oneness (*tawhiid*) of Allah threatened the local religious and economic system, based on a system of idol worship. It was at this point that Muhammad began to encounter persecution. He remained in Mecca until his life was in danger and then fled to Medina, making a miraculous escape with a few of his followers in September 622 CE (the beginning of the Islamic calendar).

He had wisely laid the groundwork for his flight to Medina through a series of treaties with the leaders of Medina. He arrived in the city as a man of influence with a considerable following of emigrants (*muhaajiruun)* from Mecca. The flight to Medina (*hijra*) was a watershed event in Muhammad's prophetic career. Medina became his outpost for the forward expansion of Islam. Muhammad gradually gained economic control of the Arabian Peninsula through raiding caravans bound for Mecca. Martin Accad comments on the importance of the *hijra*:

> The life of Muhammad is made up of two distinct periods, recognised by Muslims themselves, and separated by the dramatic event of the *Hijra*, the "migration" of Muhammad and his early followers from Mecca to Medina (two cities of Arabia) under persecution by Muhammad's own tribe, the pagan rulers of Mecca. In Medina, the host city of the "new community", the new message was able to thrive in a largely sympathetic environment. However, it was in Medina as well that the Jewish tribes ruling over the city began to awaken to the threat that the budding new religion was beginning to pose to their continued control. During the *Meccan* period Muhammad perceived himself as a messenger from God and applied himself to the proclamation of a message of repentance and "submission" (literal meaning of "Islam") of pagan Arabs to the One God of Abraham. During the *Medinan* period, however, Muhammad was

gradually becoming the leader of a growing body of follow-ers that needed political leadership.[8]

Muhammad's genius as a military strategist cannot be denied. During his first eighteen months in Medina, Muhammad sent out exploratory expeditions. The first attack on a Meccan caravan took place at his command in Nakhlah, although Muhammad himself did not participate.[9] The first real battle was at Badr (624 CE). Muhammad had amassed an army of 300 men while the Meccan caravan was protected by 950 men. Muhammad gained a tactical advantage by blocking wells and posting his army around one well that remained functional. He promised paradise to those who were killed in the battle.[10] Probably 40 to 75 Meccans were killed, as many were taken prisoner, and the rest fled. Muhammad's soldiers divided the booty among themselves. The battle at Badr changed the economic landscape in the Arabian Peninsula; Mecca's traders now knew that Muhammad and his army were a force to be reckoned with. To cope with Muhammad's sudden rise to power, they would have to attack him.

The battle at Uhud was Mecca's revenge in 325 CE. Three thousand Meccan soldiers marched on Medina and were met out-side the city by Muhammad's army. A battle ensued in which more Muslims were killed than Meccans. The battle ended as a loss for Muslims, which greatly hurt Islamic morale and the contention that Muhammad's victories were Allah's seal of approval on his prophetic ministry. The defeat, however, was explained in terms of the war-riors' disobedience to Muhammad's commands given during battle. Thus, the future success of the Islamic cause was linked to complete obedience to the Prophet. Muslims were consoled by the fact that their slain warriors were in paradise: "And what though ye be slain in

Allah's way or die therein? Surely pardon from Allah and mercy are better than all that they amass. What though ye be slain or die, when unto Allah ye are gathered?" (3:157–158). Thus the reward of those slain in jihad is forgiveness of sins and assurance of paradise.

Approximately two years passed between the battle at Uhud and Muhammad's next military encounter. During this time Muhammad was busy sending out minor raiding expeditions to break up any attempts of attack on Medina. He also allowed bands of his followers to conceal their Islamic faith in order to infiltrate the enemies of Islam and conduct assassinations. His attempts were successful in forestalling the growth of the Meccan confederation against him.

In March 627 CE the men of Mecca made one final attempt to bring Muhammad's reign to an end. They marched on Medina with ten thousand men. The Muslims remained in Medina with only three thousand men, but Muhammad realized that he could neutralize the Meccan cavalry by digging a deep trench around the exposed part of the city. The Muslims carefully guarded the trench, and the Meccans could not penetrate Medina. Their confederation, drained of resources and morale, retired and went home after two weeks. Thus the so-called Battle of the Trench was more of a standoff than an actual battle. Its importance is that it demonstrated that Muhammad could not be defeated by the more numerous Meccan army.

In the aftermath of the Trench affair, a Jewish tribe called Qurayza was massacred in Medina. Events during the Battle of the Trench led Muslims to believe they were about to be betrayed by the Jewish Qurayza. The Qurayza tribe surrendered to Muhammad inside the City of Medina. Muhammad conferred judgment of the tribe to a leading Medinan Muslim, who declared, "I give judgment that the men should be killed, the property divided, and the women and children taken as captive." Trenches were dug as mass graves. The men, numbering between six and nine hundred, were beheaded. Medina was now a Muslim city.

Muhammad's ascendancy proceeded unchecked. In 628 CE he attempted a pilgrimage to Mecca, which led to his signing a treaty with the Meccans. The treaty would allow him to enter Mecca on pilgrimage the following year. In actual fact, in 630 Muhammad entered the city as the unchallenged victor. Little blood was shed as the entire city acknowledged his supremacy. He immediately removed the idols from the Kaaba and established monotheistic worship of Allah as the one religion in this most influential city of the Arabian Peninsula. Muhammad returned to Medina and further coalesced his power by inviting surrounding tribes to Islam.

Muhammad died in 632 CE, leaving no designated successor. His close friend Abu Bakr took over the reins of power and became the first of the four rightly guided caliphs. The caliphs continued the military spread of Islam, pushing it westward into North Africa and eastward into Iraq and Iran.

In this brief review of the birth of Islam, you can see that armed conflict figured large in Islamic history. The leaders of radical Islam constantly refer to these events to justify their violence. While many moderate Muslims dispute their interpretations, it is not difficult to see why these radicals have embraced armed conflict in their attempts to reestablish the predominance of Islam and to redress wrongs they feel Muslims have suffered at the hands of Western infidels.

We do not attempt to define authentic Islam for Muslims. We simply point out that the use of the sword in defense of Islam is inherently linked to its history. Those who eschew violence—and there are many—must bear the burden of establishing their practice from the Qur'an and Islamic history. Furthermore, they have the daunting challenge of persuading nearly one billion Muslims, now desperately trying to reestablish the political and military influence of the Muslim world, that their interpretation is the correct one.

It is incumbent on Western observers of Islam to realize that bloody wars of a religious nature also plagued medieval Europe. The Muslim world was not alone in resorting to the sword for defense of the faith. The fact that Islam has never advocated a separation of religious and political powers may also temper our tendency to ascribe warlike tendencies to Islam. The wars that took place were not merely religious wars but also state wars.

We would do well to remember that separation of church and state is a relatively recent phenomenon in the course of Western civilization. The founding fathers of the United States had the advantage of hindsight, having observed the negative outcome of the imposition of a state church in Europe. The presence of multiple denominations in the United States made that a pragmatic impossibility. Additionally, the prevailing Enlightenment philosophy provided an ideological framework for toleration of divergent views. Thus the American experiment referred to by Thomas Jefferson became an experiment in all kinds of individual freedoms, including the freedom of religion—the state was not to prescribe religious belief nor meddle therein.

Islam, as a civilization, may well be in the throes of a paradigm shift. At this point, it is too early to tell if a wall of separation in the religious and political powers will be recognized as legitimate. Some have suggested that political power is in the DNA of Islam, whereas the separation of Christian faith from political power was bound to happen eventually. Time will tell. For the present, the movement of Islamic militancy is an attempt to remarry military power with religious faith in countries where a separation of sorts has been foisted upon them. The militants see their efforts as a return to true Islam and remain assured that God's blessing will crown their efforts with success.

◆ SEEKING FRESH VISION ◆

In summary, the essential elements of Islamism are the texts of the Qur'an and Hadiith. We readily admit that we, as Christians, are not the authoritative interpreters of the Qur'an. At the same time, we note that Islamists throughout the world are forging their strategy based on these ancient texts as well as the example of the prophet Muhammad and the caliphs. While their interpretation of the texts may be flawed, we are compelled to admit the force of their argument and appeal to more moderate Muslims to supply a more accurate reading of the textual sources.

Additionally, a catalyst has now been added to these essential elements of Islamism—the demonstrable decline in world influence of Islamic nations coupled with the superiority of the West. This decline became painfully evident to all Muslims throughout the twentieth century as the West demonstrated its superiority through two world wars, the fall of the Soviet Union, and wars in Iraq and Afghanistan. In its superiority the West has ridden roughshod over Islamic sensitivities. In the minds of Muslims, the list of Western transgressions is long, including a deluge of immoral media, economic usurpation of Muslim markets and land, colonialism and occupation, military presence, diplomatic inequality and—the crown jewel of Western violations—the presence of a Jewish state on land that was, until the twentieth century, under the protection of Islam, not to mention the refugee status of millions of Palestinians.

In the next chapter, we'll begin asking how a Christ-follower might respond to the complex phenomenon of Islamism.

Additional Reading for Chapter 10

Accad, Martin. "Christian-Muslim Relations." www.abtslebanon.org.

Riddell, Peter G., and Peter Cotterell. *Islam in Context: Past, Present, and Future.* Grand Rapids: Baker Academic, 2003.

Watt, W. Montgomery. *Muhammad at Medina.* Oxford: Oxford University Press, 1956.

CHAPTER 11

"THOU SHALT NOT BE TERRORIZED"

The long decline of Islamic civilization as an economic and military power base in the world is apparent. There are some signs of renewal in Islamic society. Many Muslim friends have pointed to the rapid development in the petroleum-rich Arabian Peninsula states as a sign of both the favor of God and the coming renaissance of the Muslim world. Indeed the rapid urbanization and development of countries such as the United Arab Emirates are nothing short of mind boggling. Still, Saudi Arabia's recourse to Western powers for its defense against Saddam Hussein demonstrates to many Muslims that the hoped-for renaissance remains remote.

Two world wars, the rebirth of Israel on land that had been long held by Islamic empires, Western economic and cultural expansionism in the Arab and Muslim world, the presence of Western military in Muslim lands, the overthrow of the Taliban and Saddam Hussein—all these and many more indicators point to a perceived weakness among Muslim countries that continues to fuel frustration. The decline is even more maddening for Muslims given their history of glorious exploits and phenomenal expansion under the leadership of the Prophet, his caliphs, and other noted leaders of successive Islamic empires. In the twentieth century, Muslims around the world began to ask, "What is wrong? Islam is the path of true submission to Allah. So why are we at or near the bottom of the heap?"

The question is intriguing, but for Muslims and those who live among them it is of much more than passing academic interest. Daily they see an educational system hopelessly behind the times and incompetent to produce a literate population. They witness government corruption wreaking havoc with the economy and bureaucracy crippled by fear of taking responsible action. Families cannot afford to buy meat. Young men cannot get married simply because there are no jobs, no places to live, and no hope. To you that kind of life is what you see featured in news reports on CNN or BBC, but for a good portion of the Muslim world, it is day-in and day-out reality. The question of what went wrong is the hinge on which much of the Muslim world is turning. For those who wish to open their eyes and see the Muslim world in a new way, this question incites compassion and motivates to action.

Hunger for Change

For some Muslims living through this nightmare, something needs to be done and done now! The wrongs must be made right. The corruption must be purged. Government leaders must be called to account and, in some cases, replaced. Reform, radical reform must take place.

And where do these frustrated and desperate Muslim people look to set the agenda for reform? To the foundations of their religion, of course. Very few will have implicit trust of a Western agenda for economic and governmental reform; the history between the Muslim world and the West is too jagged. Their own heritage wins their confidence (as would ours); they opt for religious reform. Much as the Reformers of Protestantism cried *sola scriptura* and *ad fontes* (to the source), many Muslims are rallying for a return to the era of the Prophet and the original caliphate of Islam. When leaders arise who sound this clarion call for purging the Islamic world of its apathy and corruption, you can be sure that many Muslims are listening. They need a solution, and they needed it yesterday!

During my sojourn among Muslim people, I felt keenly their need for societal justice, lifting of oppression and tyranny, and economic reform. While it may be difficult for Westerners to appreciate, the movement of Islamic fundamentalism must be understood through this grid. Not only does Islamism attempt to restore Islam to its position of preeminence in the world, but it also works at a grassroots level to alleviate societal injustices. The Society of Muslim Brothers (also known as the Muslim Brotherhood), with its well-worn slogan "Islam is the solution," has become a force for all kinds of social services within Egypt. It has administered earthquake relief, medical clinics, and food distribution. Having been banned as a political party, it resorted to infiltration of a vast network of professional syndicates in Egypt. Thus it has brought Islamic reform to a number of professions—medicine, engineering, law, and teaching. Is it any wonder that candidates sanctioned by the Muslim Brotherhood have had tremendous success when running for parliamentary seats in Egypt?

Hamas has played a similar role among Palestinians. While Gaza has been virtually shut down by the closing of its seaports and borders with Israel, Hamas has been able to provide some sustenance to a needy Gazan population.

In the West what is most known of these fundamentalist Islamic groups is their perpetration of violence. Certainly I do not wish to deny that violent strain. Assassinations, suicide bombings, and attacks on tourists have all been part of the fundamentalist package. Nevertheless, the movement of Islamism is multifaceted. Some Islamist movements, such as the Society of Muslim Brothers, have formally renounced the use of violent means. Others continue to hold to the necessity of a military coup to establish Islamist leadership in their countries. Some have established clear protocol for the use of violence to resist what they deem to be occupation of Muslim lands.

As Muslim peoples continue to experience the violent strain of Islamism, thousands are beginning to ask, Can this be the right way? A dear friend in Egypt who is a Christ-follower was formerly a Muslim fundamentalist, deeply committed to the violent overthrow of his country's ruling powers. When reading Jesus' Sermon on the Mount, he was confronted with the kind of God the Christians follow. This God requires that his follower turn the other cheek when struck, give to all who ask, overcome evil with good, and love one's enemies. This was his first realization that the God of Islam and the God of the Christians are not the same. Their requirements are polar opposites.

As Muslims grow increasingly suspicious and fed up with the violent response of Islamists, they are beginning to look for alternatives. Some are finding their alternative in secularism. Others are turning to materialistic pleasure. Will we as Christ-followers have anything to offer them?

Who Speaks for Jesus?

In the massive conflict of Islamic and Western values, is there no distinctive Christian voice? The primary mission-sending country in the nineteenth and twentieth centuries was the United States. Missionaries and an extensive network of Christian media (television, radio, Internet, etc.) have carried the currents of American Christianity far and wide. This reality is shifting as the axis of Christianity shifts from the Western world to the East and the Southern Hemisphere. However, the influence of American Christians is still readily felt throughout the world, and the fact that the United States remains the precarious sole superpower makes the voice of Christians in America even more pronounced.

The problem is that Christians in the United States have become enmeshed in the societal interests and political structures of their own culture. Muslims and other peoples around the world are hearing a voice from Christians that suspiciously resembles the voice of U.S. national interests. Unfortunately, Islamic terrorists have successfully terrorized Christians. Christ's simple and poignant exhortation must be heard again in our day: "Do not let your hearts be troubled and do not be afraid" (John 14:27).

It is possible that Western Christians genuinely fear for the survival of the church. If that is the case, such a fear is unfounded, as the church of Christ continues to show dynamic growth throughout the world. More likely, Western Christians are fearful of the destabilization of Western democracy and the level of affluence it has afforded the Western church. If Western democracy thrives with its protective shade spread over the church, Christians feel that their future is secure. Thus the enemy of Western democracy—Islamism—has effectively become the enemy of the church.

In a recent church meeting, I was asked if the church had any reasonable hope of survival under a nondemocratic form of government. The question itself revealed a shocking naïveté about the state of the church in the rest of the world. The facts are in, and they reveal a startlingly different reality: the church grows lax, complacent, and anemic when its interests are protected by the state. It develops muscle, both intellectually and spiritually, when there is resistance. What's more, the church's strength is not commensurate with its wealth.

It is indeed possible that the advent of Islamism will force the hand of many Western Christians. To what degree is our allegiance to our national interests, both economic and political, and to what degree is our allegiance to Christ? So Christians must ask to whose kingdom they belong. In no way do I wish to intimate that belonging to Christ's kingdom is antithetical to good citizenship and patriotism. What I am suggesting is that a proper valuing of Christ's kingdom will equip the church to stand strong even when Western democracy is threatened.

If Western Christians become overly identified with the interests of our governments and societies, we will lose that which is most beneficial to our countries—our prophetic voice—and what is most essential to Christ's kingdom in the Muslim world—the voice of Christ. The survival of Christ's kingdom is not dependent on the survival or even the continued preeminence of the United States or any Western country. Much like Augustine, who penned *The City of God* as he watched the Roman Empire disintegrate, contemporary Christ-followers must realize that empires come and go but that the reign of Christ will endure forever. This realization will stand us in good stead to encounter Islam proactively rather than reactively.

Can Islamism Destroy Us?

It is incumbent on Christians of the Western world and particularly the United States to ask if Islamic fundamentalism is capable of destroying our civilization. The intent in posing such a question is not to minimize the horrific and abhorrent effects of events such as 9/11 or 7/7 (London bombings in July 2005) on our societies. Clearly, Islamists can inflict great harm and should bear responsibility for the loss of life they have caused. The question is an attempt to grapple with the real issues in our societies that could lead to their disintegration.

The demise of the Roman Empire occurred as Germanic people were invading; however, the empire was severely weakened from within, such that one could almost say the internal weakness invited or at least encouraged an external attack. The fabric of our society has held strong through racial tensions, civil war, and world wars. Could it be that Islamic fundamentalism will bring about the demise of our Western democratic societies? I must respond to that question with an emphatic no. Our civilization, like other civilizations, will fall only as it crumbles from within.

While it may be easy to cast blame on Islamic fundamentalism, we must resist the urge to look outside ourselves for a scapegoat to our societal dilemma. A movement of radical Muslims will never succeed in destroying our civilization unless our civilization has already been undermined by a massive defection from its values and foundational tenets. Could it be that our collective awareness of this defection is a contributing factor to our fear of Muslim radicals? We fear primarily because we know we are vulnerable (much like the

Waorani tribe of Ecuador that I discussed in chapter 1). We assume the external enemy to be the great threat to our civilization when, in actual fact, the real threat is internal—it is we ourselves!

There is a corollary concept that, although asked daily by secular news sources, has received scant attention in Christian media: Is Western-style democracy the hope for the Muslim world? As a Christ-follower I have the audacity to suggest that the real hope for the Muslim world is the diffusion of the gospel of Christ and the establishment of his reign. In our attempts to establish democracy, we have spent billions of dollars and lost many lives. So far, all this has produced little hope of enduring change in the Muslim Middle East. Whether in Afghanistan or Iraq, we are discovering that the cultural roots of these ancient civilizations will not easily give way to democratic forms of government. Perhaps a humble suggestion is in order: the infusion of the gospel (in both word and deed) is the surest and best hope for positive change in any culture, including our own.

◆ SEEKING FRESH VISION ◆

It must be said that this type of radical allegiance to Jesus will not enjoy a warm welcome in many nations of the world. Just as war in Iraq and Afghanistan has had a high price tag, so the call to carry the gospel will demand the utmost sacrifice. No doubt some will give their very lives in the cause. Some already have. Christians throughout the world are shedding their blood in the cause of Christ. But I was recently informed that a U.S. seminary cannot name one single martyr from among its graduates in forty-five years of operation. In some countries that fact would seriously jeopardize the seminary's claim to be preparing men and women to serve the kingdom of

Christ. Let us not be so foolish as to think that fresh vision for the Muslim world will come easily.

So now Christians of the Western world and particularly the United States must ask how we can live as loyal citizens of the state and yet give radical allegiance to a crucified Lord. It may surprise you that the answer to that question, if we get it right, will be good for the church here in the West and good for the Muslim world also, because the only hope for America and the West and for the Muslim world is that crucified Lord.

So let's tackle that question in the next chapter.

Additional Resources for Chapter 11

Abdo, Geneive. *No God but God.* Oxford: Oxford University Press, 2000.

Jabbour, Nabeel. *The Rumbling Volcano.* Pasadena, CA: Mandate Press, William Carey Library, 1993.

Kepel, Gilles. *Jihad: The Trail of Political Islam.* Cambridge: Harvard University Press, 2002.

Article on Sayyid Qutb: en.wikipedia.org/wiki/Sayyid_Qutb.

PART V
STEPS TO INCARNATION

Jesus told his first disciples, "Follow me, and I will make you fishers of men." By following him, they chose to be on mission with him—his mission. There will be no fresh vision for the Muslim world without returning to the original mission of Christ: following him, becoming fishers of human beings. Part of Jesus' mission was to live among us humans. He sought out the lost. He healed the sick. He taught the ignorant. He rebuked the prideful and arrogant. He allowed himself, in all his holiness, to become soiled with our dirty reality.

CHAPTER 12

GOD ON MISSION, HUMAN BEINGS ON MISSION

Does God seek anything?

That's not the same as asking if God needs anything. Does he *seek* anything?

In the early chapters of Genesis, we find God's voice echoing through the ravines of Eden, "Adam, where are you?" He continues seeking human beings, who, like Adam, are also hiding themselves in shame and guilt. He seeks out a family of worshippers in Noah. He seeks out a true friend in Abraham. He seeks a people of his own in Israel and seeks his own glory among the nations of the world by indwelling that people in tabernacle and temple. He finds a king after his own heart in David. He stretches out his arms to a rebellious and obstinate people through the prophets. He sends his unique and only Son to "seek and to save what was lost" (Luke 19:10). He also sends his Spirit on the disciples, the Samaritans, and the Romans, making no distinction. He calls a Pharisee-jihadist named Saul to go and seek after the Gentile nations that had not yet heard.

Ultimately God's seeking is fulfilled when innumerable multitudes from every tribe, tongue, and nation gather around the throne, expressing their praise and worship. God *is* seeking. God is seeking human beings—men and women, boys and girls.

And our role is far from passive in all that is described above. We *are* his seeking. We are the instruments of this insatiable, seeking God as we move through a world largely estranged from him. Can you imagine? While God never limits himself to using only human beings, I find that in every case in the Bible where God breaks through to someone, he uses people! When God was pursuing a lame beggar, he used Peter. In order to get to Saul of Tarsus, he used Ananias. To get to the Philippian jailor, he used Paul and Barnabas. And on and on it goes. Truth to tell, the gospel is a virus that has infected you and me. We carry it throughout the world, and its effect just keeps growing and growing as more and more people get "infected"!

Personally, I am greatly encouraged as I hear many thoughtful Christian leaders in the United States and other countries calling us to live "on a mission with God" or, as they say it, to live *missionally*. Sounds good, huh? But the shift we are called to embrace is not so subtle. It will challenge the assumptions that, for many of us, have become second nature. In order to live on a mission with God, seeking his people in this world, we will have to lay aside much of our own agenda. In fact, what is necessary is a significant paradigm shift—a new way of thinking in terms of how we live our Christian faith in the world.

As a missionary who has recently returned to the United States, I see the need of this paradigm shift, but I must admit that I struggle with how to bring it about in my own life and in the church. Honestly, it would be much easier for me to just slide back into the old way of doing "church"; however, I don't think that's an option anymore. Some contemporary analysts of American culture and church culture have been helpful to me. In *They Like Jesus but Not the Church,* Dan Kimball writes that the following ideas underlie the philosophy of living missionally:

> Being missional means that we see ourselves as representatives of Jesus "sent" into our communities, and that the church aligns everything it does with the *missio dei* (mission of God).
>
> Being missional means that we see the church not as a place we go only on Sunday, but as something we are throughout the week.
>
> Being missional means that we understand we don't "bring Jesus" to people, but that we realize Jesus is active in culture and we join him in what he is doing.
>
> Being missional means we are very much in the world and engaged in culture but not conforming to the world.
>
> Being missional means we serve our communities, and that we build relationships with the people in them, rather than seeing them as evangelistic targets.

Being missional means being all the more dependent on Jesus and the Spirit through prayer, the Scriptures, and each other in community.[1]

The Paradigm Shift of Missional Living

Although I struggle to implement missional living, I am struck that what is described above is essentially the way I tried to live for twenty-plus years in the Muslim world. So my small contribution will be to draw a parallel between this kind of missional living and what I experienced in the Muslim world. I think you will see some very intriguing points of comparison, and I hope you will realize the enormous implications for living missionally in our culture and gaining a fresh vision for the Muslim world.

There was a time when the interests of the church and the interests of the state were so close that they became virtually one and the same. That period of time has been referred to as *Christendom*. The monarchy (the state) recognized church leaders, and the church sanctioned the monarchy, creating a dynamic tension that caused church and state to work together harmoniously. As heirs of Western European thinking, we are also the heirs of Christendom. We Westerners generally assume that the state should ensure our freedom to worship God. Until very recently, the prevailing consensus in our culture was that worship of God takes place in a Christian, or perhaps Jewish, context.

Unlike Christendom, the United States determined there will be a separation of church and state such that the state cannot meddle with religious expression. Today that separation has been driven beyond its original intention, and the result is unpleasant for many Christians. The problem is that the prevailing consensus of our culture has strayed far from its beginnings, which were much more sympathetic toward Christian faith. Typically, the moral issues of our day (sanctity of human life, marriage, etc.) form the battle lines between this conflict of Christianity and contemporary culture. I suggest that the working paradigm of many American evangelicals is that of a battlefield.

Western Christians are surrounded by a culture increasingly post-Christian that can be antagonistic to our faith as well. We view ourselves as waging a battle within our culture. Our job is to hold the lines and, if possible, even extend the lines deeper into our culture. A diagram might look something like this:

WESTERN CULTURE
CHRISTENDOM PARADIGM

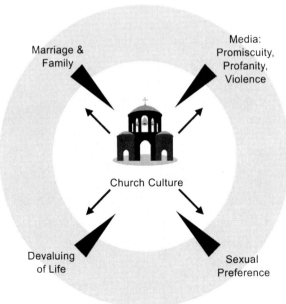

Diagram A

In diagram A the institutional church occupies the center of the culture. Its "church culture" overlays the broader Western culture, such that the two are assumed to be one and the same. Moral issues are portrayed as attacking the church culture. Indeed, in many cases the attack has been successful; churches and Christian institutions have given way under the relentless onslaught of this alternative morality.

As this happens, Christians feel compelled to react defensively. In fact, many Christian leaders expend great energy directing Christians to fight against this alternative morality. The hope seems to be that Christian values, especially moral values, can retake our culture—an attempt to preserve Western Christianity.

This paradigm suggests that a battle is raging for our culture. The battle lines, in this way of understanding, are formed by the moral issues. While this paradigm has a certain appeal, it has some real problems. I am not suggesting that the battles for the moral issues are unimportant. They are critical. However, it is important to note two facts.

The first is that some moral issues are conveniently avoided. These issues, like a deadly virus, enter into the church, weakening it from the inside and ultimately preventing it from fulfilling its purpose. They include materialism, consumerism, racism, hedonism, neglect of the environment, and the deadening of critical reasoning. Frankly, the church may be guided by its own church culture more than the Bible in determining which battles should be fought.

Second, the fact that the battle over these issues now rages within the church demonstrates the inadequacy of this paradigm. Western Christianity has been infected by values that in the view of evangelicals are opposed to Christian values. For example, mainline denominations in America are battling over ordination of homo-sexuals. Abortion has visited virtually every extended family in the nation, and families within the church culture are no exception.

All this suggests that the paradigm for how to live the Christian life within our culture should change. This change is particularly challenging for American Christians who live in conservative parts of the country such as the Southeast or Midwest. In many of these locations, church life continues much as it has for decades. Families attend Sunday worship services led by professionals in buildings designated for that purpose. "Going to church" is still recognized as a good thing to do. However, even conservative communities are beginning to get the message that the broader culture has changed. Conservative positions considered unassailable thirty years ago are now being recast in the light of our culture, which views these things with a great deal of tolerance as it places the supreme value on individual freedom. Need it be said that in our culture premarital sexual activity is assumed and homosexuality is increasingly a mat-ter of preference and orientation? Certainly we are becoming more aware that these moral issues have invaded the domain of the church culture and, in all probability, are here to stay.

The church formerly occupied a central role in the culture and largely determined its moral standards, but that role has dissolved as the church itself has been infiltrated by the presuppositions and values of the surrounding culture. It is a confusing time for many evangelicals in the United States. If the church no longer occupies the high ground, does that mean we have lost the battle? Has American culture followed Europe in becoming post-Christian?

Rather than postulate a lost battle, American Christians should come to terms with the fact that we can no longer assume a

Christendom paradigm. We can no longer assume that our culture looks favorably on the church and its doctrine, morality, and worship. The culture is seemingly more apathetic, and in some cases antagonistic, to Christian faith, especially to the institutional church. But the good news is that the church in America may be facing its greatest moment of opportunity since the Great Awakenings of the eighteenth and nineteenth centuries. Dan Kimball's book *They Like Jesus but Not the Church* develops the idea that our culture remains largely respectful of Jesus but suspicious of the institutional church; there is still a positive impression of Jesus throughout our culture. That's great news and offers immense possibilities for positive change.

Now is the time for the church to change its paradigm and learn the lesson of living missionally. That lesson may be best learned from those living in cultures antagonistic to the gospel, like Muslim cultures.

A New Paradigm for Post-Christendom

In recent years I have begun to read the writings of Lesslie Newbigin and have found him to be a deep well from which I am happy to draw. Lesslie Newbigin was an Anglican missionary who labored for long years in India—a culture antagonistic to the gospel. When he returned to his native England, he observed that the England he found was not the England he left. The culture had shifted in a marked way. Christian values and presuppositions were no longer commonly held by the English. In short, Newbigin observed that during his sojourn of forty years in India, England had shifted toward a more antagonistic posture toward the Christian faith. If it is not entirely accurate to say that England became antagonistic, you will understand, at least, that the shift was away from a Christian consensus and toward a pluralistic worldview.

Newbigin began to look at British society, analyzing it as a missionary. He asked what the church should look like in this society and how the church should conduct itself amid such a worldview. His seminal thinking provides the framework for many in our day who are asking how the church can minister in our culture in this time and place.

Newbigin exhorted the church to insert itself into the cities with a missional mind-set. He urged the church to regain its sense of mission to the British culture. He knew that the approach of the church to ministry would need to shift, and he helped the church navigate those changing waters. He encouraged ministers to view themselves as lead activists, teaching the truths of Christ not so much from a pulpit as from the head of the forward-moving line of mission.

This, in essence, is the distinctive of the new paradigm as opposed to the old. The movement of the kingdom of Jesus is forward and offensive. There are no boundaries around the kingdom because there is no territory to defend. Christ-followers invade territory, leaving in their wake the fragrance of Christ, the preserving salt and exposing light of the kingdom.

Evangelical churches in the West have understood missions since the advent of the faith mission in the 1800s. However, we have subtly embraced a watered-down concept of mission in our own culture. In all probability, this situation has devolved from a deficient understanding of the priesthood of all believers. Rather than viewing ourselves as ministers, we have tended to rely on professionals whom we pay to carry out the work of ministry. In a similar vein, we have sent paid missionaries to do in foreign cultures what we have not done in our own.

Very simply, we have failed to impact our own culture with the light of the gospel. The result is that we now find ourselves attempting to fend off the advance of our culture as seen in the previous diagram. The following diagrams are an attempt to depict how the kingdom of Christ continues to move forward despite our culture's increasing ambivalence or animosity toward the church.

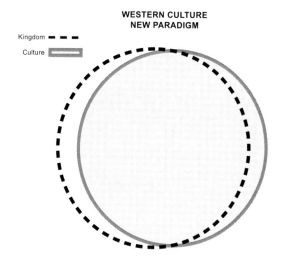

**WESTERN CULTURE
NEW PARADIGM**

Kingdom ▬ ▬ ▬
Culture

Diagram B

Diagram B demonstrates a shift as we begin to understand that the values of Jesus' kingdom are different from those of surrounding culture. This is the first step away from a paradigm of Christendom. We may still believe that our culture is pervasively influenced by the values of the kingdom, such that the overlay is as much as 90 percent. However, as we understand our culture and the values of the kingdom, we will begin to view the relationship differently, as the next diagram shows.

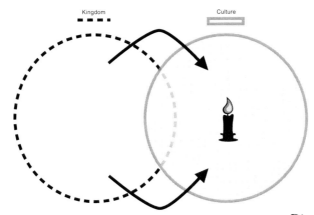

Diagram C

The fact is that the kingdom overlays our culture only minimally. However, its effect on the culture should be pronounced, acting as salt and light, preserving and enlightening the world (represented by the arrows and candles in diagram C). The dashed line representing the kingdom highlights the fact that there is movement both out of the kingdom (missionally) and into the kingdom, as people from the broader culture become reconciled to God.

We must also see that as Christians we must belong to the two realms—the kingdom of God and our own culture. It is important to seek balance in this matter of our cultural affinity. Although much in our culture may be offensive to our values as disciples of Jesus, it is important that we develop a healthy appreciation for our culture. If we do not love and enjoy the culture we are part of, we will find it impossible to act as salt and light within it. We will end up being alienated from our culture, living in a ghetto as opposed to being sent into our culture. Often my Middle Eastern friends would complain to me about a foreigner living among them who did not appreciate and enjoy their culture (their food, customs, language, films, etc.). In much the same way, if Christians reject their culture as a source of ungodliness, they will quickly find that their ability to impact the culture is greatly diminished. Living missionally will involve loving our culture and its people while also feeling the pain of its estrangement from God.

As we understand that our culture is quite distinct from the kingdom, we will also see that other cultures, although distant from our own, may have as much overlay with the kingdom as our own. This will help us progress in our understanding that the kingdom welcomes diverse cultures and peoples. The multicultural nature of the body of Christ will begin to feel natural to us. In the next diagram, the "other culture" could be an Islamic culture, a Buddhist culture, or even a secular culture. The kingdom will relate to other cultures much as it does to our own—it will become salt and light to these other cultures. And you will see in a moment that diagram D bears a strong resemblance to the diagram of the life of the church in an antagonistic culture (diagram F).

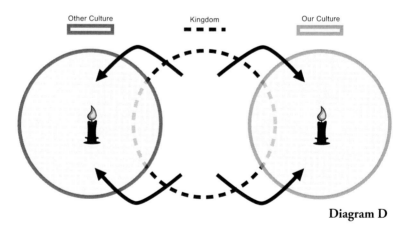

Diagram D

You might ask, "Where is the institutional church in this new paradigm?" The institution of the church is not a place to retreat out of the world. Rather, the church is a strong springboard for an effective infiltration into every area of life. Christ-followers do not see the church as an oasis to which they retreat but as a fueling station that equips them to enter the world with a renewed kingdom perspective. The kingdom of God is taken to the world on a daily basis by his ministers—those Christ-followers who take him into their various spheres of activity. In the best-case scenario, the institutional church acts as a missional conduit for the kingdom into the culture. Inevitably, the church's institutional presence moves to the periphery of our culture (as in the next diagram), but the kingdom of God becomes even more pronounced as it infiltrates every area of public life through the movement of Christ's disciples.

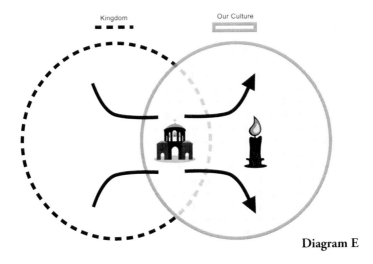

Diagram E

I stress that diagram E is a best-case scenario. Unfortunately, much of the institutional church is disengaging from the kingdom of Jesus. When this happens, the church remains in "our culture" but is no longer actively involved in the kingdom; thus it becomes little more than cultural decor.

Note also that the moral issues that figured so large in the former paradigm are hardly visible here. They have not disappeared, of course, as the church continues to address issues of moral concern, influencing legislation and addressing societal evils. However, they cease to be the defining element of the church's mission. That mission becomes more holistic, concerned to glorify Christ in every imaginable sphere: the arts, justice issues, education, labor laws, and medicine, for example.

Missional Living in Antagonistic Cultures

Consider the paradigm of a culture that is non-Western and antagonistic toward Christianity, such as a Muslim culture. Some of these cultures will have a minority Christian population, but the prevailing sentiment is antagonistic to Christianity. In these cultures, true Christians will not see the "church culture" in a position of power—a Christendom paradigm. They are more likely to see their culture as an area devoid of Christ's light into which they are sent as his representatives. They are, so to speak, on a mission with God to bring the light and truth of the gospel to their culture. Diagram F shows how this society might be depicted.

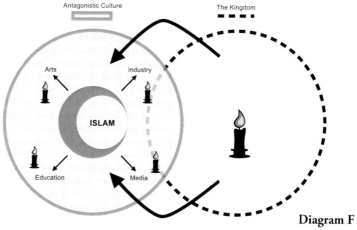

Diagram F

The society, as a whole, is estranged from the light of Christ. Therefore, Christianity occupies no "territory." It has little or no institutional presence in the society. It does exist, however, as the kingdom of Jesus Christ in the hearts and lives of his people (represented in the diagram by the candles). These people carry his light into their various spheres of influence. As they begin to reflect Christ's love and truth in their various spheres, those spheres can be transformed or at least impacted in such a way that Christ's glory will be seen and felt. This diagram cannot depict all that is true of such societies. Even in antagonistic cultures, the people of Jesus do gather, forming a church. However, the church is not seen as having authority or power within the culture. Often it is noninstitutional in nature. It does not enjoy a cozy cohabitation with the state. Its existence may well be underground or an unwelcome, although legal, presence.

Think for a moment about the implications of living in such a society. Here, one is not surprised to discover that a colleague holds views that are antagonistic to Christianity. It is, in fact, the norm, as another faith (in this case, Islam) holds the primary place of influence and power in the culture. This clear demarcation of the kingdom from the prevailing cultural values allows Jesus' disciples to demonstrate their distinctiveness as salt and light. The disciple of Jesus in such a society is not deluded to think that the state will protect his right to exercise his Christian faith. On the contrary, the state may well be explicitly prohibiting his most deeply held convictions.

The result, inevitably, is tension, resistance, friction. This tension might be more subtle, taking the form of discrimination, or it might be overt and explicit, moving into the realm of persecution. In any case, living as a Christ-follower in an antagonistic culture demands that one count the cost each day. There is a price to pay.

In such a culture, the words and actions of a Christ-follower are marked by a clear distinction between him or her and the surrounding culture. For instance, in Muslim cultures it is very common to swear. A common expression is *wallahi* (by Allah). The phrase is used to affirm and insist on the veracity of what one is saying. Christians in these societies avoid this expression and many others like it. Thus there are immediate indicators that something is different about this person. Christians in the Coptic Orthodox Church in Egypt make a clear external distinction between themselves and Muslims as they tattoo a small Coptic cross on the inside of their wrist. Thus they are marked as Christian people. I do not suggest we need go that far, but the principle is clear. Living in a culture antagonistic to the faith provides opportunity for Christians to stand out by their distinctive behavior and language—that is, if it is distinctive. High school and college-age Christ-followers, for example, can have an immense impact on their culture by remaining sexually abstinent with a reasoned defense for going against the grain of their culture.

The life of the church also takes on new realities. Allow me to describe some of the distinctives of the underground church such as my family and I were involved in. Very often these churches do not have legal status in their societies, particularly those churches that are made up of Muslim-background believers. The right to convert is not recognized, much less a church made up completely of converts.

First, the leaders of the churches are normally nonprofessionals. That means they are not paid to lead the church; it does not mean they are not trained. Their training, however, is typically of an informal nature. They may have read extensively or been mentored by other leaders. Their exercise of leadership will be in proportion to their influence on their peers. Often the church will have multiple leaders with no clear "senior pastor." The leaders may have no title, or some generic title such as "elder" may be used.

Second, the church in antagonistic cultures does not normally have its own building designated for the functions of worship. Most often homes are used for this purpose. Naturally, the meetings accommodate a smaller number of worshippers, but they provide an informality and intimacy rarely experienced in larger churches. Normally we did not call our gathering a "church." We called it simply the gathering or the meeting so as not to attract attention from anyone who might be listening to our phones or overhearing our conversation.

The house meetings I have attended lacked the note of professionalism in music and preaching. A guitar or recording might accompany the singing. Food is served and enjoyed in an atmosphere of informality. Often the real problems of the worshippers are discussed before, during, and after worship. As a Westerner attending these meetings, I admit being bothered at times by the informality. It was difficult to discern if we were worshipping or just visiting. In fact, we did worship but not according to a program or plan. We set our meeting time, and when we got together, each one would bring a song, a question about the faith, a word of exhortation. (Sound familiar?) Oh, one other thing—kids. We had kids running in and out of the meeting. Sometimes they stayed. Sometimes they played in the next room, but they always belonged. At times, we tried to provide a lesson for them. At other times, they just came and went as they pleased.

All of that might sound rather quaint and primitive, like the book of Acts. I can assure you that we experienced all the normal problems that exist in any church and then some. There were times when all of us wanted to give it up. We persevered through the challenges, and some of us found it to be a very satisfying experience of Christian community.

After having enjoyed this kind of fellowship, I can see that house churches have drawbacks as well as advantages in respect to the larger churches of the West. For instance, you might assume that meeting in a home allowed us to invite many friends and colleagues. However, the dynamics of Islamic society were such that it was quite dangerous and risky to invite unknown people to the meetings. In the house churches I experienced, spontaneous growth was not as you might expect. Therefore, I do not wish to advocate a wholesale abandonment of the way church is done in the West. I do believe that American and European Christians can learn from the house churches of antagonistic cultures such as China, India, and the Arab world. I also feel they can learn some things from us.

In my opinion, Christians of the West should avoid looking at Christians of antagonistic cultures as the real paragons of faith; that is counterproductive for them and for us. It elevates them to an imagined status they simply cannot maintain. It also afflicts us with a spiritual inferiority complex that cannot lead to the true humility of faith. Some of my best friends in the Arab world have been imprisoned for their faith and endured police brutality as severe as any you might have heard or read about. Still, they are just men and women who struggle in their daily lives and look to their brothers and sisters for help and support. We have only one Hero, and his final appointment on this earth was a cross. He taught us that we should call no one on this earth our teacher or our father. He did that because he understood human nature. As long as we are human beings, we need to have a sober assessment of ourselves and others.

Implications for the Muslim World

Our pursuit of fresh vision for the Muslim world has taken a strange turn. In this chapter, rather than look only into the Muslim world, we are attempting to look at our world as well. I believe that this change of paradigm is absolutely fundamental to our future as the church on mission within our culture. Allow me to suggest a few implications if we lay hold of this change of paradigm.

Political Alliances Yield Diminishing Returns

I received a letter yesterday from an American friend in the Middle East. He spoke of the pressure he felt because of the recent war in Lebanon. He described feeling "smothered" by the anti-American sentiment in the air and expressed relief that, now that the war is over, he can catch his "emotional breath." Many Americans take offense that such animosity would be displayed against our country during a war in which we had no direct involvement. However, I have come to believe that this interconnectedness of our government's policies with conflicts throughout the world is more real than imagined. Be that as it may, the point is that if American Christians are overtly aligned with the policies of their government, their missional impact around the world and in America will be diminished.

I recently overheard a conversation in the gym where I work out. A Christian was trying to persuade an unbelieving colleague to consider the faith. I was stunned at how quickly this unbeliever associated Christianity with conservative politics, steering the whole dialogue off course. I waited for the Christian to deny, or at least challenge, the association. I was disappointed to find he did no such thing. Rather, the conversation left the substance of the Christian faith entirely, taking on the appearance of a CNN or Fox News editorial analysis. It seems the believer shared the assumption of the non-Christian, that to be a Christian one had to be unswervingly committed to a conservative political perspective. It would have been refreshing for me and eye-opening for him if the unbeliever had heard that Christians are open to examining all truth claims in the light of Scripture, that being socially conservative and politically conservative are not necessarily prerequisites for the Christian faith.

In much the same way, people of other cultures and lands want to see that Christ-followers are willing to examine the policies and practices of their government as well as the assumptions of their culture in the light of the teachings of Jesus Christ. If we are willing to release the battlefield paradigm for an incarnational and missional vision, then we will find ourselves less inclined to cling tenaciously to our government's policies and our cultural presuppositions. This will be good for our government, as it will be called to task by our active involvement in the political realm. Incarnational ministry will lift up the downtrodden and restore justice to the oppressed of our society. Without jettisoning Christlike morality, we can gain Christlike influence by seeking and saving that which is lost. Our voice in the culture will no longer be condescending but healing to the broken and simultaneously convicting to the practitioners of injustice. Regaining our prophetic voice with regard to the entire spectrum of moral issues can do much to restore credibility to the church. How? Our light must be seen more than our voice is heard. Our culture must see our thoughtful engagement with it and recognize our acts of mercy and love rather than hear our words of self-righteous condemnation.

The unfortunate fact is that much Christian media serve to propagate a conservative political and military agenda, deriving from the battlefield paradigm, that has very little to do with extending the kingdom of Christ. In my opinion, these media ministries have done great harm to the cause of Christ in the Muslim world. They have thoughtlessly affiliated the Western church with a militaristic and political Zionist agenda. Muslims have watched Christian satellite stations with astonishment as arenas packed out with American Christians break into spontaneous applause when a presumptuous preacher declares that God is unequivocally on the side of Israel. Embracing a new paradigm for the church—a missional paradigm— is vital because it can help to correct these unfortunate and destructive generalizations.

A Church of All Nations

A further implication of living missionally in antagonistic cultures is that Western Christians will rediscover the multicultural nature of the body of Christ. A unique thing has transpired in our day: the geographical axis of the Christian faith has shifted out of the Western industrialized world and into the Southern Hemisphere and developing countries. More and more missionaries are being sent from countries such as Brazil, Argentina, Nigeria, Kenya, Korea, and Singapore. I have marveled many times at the fervent prayer life of the Koreans, the simplicity and spontaneity of the Brazilians, the willingness of the Nigerians to endure deprivation for the cause of the gospel, and the selfless service of the Filipinos. I will never forget the thrill of belonging to an international church in Cairo. Our worship team was enriched by a Nigerian drummer who occasionally emitted yelps of glee as he beat out his African rhythms to our delight! The other vocalists and musicians were from all over the globe. In that context, I needed to learn to lay aside the fact that I had benefited from a full seven years of undergraduate and graduate education in biblical studies and theology. The fact is, I needed to learn from these brothers and sisters. Of course, they had things to learn from me as well.

Let's try to work out this implication a bit further. If we can release our battlefield mentality and come out of our fortress, we may find ourselves deeply enriched by the diverse cultures and traditions of the international church of Jesus Christ. Worship, preaching, education, outreach, and prayer will all be different than we are accustomed to, and we should allow ourselves to be affected and enriched by this glorious diversity. Friends in France and England assure me that revival in their countries may be instigated by the immigrant churches, largely African. In our own country, we have a ways to go in realizing our kinship to our Hispanic brothers and sisters or our need to embrace the rich traditions of African-American Christianity. If our faith disengages from white-collar conservatism, I believe that our testimony will be greatly enhanced.

The Muslim world may yet see a faith that transcends cultural and ethnic differences. If, on the other hand, our religious beliefs are inextricably linked to our political and cultural preferences, we will incur the disdain of the Muslim world along with much of the developing world.

The Global Village

Finally, if Western Christians are able to bid farewell to our fortress mentality, we will find that our countries have already become exceedingly accessible and potentially fruitful mission fields. While American foreign policy now is despised throughout much of the world, for example, the American educational system still enjoys worldwide prestige. Intellectuals from every corner of the globe go to the United States to obtain advanced degrees. They return to their homelands to occupy posts of influence. Not all immigrants are students, of course. Many asylum seekers and those who are simply seeking a better life relocate to the United States and other Western nations.

While the reality of the 10/40 window[2] has brought home the vast needs of that part of the world, the truth is that mission is less and less limited by geography. Our world is becoming increasingly mobile as great urban centers act as gathering places for minority groups from every continent. A friend of mine returned from his Latin American mission field to labor in New York City. He told me that from his position he is able to assist church-planting movements throughout Europe and Asia! A missionary formerly in Somalia now finds that his most fruitful fields of labor are in the great cities of the northwestern United States! Yemenis congregate in Detroit and Egyptians in Jersey City. Moroccans and Chinese have occupied Boston. It is a day of unparalleled opportunity if we will lift up our eyes and look at the harvest.

◆ SEEKING FRESH VISION ◆

The same challenge that Jesus put before the apostles stands before us today. Are we willing to step outside our cultural assumptions? Are we prepared to see the Samaritans not as those who hatefully pervert our cherished faith but as the Father's delight? Are we willing to find our joy in seeing the gospel of the kingdom penetrate a new Samaria?

I contend that our reaction to the Muslim world should not be viewed as a peripheral element of the life of the church in the United States. How we respond to the Muslim world is intricately linked with our response to those who are antagonistic to the faith or apathetic toward it in our own culture. If we are prepared to give up the defense of our battle lines and move forward in an intentional and peace-promoting incarnation of Christ's love into our culture as salt and light, we will learn much that will enhance and further our witness in the Muslim world. That is an incarnational vision of ministry—the outworking of Jesus' teaching that he would send his followers just as he was sent by the Father. Jesus warned that his followers would receive a similar reception to his own, so we should be forewarned that this shift to a missional paradigm will cause us to encounter resistance. We just may discover that the ministry of the gospel in our culture is not so different from ministry in the Muslim world after all!

Finally, all this talk about disengaging from our cultural and political presuppositions needs to go beyond the level of a stimulating intellectual discussion. The renewal of our churches is dependent entirely on the work of the Holy Spirit. As we realize our dependence upon and interconnectedness with the global church of Christ, we will release our cultural, political, and economic pride. The result will be an authentic humility—the necessary preliminary for an outpouring of the Holy Spirit on the church. In essence, the call to live incarnationally and missionally is also a call to repentance of pride and judgmentalism toward other cultures and our own.

Additional Resources for Chapter 12

Guder, Darrell L., and Lois Barrett, eds. *Missional Church: A Vision for the Sending of the Church in North America.* Grand Rapids: Eerdmans, 1998.

Kimball, Dan. *They Like Jesus but Not the Church.* Grand Rapids: Zondervan, 2007.

Kinnaman, David, and Gabe Lyons. *UnChristian.* Grand Rapids: Baker Books, 2007.

Newbigin, Lesslie. *The Gospel in a Pluralist Society.* Grand Rapids: Eerdmans, 1989.

CHAPTER 13

LIVING THE KINGDOM, EXTRACTING THE EMPIRE

We've been over a lot of territory in the preceding chapters. I make no claim to have covered it exhaustively. My hope is that this book might open the conversation about how Christ-followers in today's world should be looking at the Muslim world.

In the last chapter, I tried to make the point that our vision for the Muslim world and how we interact with that world will have definite ramifications for how we view Western society, which is drifting away from its Christian moorings. In previous chapters, I attempted to articulate a view of Islamic fundamentalism that neither sensationalizes the threat nor belittles it. We also took a long look at the little country of Israel and how it should figure into a vision for the Muslim world. My hope is to refine our vision and affection for Israel as we lift up our eyes and look on the many Muslim nations

that surround it. I attempted to open a window into the real world
of Muslims who choose to follow Christ and remain in their Islamic
societies. I've also sought to provide a mountain-peak perspective
on Islamic history and theology, believing that any vision must be
sustained by a sober assessment of reality.

In chapter 1, I sought to find the groundwork for fresh vision
for the Muslim world in Jesus' reaction to a despised people group of
his day, the Samaritans. In that chapter we arrived at the conclusion
that Jesus' approach was to live among the Samaritans, talking to
them, eating with them—in brief, sharing their lives. I used the word
incarnation to describe this model of bringing the kingdom of Jesus
into a people group and the term *missional* to describe the movement
of Jesus' kingdom through his people into the surrounding culture.

Kingdom or Empire?

Jesus' kingdom is wonderfully designed to infiltrate and impact
the many cultures of our world. However, our hearts and minds are
often enticed away from the kingdom as we become enamored with
the empires of this world. By *empire* I do not mean a particular state;
I am referring more broadly to institutional systems that are self-
defending, self-promoting, and self-serving. Jesus said very clearly
that his kingdom was not of this world. Thus we are faced with a
dilemma: How do we live in the world with its empire-like systems
and institutions and still maintain our primary loyalty to the kingdom of Jesus?

A fundamental concept that continues to fuel much of Islamic
fundamentalism is the concept of *dar al Islam* (house of Islam),
understood to mean the territory ruled by Muslims. For Muslims,
it is implicitly understood that once an area has been taken over by

Muslim rulers, that area is forever consecrated to Allah and to the Islamic faith. With this concept as a given, it is not hard to understand why Muslims are irate that Israel and southern Spain are no longer in the fold of Islam. The military occupation of other Islamic lands causes great concern for Muslims.

Based on this concept, I have pointed out to Muslim friends that Islam conceives of itself as an empire—a God-ruled earthly empire with geographic borders under the authority of a caliph or imam. Moderate Muslims deny this, insisting that Islam is tolerant and accepting of other faiths and needs no political power to exist and thrive. Nevertheless, Islam existed through the centuries as an empire. It ruled over a well-defined territory and held political authority. We do well to recall that Christendom was essentially the same—an empire sanctioned by the Christian faith. Just as Christendom benefited the church economically and politically, so the empire phase of Islamic history brought in great revenues to the Islamic state. Many Muslims would like to see a return to the caliphate or the political rule of Islam over the *dar al Islam*. I think that is perfectly understandable because, in my opinion, Islam conceives of itself as an empire. The political function of the religion is not separate from the spiritual, moral, and social.

Christendom is now a thing of the past. That suits me fine. Jesus Christ never conceived of his kingdom as an earthly based political power: "My kingdom is not of this world" (John 18:36). Admittedly, Christendom contributed much to our contemporary culture and way of life. Still, the demise of Christendom presents us with an opportunity to recapture the nature of the kingdom as Jesus intended it to be lived out in this world, if we are willing to do that as he taught us—serving the world rather than exercising power over it. Unfortunately, our tendency is to revert to Christendom, to empire. After all, losing power leaves us vulnerable. It is destabilizing to embrace the other and serve. It requires us to take up the basin and towel and lay aside the money bag and sword.

What is at stake here is huge. We have a tremendous opportunity to get it right and, in so doing, to live out the kingdom in full view of the Muslim world, which is still largely thinking of its submission to God in empire-like terms. We have a chance to model the kingdom to 1.4 billion people of the world who are estranged from it! I believe that if we live the reality of that kingdom well, many Muslims will be attracted to it.

Extracting the Empire

The problem is that culturally we have "empire reflexes." We want to preserve "our way of life." Subtly, it is advantageous for us to discredit the "other" in order to establish our rights and our vision for the good life. It is an innate tendency toward self-preservation—entirely natural, but most unbecoming of the kingdom of Jesus. The truth is that empire-like activities are needed in the world to keep order. However, the kingdom is not intended to engage in empire building. When you and I become complicit in the building of the empire, we unintentionally act in a way that betrays the kingdom.

Our role in the world is distinct. Even those who find themselves in empire-preserving occupations such as politics, police, or military must constantly be reminded that the kingdom is distinct from their legitimate professional pursuits. In order to incarnate Christ's kingdom in this world, we will need to extract the empire from our thinking and acting. What follows are some ideas derived from the story of Joseph as well as from Jesus' teaching in Luke 13, specifically his reference to the Galilean Jews killed by Pilate and the parable of the mustard seed. These ideas are an attempt to juxtapose the kingdom with the empire. I hope this will enable us to see more clearly where our thinking has left the realm of Jesus' kingdom and wandered into the realm of empire.

Empire Combats Evil; Kingdom Absorbs and Transforms It

Joseph experienced terror. His brothers abused him, sold him into slavery, abandoned him. He made the best of it and rose to a position of honor. He was falsely accused and put into prison. Again, he rose to a position of honor. He interpreted dreams and was not rewarded. You know the story.

In an incredibly moving scene, Joseph reveals himself to his brothers with loud wailing, such that the Egyptians outside could hear what was going on. "You intended to harm me, but God intended it for good," he said (Genesis 50:20).

While in Iraq, I met a pastor of one of the new churches in Baghdad. While Saddam Hussein was still in power, this man had moved out of the established church because it was clear to him that government informants had infiltrated. As a result, he came under suspicion and was imprisoned before the Americans invaded. He was released just before the invasion. He now pastors a rapidly growing church in Baghdad and will certainly be one of the key leaders of the church in that country. He is a shining example of a person who absorbed evil and transformed it into a good and beautiful end.

Sometimes the distinction is subtle, but it is generally true that empire goes to war against evil (or what it perceives as evil or different from itself), while the kingdom absorbs evil, transforming it.

Empire Is Power Oriented;
Kingdom Is Change Oriented

The first part of Luke 13 refers to an enigmatic incident. We don't have any extrabiblical data about this event, but you can be sure of one thing: it was the buzz. People were fired up and talking about it. Pilate, the Roman governor of Judea, apparently had killed some Galilean Jews "whose blood [he] had mixed with their sacrifices" (v. 1), which suggests that he killed them while they were in the act of worship. Now, given the background of Roman occupation of Judea and Pilate's treachery, which is well established, you can bet the Galileans were upset.

The amazing thing is that Jesus resisted any urge to ride the wave of this anti-Rome enthusiasm. There's no criticism of Pilate. There's no warning for corrupt political leaders. Nothing like that. He turned the tragedy of the event into a call to repentance. He warned the people that the same fate could await them—not the most endearing message, you might say.

He resists the urge to destroy the empire. Here was the perfect opportunity. The Romans were illegal occupiers of the land. Apparently, they weren't allowing the Jews freedom to worship. Worse than that, they were mingling Jewish blood with the blood of sacrifices. But there's no hint of mobilization for the destruction of the empire, nor is there any indication that Jesus was building an empire that would be in competition. Incidentally, the Roman Empire came and went, but Jesus' kingdom lives on.

But there are urgent matters in our day. The big matters of our day internationally are Iraq, the threat of Iran, Islamic fundamentalism, and the Israel-Palestine situation. Domestically, countries deal with other issues—health care, immigration, border security, the economy.

All of these issues and many others are producing a great deal of insecurity in our day. Because I've been in the Muslim world a long time, I get asked about Islam everywhere I go. The sense of fear, concern, almost panic, is palpable. I appreciate that we need some perspective on these issues, but may I suggest that one of the reasons we're so concerned about these things is because we still live with an empire mentality. Similar to the Jews of Jesus' day, we feel our security and our territory being threatened—our way of life, our prosperity, our freedom.

How might Jesus respond? "Unless you repent . . ." (Luke 13:5). Repentance is not just getting on our knees and weeping, coming to the front of the church to confess, or some other show of emotion. It's a total reorientation of life; it's a change of direction.

The "God empires" of this world just aren't working—whether they are the Abbasids of Baghdad or the Holy Roman Empire of Europe, whether they are Jerusalem or Mecca or Rome or Washington DC. The *kingdom* of God is being worked into this world, and Christ is its King. When he returns, he will bring the kingdom fully to earth. Until then, empires will continue to come and go.

So Jesus seemed indifferent to the political realities (the empire) of his day. He displayed little concern for power but called his people to change—repentance.

Empire Is Territorial
Kingdom Is a Permeating Presence

Yeast is small. It works invisibly. Yet its effects permeate.

As usual, Jesus is countercultural. In Western culture, you make an impact from the top down. It's a hierarchy, a pyramid—the trickle-down effect. Jesus opts for permeation, infiltration, invisibility, and effect from within.

Empire is a concern for territory. Most often, territory is "our rights, our way of life, our understanding of truth," but it may at times be actual land. They both concern power. Jesus' expression of power is kingdom power. He never uses power to hold sway, to establish himself, to defend himself, to defend the disciples. He uses power in a godly way to lift up the downtrodden, mend the broken, heal the sick. Jesus stays clear of empire even in his use of power. One could say that Jesus' power, as opposed to seeking a peak from which to perch, flows to the lowest point. His power extends to needs, not to establishments. He promotes healing, not superiority.

The good news is, despite all our mistakes carrying out the life of the kingdom, it seems to be working. The Christian faith has spread everywhere in the world. The number of Christ-followers is growing, although world population seems to be growing at a faster rate. About one-third of the world is Christian of some variety. While there clearly is a *dar al Islam*, there clearly is no corresponding territorial "house of Christ." The kingdom of Jesus, rather than claiming territory, permeates. It extends to every tribe, tongue, and nation—an incredibly attractive reality!

The kingdom of Jesus as opposed to empire is not concerned in the least about the political boundaries of a country. It is a reality that overlays the political boundaries because it permeates peoples and cultures and transforms them to the glory of Christ.

Empire Defends Identity;
Kingdom Invites and Protects All

Finally, though the kingdom starts small as a mustard seed, it becomes like a large plant (ten to fifteen feet tall) that acts as a shelter and resting place for many diverse peoples of the world. Most commentators draw on Old Testament imagery to say that Jesus, in the parable of the mustard seed, was suggesting the multicultural dimension of the kingdom—people of all tribes and tongues and nations represented by the birds of the heaven who come to rest in the branches of the mustard plant. This kingdom is a place of welcome and equal access for all peoples of the world.

Recently I was on the campus of the University of Illinois in Champaign. An Asian-American church invited me to come and speak. I watched while about eight hundred Asians worshipped, prayed, praised, and received teaching with all their hearts from 7:00 to 11:30 at night. These guys were serious. As I looked on, it occurred to me that my homeland was indeed honored to have become the home of these Asian Christians. They were immigrants to the United States, but there are no such things as immigrants in the kingdom. All are sons and daughters.

I've lived as a foreigner for most of the past twenty-two years. Egyptians have a word for someone who is a non-Egyptian—*khawaga*. I got very tired of being called a *khawaga*. But when I was with brothers and sisters in Christ in Egypt, things changed. They included me in their jokes and explained them to me when I didn't understand. They asked me to teach and pray with them. They listened to my opinion. Pretty soon, I didn't feel like a *khawaga* anymore.

The African-American Muslim leader Malcolm X had been steeped in the racist views of the Nation of Islam. When he went on pilgrimage to Saudi Arabia, his racist views changed as he saw Muslims of many colors and nationalities praying together and circling the Kaaba in the Great Mosque of Mecca. That vision of a multicultural Islam transformed him and provided powerful impetus to transform the entire Muslim community in America.

The world is waiting for that entity that will break down the barriers. Malcolm X found it as he was circumambulating the Kaaba—at least he thought he had. I believe the reality of the multicultural and multilingual body of Christ has yet to be realized fully in our world. When we take hold of it, we may see an amazing forward thrust of the kingdom as people of all the various tribes and nations of the world assemble in great praise to our great King.

Living the Kingdom

Extracting the empire will necessarily result in living the kingdom. As we draw to a close, I will offer a few suggestions as to how we might incarnate the kingdom of Jesus among Muslims in our own day. Of course, these suggestions won't be exhaustive. I hope others will add to them in an ongoing conversation. Nevertheless, perhaps by adopting some of the principles listed below, you can begin to share the elation of Jesus, who referred to his conversation with the Samaritans as "his food."

Linger by the Well

Jesus did. He had time to listen to an immoral Samaritan woman ask questions. He even incited the dialogue and progressively moved this woman toward a fuller understanding of himself.

We live in a world of walls. There are walls between East and West, walls dividing Christians from Muslims from Jews from Buddhists from atheists from . . . There are linguistic barriers, political barriers, cultural barriers, educational barriers, race and gender barriers. One lesson that screams at us from Jesus' encounter with the Samaritan woman is that he felt it important to overcome the barriers separating him from that woman. In order to overcome the barriers, Jesus lingered for a while. He actually had a conversation—something of a rarity in our day and age. The disciples had gone ahead to get food. He just lingered. He waited.

More and more of us will be encountering Muslims in the coming months and years. They are flocking to the West in search of education and employment. Many of them will be intimidated by their new surroundings and quite fearful that their Islamic faith will put them in jeopardy. Some, no doubt, will seek to barricade themselves in the American or European Muslim community with as little contact as possible with those who are outside the walls of that community. It will take some effort to linger by their well.

Perhaps you are anticipating that I am encouraging you to have these conversations with Muslims so you can share your faith. May I surprise you by saying that's not my intention; rather, I think it imperative that Muslims experience genuine concern and care from a Christ-follower. The facts of Christ's death and resurrection are easy enough to rehearse. What is indeed rare in our day is an extended hand, a caring smile, someone who is willing to go the extra mile to help someone in need. When Muslims see these things, barriers are broken down and life is transformed. A true conversation can take place that will no doubt reference our faith, but not only that. Linger by the well.

Ask Questions

Jesus simply requested some water. It was the most immediate presenting need. He allowed the Samaritan woman to meet his need and thereby opened a door that radically changed her life.

Asking a question puts us in a state of vulnerability, provided we're asking sincerely (not just to confirm our suspicions). Questions allow others to correct our impressions, to serve us, to teach us, to inform us. They also show genuine interest in the person we're speaking with. Questions are the hinges that relationships turn on.

Occasionally I have surprised a Muslim acquaintance by simply asking, "What's your opinion about the world?" More often than not, he can give me an earful. I often discover that he and I have a lot more in common than either of us would have believed before the discussion. I also ask questions like, "What do you hope to do with your degree? What are your top three objectives in life? How do you please God? Can you know that God is pleased with you? What do you talk to God about? How can you know God listens?" Ask questions.

Share Some Food

To share food with a Middle Easterner is almost sacramental. It creates a bond between you, particularly if you have prepared that food and served it with your own hands. There is a saying in the Middle East that by eating "bread and salt" with someone you become bonded for life. It is true; once we invite people into our homes, we have entered into a type of covenant with them. We have allowed them to see us in our intimate surroundings.

Are our homes and kitchens open so that people feel secure and welcome there? I think it is no accident that the first believers in Acts took their meals together with joy and broke bread from house to house. That produced an intimacy we seldom achieve in our larger institutional churches today. By returning the faith to our homes, we will prepare the way for Muslims to experience it. If our home is a "warm center" where Christ's people find love and acceptance, a Muslim will be able to sense that. The reality of the Christian community can be very attractive.

Talk about Jesus

In our post-Christian society, talking about Jesus directly is often viewed suspiciously. We feel almost unnatural interjecting his name into our conversation or making reference to his teaching. Ironically, we find it easier to talk about our church or the faith of some noted religious or political leader. Some recent studies show that Jesus' popularity is increasing in our culture. Talk about him. That's the safe ground. Most Muslims I have met are not ill at ease talking about matters of faith. They quote religious texts liberally and make constant reference to their prophet.

I believe that Muslims should hear the name of Jesus on our lips very early in our relationship. I find it helpful to mention his name almost casually. That establishes the fact that I am a Jesus-follower, yet it doesn't feel preachy. I just make reference to one of his teachings, such as, "What shall a man give in exchange for his soul?" That lets the Muslim know I am serious about following Jesus.

Furthermore, Muslims should know that they have an open invitation to come to our homes and read the Scriptures with us. One friend, who labored long years in North Africa, said that every Muslim who completed a simple question-and-answer study with him through the book of Luke became a disciple of Jesus. That's quite amazing! Talk about Jesus.

Practice Holistic Ministry

Jesus' ministry involved feeding the hungry, healing the sick, and ministering to the oppressed and afflicted. Much of the Muslim world (indeed the whole world) is in dire need of this holistic ministry. There need be no demarcation between what has been called social ministry and evangelistic ministry. Our motivation is not merely to incite conversion but to glorify God by caring for that part of his creation created in his image—human beings. Muslims are well acquainted with the injustices of their homelands. They will sense if our discipleship has sufficient integrity to reach out to a broken and hurting world.

Beware of Slogans, Sound Bites, and Bandwagons

Politics used to be the furthest thing from my mind, at least I naively thought so. A few years in the Muslim world convinced me that policies have implications on people. As such, our politics are intimately connected with our faith. The problem is that normal politics are incurably dedicated to promoting the interests of the group in power. What that amounts to is oppression of the disempowered, the disenfranchised. Living in a foreign culture helped me see that even here, in our own culture, the politics of the powerful often run roughshod over the weak.

Muslims must see that we are willing to reexamine our political slogans and party lines in order to ensure, to the best of our ability, that justice is served for all people, including the weak and disempowered. If Muslims see our policies as promoting raw American or Western consumerism at the expense of poorer societies, our Christian faith will ring hollow or worse. In a word, we must be more excited and convinced about the reign of Jesus over all nations and peoples than we are about our current political affiliations. So beware of those slogans, sound bites, and bandwagons.

Get Up to Speed

I find it incredible how few of our theological seminaries offer any formative courses on Islam or any other major world religion. The sheer demographics of Islam make it imperative that we understand it. Islam is growing in Western Europe. It is expanding into sub-Saharan Africa. It is a vital movement within our nation's prisons, and entire sections of major cities have become Islamic. Beyond that, we have the realities of a post-9/11 world, which make it incumbent that we begin to understand Islam.

I have a Lebanese friend who has dedicated his life to telling Muslims about Jesus. He has read the Qur'an fourteen times! Maybe that's more than you feel called to do. But learning about a person's faith is a way of loving that person. I am challenged by the example of Daniel, whom I consider to be the preeminent Old Testament missionary. He excelled in the learning and literature of the Chaldeans—the people who had carried him into exile! As a result he was used of God to bring kings into a relationship with the God of Israel. Perhaps we would find more Muslims showing interest in the gospel if more Christians knew the Islamic faith.

Support Ministry in the Muslim World

The United States is currently pouring billions of taxpayer dollars into the Middle East in an attempt to establish the legitimacy of democracy in that part of the world. In my opinion, it is at best a distant and faint hope. The gospel does produce change from within. The amount of money contributed by Western churches to ministry among Muslims has increased in recent years, but it remains scandalously low. In many situations we can partner with churches and national Christians who are laboring in Muslim countries. These brothers and sisters have much to teach us about how to carry out ministry in their part of the world. In other places the best option will be to send a gifted cross-cultural missionary.

In any case, it is clear that many Muslims are turning to Christ from all over the Muslim world. If our churches in the West cannot wake up to this reality, Christ will reap his harvest in the Muslim world, but what part will we play? Will we have the privilege of sharing in his harvest? Support ministry in the Muslim world.

Pray with Faith

Do you sometimes think we've forgotten this? Are we willing to take what we hear in the news and turn it back to our Father in Spirit-led prayer? Recently our church prayed for a believer in Eritrea who was being asked to recant her Christian faith. She was imprisoned with her six-month-old child. She was released on the very day of our prayer meeting! Prayer is a nonviolent weapon. It allows us to participate in the forward momentum of Christ's kingdom even if we never travel to a predominantly Muslim country. Pray with faith.

Be an Advocate for Muslims

Paul says that love "bears all things, believes all things, hopes all things, endures all things" (1 Corinthians 13:7 NASB). I recently heard a story of a young girl who saw a veiled Muslim woman in her

LIVING THE KINGDOM, EXTRACTING THE EMPIRE

neighborhood. She turned to her mother and asked, "Mommy, why does that lady cover her head?" The mother replied, "It's because she loves God, honey." Later when the mother and daughter were out together, they saw another woman wearing the Muslim veil. The daughter called out at the top of her lungs, "Look, Mommy! She's wearing the scarf because she loves God." The Muslim woman, who could not help but overhear the comment, was so taken aback that she approached the woman and profusely thanked her for teaching her daughter such things about Islam.

Muslims are keenly aware of the prevailing sentiment about them in the West. They will not fail to notice when we have a genuinely different spirit—a charitable attitude that believes the best about them, defends their right to worship as they choose, and practices advocacy for causes that concern them in our society. I am fully aware that there are homegrown terror cells in the United States. Obviously, we need discernment so that we do not lend support to those who would harm others. But let's remember that the majority of Muslims in America and other countries have never considered acting out a terrorist plot. They are concerned with getting ahead in life, making a better wage, and finding a good school for their kids. Whether they choose to follow Christ will be their decision, but we will have served them in Christ's way of love if we can be an advocate for Muslims.

◆ SEEKING FRESH VISION ◆

I have a neighbor who doesn't preach or lead Bible studies. She's a kind and gracious woman who lived through a tragedy. Her son was in one of the towers that went down on September 11, 2001.

When I stop to think about it, I honestly don't know how I might react if a similar tragedy befell my family. I'm sure she has struggles to leave the past behind and move forward in faith. What strikes me about her is that she has focused on getting to know Muslim people in the community, praying for them, inviting them into her home, and helping them in practical ways.

In Matthew 18, Jesus tells a parable about a king who forgave a huge debt to one of his slaves. That slave, after being released of his debt, turned to a fellow servant and began to choke him in an attempt to secure what was his. His master had forgiven him completely, but he was unable to extend the same grace and forgiveness to his fellow servant. How quickly his heart moved out of the realm of grace and into the realm of self-promoting power! When the forgiving king heard about this, he asked him, "Should you not also have had mercy on your fellow slave, in the same way that I had mercy on you?" (v. 33 NASB). My neighbor gives me tremendous hope. She reminds me that the love of God is real. It lives in her. She has been devastated by the worst possible expression of fundamentalist Islam, yet her life continues to emanate an aroma of grace, peace, and forgiveness.

Is there any hope? Will the Muslim world be transformed by a free-market economy? A democratically elected president? A new level of prosperity? An infusion of human rights?

Just a little yeast leavens the whole lump.

"As the Father has sent me, I am sending you" (John 20:21).

NOTES

Chapter 1, Casting a New Kind of Vision

1. Elisabeth Elliot, *Through Gates of Splendor* (Grand Rapids, Fleming H. Revell: 1970), 272.

2. C. S. Lewis, *The Lion, the Witch and the Wardrobe* (New York: Scholastic: 1987), 76.

Chapter 2, A History of Complicity: Who, Me?

1. Ibn Hisham, *As-Sira An-Nabawiya*, 1:217–218.

2. *Hadiith* is an Arabic word meaning "speech." The Hadiith is a collection of literature that relates the sayings and events of Muhammad's life and that of his companions. Muslims view Hadiith as authoritative, second only to the Qur'an. The primary collections of the Hadiith are the al-Bukhari and al-Muslim collections.

3. Sahiih al-Bukhari, 1:3.

4. The word used for Waraqa's conversion is *tanassar*, derived from the normal word used for Christians in the Qur'an, *nasaara*, which probably comes from the city of Jesus' upbringing—Nazareth (*Nasr* in Arabic).

5. Sahiih al-Bukhari, 1:4.

6. Nestorianism, named after a patriarch of Constantinople in 428 CE, became the title of a view of Christology in the ancient church associated

with Antioch. This view emphasized the reality of Christ's humanity and was wary of the communication of the attributes from one nature (divine) to the other (human). Nestorians opposed the title *theotokos* (God-bearing) applied to the Virgin Mary. See *Evangelical Dictionary of Theology*, 2nd ed. (Grand Rapids: Baker Academic, 1984), 823.

7. Kenneth Scott Latourette, *A History of Christianity* (San Francisco: Harper, 1975), 1:282. Jacob Baradaeus, born in 490, an active missionary roving from Mesopotamia to Alexandria, had fluent use of Greek, Arabic, and Syriac.

8. Ibid., 788. Monophysitism developed in Alexandria in the fourth century, viewing Christ as having "only a single, divine nature clad in human flesh." Note that contemporary Coptic Christians deny being monophysite as it was defined by the Council of Chalcedon: "Copts believe that the Lord is perfect in His divinity, and He is perfect in His humanity, but His divinity and His humanity were united in one nature called 'the nature of the incarnate word,'" www.coptic.net/EncyclopediaCoptica.

9. Samuel Hugh Moffett, *A History of Christianity in Asia: Volume I: Beginnings to 1500* (Maryknoll, NY: Orbis Books, 1998), 332.

10. Latourette, 288.

11. Robin Daniel, *This Holy Seed: Faith, Hope and Love in the Early Churches of North Africa* (Harpenden, UK: Tamarisk Publications, 1992), 29–35. Daniel provides a more detailed version of this account.

Chapter 3, Give Back My Holy Land!

1. Interestingly, the Dome of the Rock is lined with Arabic calligraphy, which is our most ancient architectural testimony of early Islamic teaching. The irony is that the Qur'anic verses lining the Dome all have to do with the Islamic view of Christ. See Daniel Brown, *A New Introduction to Islam* (Malden, MA: Blackwell Publishing, 2004), 43–47.

2. This was not always the case. There were periods in which overt discrimination against Christians was apparent. For Jews, however, life was more tolerable in Baghdad than in Europe. See Peter G. Riddell and Peter Cotterell, *Islam in Context: Past, Present, and Future* (Grand Rapids: Baker Academic, 2003), 90–91.

3. Catholic Encyclopedia Online, www.newadvent.org/cathen/06221a.htm.

4. Riddell and Cotterell, 125–126.

Chapter 4, Two World Wars and a New Reality

1. Bernard Lewis, *The Crisis of Islam* (New York: The Modern Library, 2003), xv.

2. Ibid., xv–xxii.

3. Samuel P. Huntington, *The Clash of Civilizations and the Remaking of World Order* (New York: Simon & Schuster, 1998), 247.

4. Lewis, 4. I am using the term *Christendom* broadly as the wedding of religious faith with political power as was common in medieval Europe, seen in the coronation of the Holy Roman Emperor Charlemagne in 800 CE, the Spanish Inquisition, the Crusades, and various other attempts of Christian powers to wield governmental authority.

5. Muslim scholars speak of both *offensive* jihad and *defensive* jihad. Defensive jihad involves defending Muslim territory (*dar al Islam*) against non-Muslim forces. Israel, Iraq, and Saudi Arabia are often identified by jihadists as legitimate areas for defensive jihad, as there are non-Muslim forces present in those areas that have historically been Islamic territories.

6. en.wikipedia.org/wiki/Abeer_Qassim_Hamza_murder.

Chapter 5, Your Truth or Mine?

1. Admittedly, this is something of an oversimplification. God in the Old Testament was with his people as they moved about in the desert. He dwelt among them first in the tabernacle and then in the temple. The incarnation of Christ, as seen in biblical perspective, is the fulfillment of God's immanent presence among human beings, not the beginning of it.

2. Space prohibits dealing with the issue of Sufism. The Sufis are a mystical strain of Islam. They seek union with Allah through various forms of dance, recitation, and meditation. Generally, Sufism is eschewed by classical Islam as a deviation. However, it has had significant appeal throughout the centuries and produced some remarkable examples of godliness among its practitioners.

3. Some have asserted that Islam is incoherent with Western-style democracy. I do not wish to make that assertion here. In fact, many Muslim leaders have distinguished themselves by their democratic principles.

4. The common understanding of Muslims is that Muhammad was illiterate. Some Muslims allow that he must have been somewhat literate to be a caravan leader and engaged in significant business dealings.

5. Yet again, there are exceptions to this general rule. Many Islamic peoples in Asia and even American Muslims insist that the Qur'an must be translatable.

Chapter 6, Jesus' Kingdom in the Muslim World Today

1. Read the story of Farah's father here: www.islameyat.com/english/books/ishmael/ishmael1.htm#8.

2. Read Jasmine's story here: www.islameyat.com/english/books/ishmael/ishmael1.htm#2.

Chapter 7, The Israel of God

1. I have benefited from learning to read the entire Bible as the story of God's unfolding mission to reconcile humanity to himself. One excellent book written in this vein is *The Mission of God: Unlocking the Bible's Grand Narrative* by Christopher J. H. Wright (Downers Grove, IL: InterVarsity Press, 2006).

2. M. Harlan's article listed in the additional readings of this chapter holds that there is a future, literal fulfillment of the Old Testament promises for Israel. He points out that there are both conditional elements and unconditional elements of God's promises to the Jews of the Old Testament. His article supplies important theological nuances for anyone considering the role of modern-day Israel in relation to the biblical promises.

3. Even the Old Testament covenant people of God were not defined merely by ethnicity. Non-Jewish proselytes were allowed to partake of Passover by becoming circumcised (Exodus 12:48).

4. Colin Chapman, *Whose Promised Land?: The Continuing Crisis over Israel and Palestine* (Oxford: Lion Adult, 2002), 153.

5. M. Harlan, "Violence in the City of Peace," unpublished article.

6. See Robert L. Dabney's *A Defence of Virginia, (and Through Her, of the South) in Recent and Pending Contests against the Sectional Party* (University of Michigan Library, 2006).

Chapter 8, What's Next or What's Now?

1. Other millennial views hold that the seventy weeks of Daniel were completed during the era that Christ lived on earth. They advocate the finalization of the period before 70 CE when Jerusalem was destroyed by the Romans and the Jews were dispersed.

2. Lesslie Newbigin, *The Gospel in a Pluralist Society* (Grand Rapids: Eerdmans, 1989), 84.

3. *NIV Study Bible* note on Romans 11:17. The common practice would be to graft a cultivated olive branch into a wild olive tree. The exact opposite was done here, suggesting that though this is contrary to what would have been expected, it has been successful and fruitful.

Chapter 9, Perspective Makes All the Difference

1. The history of this important era shows that Christian emperors did not treat the Jews favorably. Some attempted to convert the Jews to Christianity by force.

2. www.jewishvirtuallibrary.org/jsource/History/Human_Rights/geneva1. html.

3. www.untreaty.un.org/cod/repertory/art36/english/rep_supp6_vol3-art36_e_advance.pdf.

4. Elias Chacour with David Hazard, *Blood Brothers* (Grand Rapids: Baker House, 1984). Fr. Elias recounts his story in painstaking detail in his book. Some have disputed his claims, but his story stands as a rebuke to the heartless displacement of thousands of Palestinians that continues until the present day.

5. Gary M. Burge, *Whose Land? Whose Promise?* (Cleveland: The Pilgrim Press, 2003), x.

6. Ibid., 8.

7. Amnesty International Executive Summary, December 1999. Cited in Burge, 7. See www.amnesty.org/ailib/aipub/1999/MDE.

8. E. Walter Laqueur and Barry Rubin, eds., "The Balfour Declaration," *The Israel-Arab Reader: A Documentary History of the Middle East Conflict* (New York: Penguin, 1998), 16–17.

9. Donald Wagoner, "Bible and Sword: US Christian Zionists Discover Israel," www.informationclearinghouse.info/article4950.htm.

10. B. Morris, *Correcting a Mistake—Jews and Arabs in Palestine/Israel 1936–1956* (Tel Aviv: Am Oved Publishers, 2000). Cited in Burge, 40.

11. Chacour, 44–45.

12. www.ifamericansknew.org.

13. http://en.wikipedia.org/wiki/File:US_aid_to_Israel.gif.

14. www.seruv.org.il/english/combatants_letter.asp.

15. www.informationclearinghouse.info/article2000.htm.

Chapter 10, Reformation à la Islam

1. http://academic.udayton.edu/Race/06hrights/GeoRegions/Africa/Rwanda01.htm.

2. http://edition.cnn.com/2003/WORLD/asiapcf/south/07/07/india.infanticide.pt1/index.html.

3. It is of interest that some Muslims are calling for a return to the Qur'an only, apart from the Hadiith, as the source of their authority. Although the Hadiith has been an integral part of Islamic jurisprudence and life for centuries, there is a movement afoot within Islam to limit the sources of Islamic reform to the Qur'an alone without the Hadiith. Although it is hard to see how these reformers will overcome the edifice of Islamic clerics, it is a movement that merits careful attention.

4. The commentary of Ibn Kathir (a very respected commentary in Islamic tradition) states: "What we transfer of the judgement of one verse to another (verse), we substitute it, we change it. This by exchanging the permitted to forbidden and the forbidden to permitted . . . and this takes place only in the case of commands and prohibitions . . . as for events, there can be no abrogation" (author's translation: Tafsiir al-Qur'an al-'adhiim li Ibn Kathiir, p 194).

5. The Arabic word for the verse that abrogates is *naasikh* (abrogator), while the verse that is abrogated is *mansuukh* (abrogated).

6. Cyril Glasse, *Concise Encyclopedia of Islam* (San Francisco: Harper & Row, 1989), 209.

7. www.submission.org/war.html.

8. Martin Accad, "Christian-Muslim Relations," www.abtslebanon.org/Default.asp?PN=Level1Page&L=0&DivisionID='1496'&DepartmentID='&SubDepartmentID='&PageID='2204'&ToggleSideNav=ShowAll.

9. W. Montgomery Watt, *Muhammad at Medina* (Oxford: Oxford University Press, 1956), 5. See Watt for a much more detailed account of the raids.

10. Ibn Hisham, As-Sira An-Nabawiya, 2:239.

Chapter 12, God on Mission, Human Beings on Mission

1. Dan Kimball, *They Like Jesus but Not the Church* (Grand Rapids: Zondervan, 2007), 20.

2. The 10/40 window is the geographic area between 10 and 40 degrees latitude stretching from North Africa on the west to Southeast Asia on the east. Missiologists have pointed out that the majority of the world's peoples who have yet to understand the gospel reside in this area.